T0353081

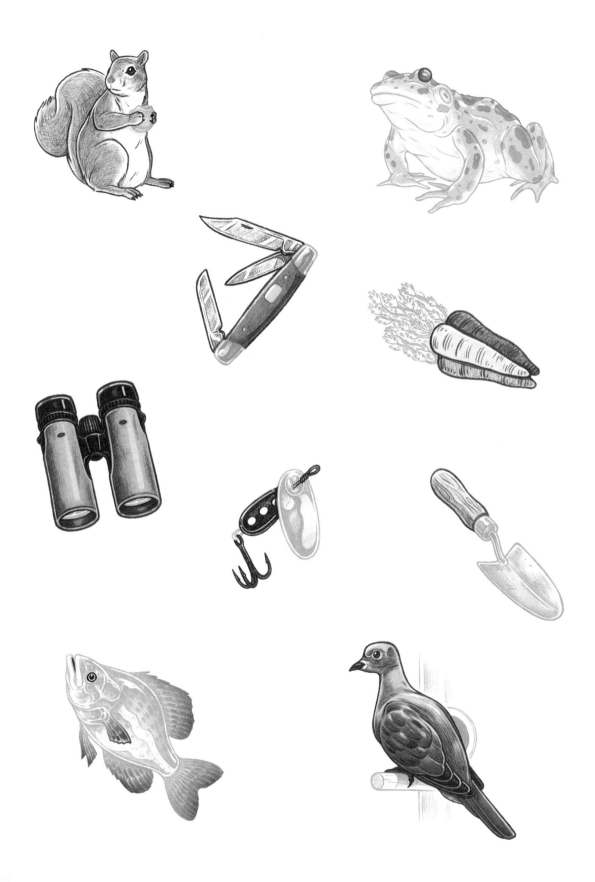

BY STEVEN RINELLA

CATCH
A CRAYFISH,
COUNT THE STARS

CATCH A CRAYFISH, COUNT THE STARS

Fun Projects, Skills, and Adventures
for Outdoor Kids

STEVEN RINELLA

with Brody Henderson

Illustrations by Max Temescu

RANDOM HOUSE

NEW YORK

Published in the United States by Random House, an imprint and
division of Penguin Random House LLC, New York.

RANDOM HOUSE and the HOUSE colophon are registered
trademarks of Penguin Random House LLC.

LIBRARY OF CONGRESS CATALOGING-IN-PUBLICATION DATA
Names: Rinella, Steven, author.
Title: Catch a crayfish, count the stars: fun projects, skills,
and adventures for outdoor kids / Steven Rinella.
Description: New York: Random House, [2023] | Includes index.
Identifiers: LCCN 2023001465 (print) | LCCN 2023001466 (ebook) |
ISBN 9780593448977 (hardback: acid-free paper) |
ISBN 9780593448984 (ebook)
Subjects: LCSH: Outdoor recreation. | Outdoor life. |
Handicraft for children. | Creative activities and seat work.
Classification: LCC GV191.6 .R56 2023 (print) |
LCC GV191.6 (ebook) | DDC 796.5—dc23/eng/20230404
LC record available at https://lccn.loc.gov/2023001465
LC ebook record available at https://lccn.loc.gov/2023001466

Printed in the United States of America on acid-free paper

randomhousebooks.com

3rd Printing

First Edition

Book design by Caroline Cunningham

Dedicated to all you kids who love nature.

Tomorrow, it will be your job to protect it.

CONTENTS

II. COLLECTING AND FORAGING

III. FISHING, HUNTING, AND WILDLIFE

IV. GARDEN AND HOME

INTRODUCTION

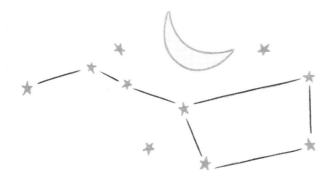

You're probably the kind of kid who dreams of having a lot of adventures in the outdoors. That makes total sense to me. Nature is exciting and full of surprises and lessons. I've been charged by grizzly bears and got zapped by an electric eel. I've watched ospreys swoop down from the sky and catch trout from mountain lakes. One time, I saw a catfish rise to the surface of a river and snatch a mulberry that fell from a tree. I've traveled in the jungles of South America with Indigenous peoples, eating foods that we caught ourselves by hunting and fishing. In Arctic Alaska, I found a spear point that was made by an Ice Age hunter. I'll never forget any of that stuff. Those memories make me happy. They make me who I am.

I got my start having these adventures when I was a kid like you. The thing I loved more than anything else was being outside doing stuff like hunting, fishing, canoeing, exploring, making forts, and sneaking up on birds and animals. Back then, my dad gave me an important piece of advice. "You're gonna spend a third of your life working," he told me. "So you better find a job that you love." It was the best piece of advice I ever got, and he repeated it about a hundred times. That's how I eventually got one of the coolest jobs in the world, which is being a writer. My job is to have great outdoor adventures and then share my stories with other people. If I hadn't learned how to do the kinds of things that you're going to learn in this book, I wouldn't be doing the awesome things that I get to do now.

Not all of the advice you get from grown-ups is as good as the advice that my dad gave me. In fact, some of it's pretty dumb. I once had a grown-up tell me that I shouldn't try to become a writer because it wasn't a realistic goal. If I saw that person now I'd just have to laugh. I've also seen a lot of grown-ups try to discourage kids from experiencing nature in an up-close and personal way. It seems that some of these grown-ups have forgotten that humans are animals, too. They think that we mostly belong indoors, and that participating with nature is bad. They think hunting and fishing for your own meat is cruel, even though they'll happily buy meat from a grocery store without even thinking about where it came from. They think that trying to sneak up on a deer is mean, even though deer spend their whole lives evading predators and think no more about it than you'd think about checking for traffic before crossing the road. They think that dirt and bugs and frogs are gross and will make you sick. But when you ask which bugs or frogs will give you which sickness, they have no idea. One time, I watched a kid take a shrimp that he was using for fishing bait and throw it to a great blue heron that was fishing just down the beach from him. The heron gulped the shrimp down. Meanwhile, a grown-up ran over to yell at the kid. She said the kid was "interfering with nature." It scared the kid and made him confused and sad. If that heron could have talked, I'm guessing it would have told the woman to mind her own business. The woman eventually left the heron and the kid alone, and they went back to fishing. It made me wonder who, exactly, was interfering with nature.

While it's good to live a close, hands-on relationship to nature, it's even more important that you love and respect it. When you think of Earth, don't just think of it as a giant sphere made of rock and dirt that is home to plants and animals. Instead, try to imagine the earth as a thing that *is* alive. Imagine that water is the earth's blood. Its rivers are veins. The soil is its skin. The wind is its breath. The mountains are the earth's bones sticking up under the skin. It is covered in fur made of trees and grass. As for yourself, imagine that you're a creature that has been given a home on the surface of this giant, beautiful creature. You ride on its back. This might seem like a crazy idea, but please try to keep it in mind while experiencing the adventures inside this book. Thinking this way can make you feel happier and stronger.

As for grown-ups, they're probably gonna look at what you're reading and see the words *hatchet* or *saw* and get worried that you'll hurt yourself. First off, you should tell them a few facts. Camping-related activities aren't nearly as dangerous as football and cheer-leading. Even hunting with a firearm, which might seem extremely dangerous, is actually a very safe activity. If grown-ups don't believe you, you can tell them that tennis, mountain biking, and golf all have a higher rate of injury than hunting with a firearm. In fact, billiards is the only sport that is safer.

Whatever the statistics say, you shouldn't use them as an excuse for being a knucklehead. A careless or inexperienced person can easily hurt themselves with a hatchet or saw. You could get cut bad enough to need stitches. Being careless with a homemade blowgun could lead to a serious eye injury for a friend or sibling. They could even lose an eye. Eating wild mushrooms you found in the woods without verifying their identity with the help of a responsible and knowledgeable adult could put you in a hospital.

To avoid risk and danger, you need to practice something called situational awareness when doing the projects in this book. Practicing situational awareness means paying close attention to everything that is going on around you. It means understanding what's happening around you and predicting what might happen next. Let's say you're wading in a creek and trying to catch a tadpole in a net. If you're not practicing situational awareness, you might be so focused on the tadpole that you don't notice the deep water to your right or the snake to your left. Another example would be trying to light a campfire in a field of dried grass. A kid with good situational awareness would recognize the risk of the fire catching the grass and spreading out of control. They'd know not to risk it, and that they need to find a safer place or else not light a fire at all. As you explore this book, make sure that you have your own situational awareness turned up to full blast. This book should be fun and relaxing, for sure. But most important, it should be safe.

NOTE TO PARENTS

Some of the projects in this book are potentially dangerous and require adult supervision. Other projects assume that young readers will explore with some degree of independence. Depending on household rules and your child's age and experience, you may want or need to be an active participant throughout.

In places, children may need some help following instructions. They may also need guidance and oversight to ensure they're using tools safely and venturing outside with appropriate caution and preparation.

If you have kids who require extra guidance, it's not a bad idea to scan through these projects together. Mark the ones they can do by themselves, and take note of the ones that they'll need help with. Learning to work together as a family is just as important as learning to work independently. Good luck, stay safe, and have fun.

CATCH
A CRAYFISH,
COUNT THE STARS

NAVIGATION AND EXPLORATION

Ever wondered if you have what it takes to survive in the wilderness? That's what the projects in the first part of this book are about. You'll learn how to use the night sky to find your way home, follow the tracks of animals, build shelters out of natural materials, and start a fire that will heat and light your campsite. The more you practice these skills and the others in this section, the more comfortable and capable you'll become in the outdoors.

BUILD AN EXPLORATION KIT

Early American explorers on the Great Plains were amazed to see that Native Americans could make boats big enough to carry an entire family using nothing but a knife and natural materials found along the riverbanks. They could turn the skin of a drowned buffalo into a boat by attaching the hide to a frame of willow limbs secured with cord made from the buffalo's skin, sinews, and tail. If they needed to hunt for a buffalo, they could make arrow points from special types of stone known as flint, chert, and obsidian. They'd start by banging two stones together in order to chip away a piece that was the right shape and thickness. Then they'd shape and sharpen the piece into an arrowhead by carefully flaking away chips of stone with a sharp deer antler, a process called knapping.

What could you accomplish in the wild, with the right tools and skills? The saw on a multi-tool could help you make a spoon out of a deer bone. A flashlight would let you see down into the burrow of a ground squirrel, so you could learn about how these animals prepare for winter—and maybe "borrow" a little dried grass for an emergency fire-starter. A water bottle is essential for hydration, and it's also a great place to store wild blueberries. With the right pieces of gear, you can be ready for all kinds of adventures in the great outdoors. Whether you're going on a big camping trip with your family or just riding your bike to the playground to meet a few friends, it's a good idea to be prepared for whatever Mother Nature might send your way. That's why the first project in this book is to build yourself an exploration kit. To keep things organized, pack the kit inside a small stuff sack or a big ziplock bag. Keep the kit in your backpack so it's ready to grab the next time you head outside. Over time you'll want to customize your kit, but here are some useful things to get you started.

- **Picture of family and parent contact info.** Keep a picture of your family with your parent's contact information written on the back in case of emergency.
- **Water bottle.** It's important to stay hydrated, and wide-mouth water bottles also make great containers for edible berries—or for a grasshopper that you might want to carry along with you as a pet for the day.
- **Snacks.** You'll need lots of energy for outdoor adventures. Always keep your backpack loaded with extra snacks like trail mix, cheese sticks, dried fruit, and jerky. Some explorers will throw in a couple of pieces of candy, but stay away from anything that will turn into a gooey mess in high temperatures. There's nothing worse than opening up your pack and finding that everything is all sticky and messed up.
- **Extra baggies or container.** Carry an empty medicine bottle or

a 1-gallon ziplock baggie for gathering any interesting stuff you find along the way. That could be rocks, flowers, seashells, or anything you like.

- **Small aquarium net.** These are more useful than you might guess. Use them to catch insects or scoop up crayfish and minnows from creeks and ponds.

- **Rope.** The best kind of all-purpose rope is called 550 paracord. It became popular among soldiers during World War II, when they'd scavenge the cord from old parachutes and use it for boot laces, lanyards, and even belts to hold up their pants. It has a minimum breaking strength of 550 pounds, which means it could support the weight of three grown-ups without breaking, even though it's only about as thick as two or three spaghetti noodles put together. Twenty feet of cord is more than enough to build a fort or make a stringer that can carry home a batch of fish.

- **Flashlight.** Pack a small flashlight or headlamp for exploring at night, or in case you get unexpectedly caught out after dark. Rechargeable flashlights are great. For lights powered by disposable batteries, try to get one that uses AA batteries. Those are usually easy to find.

- **Field guides.** Books like *Peterson's Field Guides for Young Naturalists* and the Smithsonian *Fossil and Rock Hunter* and *Bug Hunter* will help you identify the plants, animals, rocks, and insects you see outdoors.

- **Binoculars.** A pair of compact binoculars with 7- or 8-power magnification will let you closely examine birds, animals, and other far-off objects.

- **Waterproof notebook and a space pen.** Use them to draw pictures of what you see outside, or write notes about your day to your family and friends. You can also write down a list of things that you need to add to your exploration kit. (P.S.: They're called space pens because they're what astronauts use in outer space—they work in zero gravity or upside down, they're waterproof, and they don't leak ink.)

- **Magnifying glass.** Useful for getting a close-up view of insects, grains of sand, and other tiny natural wonders. On a sunny day, you can even use one to start a campfire by aiming a beam of light at an old bird's nest or a pile of dried grass.

- **Multi-tool.** A small multi-tool will probably become the most important part of your exploration kit. You can pull splinters with the pliers, cut sticks with the saw, take apart equipment with the screwdrivers, and clean fish or dissect big bugs with the knife.

- **Rain jacket.** The weather can change without warning from warm and sunny to cold and rainy. Always pack a rain jacket or poncho.

- **Medical supplies.** If you fall and get a scrape or cut, you can patch yourself up and get back to having fun if you keep some basic first-aid supplies like Band-Aids and antiseptic wipes inside a plastic baggie in your backpack.

- **Odds and ends.** A proper exploration kit should be small enough to carry around all day but should still have everything you need. Depending on where you're going, what you're doing, and the time of year, you might want to add a warm hoodie, a hat, an emergency space blanket, whistle, bug spray, sunglasses, sunscreen, trail maps, or even an extra inner tube for your bike tires.

MAKE A MAGNETIC COMPASS

When compasses were first invented, a couple of thousand years ago, the instruments didn't immediately replace the stars as the main tool for navigators. But they were helpful to sailors and other travelers at times when it was too cloudy to see the stars at night, or in the daytime when the sun was shining. Eventually they came to be one of the primary means of navigation, used in combination with paper maps.

The way traditional compasses work is pretty cool. We don't feel it in our bodies, but the earth is actually magnetized, due to the flow of liquid metals in the planet's outer core. And compasses contain a metal needle or pointer that responds to the earth's natural magnetic field by pointing toward north. This part gets a bit confusing, but compasses are pointing toward something called the magnetic north pole. Unlike true north, which is based on the permanently fixed location of the North Pole, the magnetic north pole moves around slightly as the earth's magnetic field shifts. That doesn't usually affect navigators, since magnetic north is close enough to true north that compasses can be used to navigate in any direction, especially over short distances. (But if you want to learn about something really crazy, you should do some research on how the earth's magnetic poles will shift from time to time. There have even been periods in the past when your compass's needle would have pointed to the south!)

Once you know where magnetic north lies, it's very easy to roughly determine the other three cardinal directions. If you're facing north, south lies directly behind you, east is directly to your right, and west is directly to your left. Some people like to use the saying "never eat sour worms" to help them remember the order— north, east, south, and west, working clockwise from north.

Whenever you're outside and in unfamiliar territory, it's always a good idea to know the cardinal direction of your destination, along with what direction would lead you to safety if you got lost. Start by studying a map of the area before a trip into the outdoors (an adult can help with this step!) and make a note of which direction you'll be traveling. Use your compass to periodically determine the location of the four cardinal directions while you're out exploring so that you're always aware of which direction you're going and which direction would take you back to your car or to the nearest trail, road, or town.

For less than $10, you can buy a very good compass to clip onto your backpack, and it's a good idea to do that. But as a fun experiment, you can see the earth's magnetic field at work by building your own compass with just a few materials. Here's how to do it.

What You'll Need

- Small magnet
- Scissors or box cutter
- Sewing needle or a small thin nail
- Small plastic bowl or cup
- A foam cup or a small bottle cork
- Water

Building Steps

1. Fill the plastic bowl about half full of water.
2. Magnetize your compass pointer: Run your magnet along the length of the needle or nail, from the back to the point, fifty times. (Don't move the magnet back and forth while you do this! In order to magnetize just the pointy end of your needle or nail, it is important to run the magnet in only one direction.)

3. Cut out the bottom of the foam cup to create a flat disc.
4. Place the needle on the foam disc, making a line through the middle of the circle, and float the disc in the bowl of water.
5. After several seconds, the disc should begin to move slowly back and forth, and then it will stop moving. When this happens, your compass is working! The tip of the needle is reacting to the earth's magnetic field by pointing toward magnetic north.

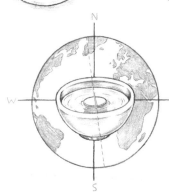

You can verify that your compass is working correctly by comparing it to a commercially made compass. In order for your compass to work properly, you'll need to keep it out of the wind and away from metal objects or electronic devices, which can interfere with the earth's magnetic field. Our planet's magnetic field is relatively weak and is able to move the point of the needle only if there is very little resistance—that's why you need to float your compass on water.

In an emergency, you can make a simpler version of this compass by using a small, wiry piece of metal, your water bottle or a small, calm puddle, and a leaf to float your compass needle. If you don't have a magnet, you can magnetize a needle with static electricity by rubbing it carefully against your hair or wool socks.

MAKE A SUN COMPASS

The stars and constellations can be used to navigate at night. During the daytime, you can use the sun. It might seem like the sun is moving across our sky slowly throughout the day, but it's actually the earth that is moving, spinning like a top in a complete circle every 24 hours. Because of this daily rotational pattern, the sun always rises in the eastern sky and always sets on the western horizon.

This knowledge alone is enough to allow you to distinguish east from west early in the morning, when the sun is rising, or in the evening, when the sun is setting. But even in between dawn and dusk, as the position of the sun changes very slowly in the sky throughout the day, shadows follow a predictable path that can be tracked and used just like a compass. Following the instructions below, you'll be able to make a simple but very accurate sun compass using just a few materials.

While you may not be embarking on a monthslong voyage, many historians believe that Viking cultures used sun compasses to avoid getting lost on long voyages across the sea. The Vikings were fierce warriors, but they were also skilled mariners and explorers who navigated the open ocean without getting lost. A thousand years ago, they traveled hundreds of miles by boat from Europe to North America. In fact, the Vikings navigated across the Atlantic Ocean hundreds of years before Christopher Columbus landed in North America!

What You'll Need

- Pocketknife
- Two sturdy sticks, 2–3 feet in length
- Four small rocks, acorns, or pine cones—something about the size of a golf ball is perfect
- A hammer or hand-sized rock

Building Steps

You can do a test run in your backyard, but making a sun compass is so easy that you can also just give it a try the next time you're out on a hike in the woods. Check the weather forecast and pick a bright, sunny day—you won't have much luck on cloudy days without shadows. For the best results, start either around mid-morning or later in the afternoon when the sun isn't high overhead.

1. First, use your knife to sharpen one end of one of the sticks into a stake with a rough point.

2. Next, find a flat, open area with soft soil that is exposed to the sun. Use a hammer or rock to pound the stake into the ground so that it's firm and won't move.

3. Find the very end of the shadow cast by the stake and mark it with one of your small rocks.

4. Wait 15 minutes, then mark the new position of the end of the shadow with a rock. Repeat this process until you have marked four spots with small rocks.

5. Use those four rocks to make an imaginary line like a connect-the-dots drawing. This line marks east and west. The last rock you placed will point west, and the first rock will point east.

6. Stand between the stake and the line, and lay your second stick across the line at a 90-degree angle. The top of the stick will point north, and the bottom will point south.

That's all it takes to make your own stationary compass! If you don't believe it, check your sun compass results against the compass app on a smartphone.

IDENTIFY A CONSTELLATION

Astronomers estimate that earthlings can see about 9,000 stars from our planet with just our naked eyes—that is, without using a telescope or any other tools that might help us see better. Beyond those visible stars are billions more that we can't see. The closest star is the sun, and it's 92 million miles away. Yet when a ray of light leaves the sun, it only takes about 8 minutes for it to get here. Many of the other stars are not just billions of miles away, but trillions. We're able to see them at night because of their enormous size and brightness. You could fit about 1 million earths inside of the sun, and many stars are much, much bigger.

Some stars are clustered together in groups that form a pattern when viewed from earth. These patterns are known as asterisms. Connecting the dots on these asterisms sometimes creates a simple picture called a constellation, though it can take a bit of imagination to spot one.

Humans began giving constellations names based on their appearance thousands of years ago, and today there are eighty-eight constellations named after everything from animals to mythological heroes. Because the locations of many constellations are either fixed or moving in a predictable direction across the night sky, people have been using them as navigation tools for centuries. Long before there were magnetic compasses and detailed maps, humans used the position of the stars in the sky to find their way home or explore new and unknown places. Today, we have high-tech GPS navigation smartphone apps to find our way, so we don't need to use the stars as a celestial compass like ancient sailors and explorers did. But because phones and other devices can break or run out of battery power, celestial navigation is still a worthwhile skill to develop. Plus, it's a lot of fun to create imaginary pictures by turning the stars into a connect-the-dots drawing.

You can start your stargazing journey by finding some of the easiest constellations to identify. Keep in mind that the constellations you can see will depend on which hemisphere you live in. If you live north of the equator, in places such as North America and Europe, you're in the Northern Hemisphere. If you live in Australia, your home is in the Southern Hemisphere. Here are some good ones to begin with.

Big Dipper

Many adventurers regard the Big Dipper as the most important constellation in the Northern Hemisphere. It's part of a larger constellation called Ursa Major (the Big Bear), named by the ancient Greeks after a mythological character who was turned into a bear. But the reason the Big Dipper is so important is that it can help you easily find the North Star. And if you can find the North Star (which

is located in the Little Dipper, a neighboring constellation), you can figure out what direction you're facing. The best way to spot the Big Dipper is to look for a large cup with a long handle. The stars in the cup are brighter than the other stars around them, so they're easy to spot, and the two stars that form the end

of the cup point toward the North Star. You can find the Big Dipper all year, but during fall and winter it will be close to the northern horizon. During spring and summer it is much higher in the sky and will appear upside down.

Little Dipper

Made up of seven stars that form the image of another cup or ladle with a long handle, the Little Dipper is one of the most easily recognizable constellations. Like the Big Dipper, it is part of a larger constellation called Ursa Minor (the Little Bear). The Little Dipper's cup is nested in the bear's head, while its handle runs the length of the bear's body toward the back of its hips. The North Star, also

known as Polaris, is located at the end of the ladle's handle, and it is the brightest star in the Little Dipper. Because the star hovers over the North Pole, it is a very reliable navigational tool. The Little Dipper is visible throughout the year in the Northern Hemisphere, but it is brightest around the summer solstice in June. Look toward the northern horizon to find it.

Orion

One of the biggest and brightest constellations, Orion has been known by many names and through several myths in various ancient cultures. In ancient Greek mythology, Orion was an incredibly strong giant and a hunter who carried a bow and a club. Chinese astronomers also saw a hunter in the shape of the constellation, which they called Shen Xiu (Three Stars). For the ancient Egyptians, the assortment of stars held the soul of the sun god Osiris. And in a cave in Germany, archaeologists discovered the image of Orion on a 30,000-year-old relic: a piece of mammoth tusk with a carving of the constellation dating back to the Stone Age.

In the Northern Hemisphere, Orion is located in the southern sky, but you can only find it during winter. It is easy to locate if you know what you're looking for. Much like the sun, Orion rises in the east and sets in the west. The entire constellation includes about twenty stars, but look for the three bright stars that form the line of Orion's Belt. Surrounding the belt, you will see several other stars that form the rough shape of an hourglass. When you connect these asterisms, they form the shape of a man holding a bow and a club. Two of the brightest stars in the sky, blue Rigel and red Betelgeuse (pronounced "beetle juice"), are part of the Orion constellation—look for Betelgeuse in Orion's raised arm and for Rigel in his front foot. You can find Sirius, the brightest star in the sky, by following the direction of Orion's belt downward and to the left.

Gemini

If you have ever drawn a stick figure, you'll have no trouble spotting the Gemini constellation. Gemini, also known as the Twins after the Latin translation of the word, looks just like two human stick figures standing side by side and holding hands. The two brightest stars in Gemini are Pollux and Castor, so named after two brothers from Greek mythology. Another fun fact about this constellation:

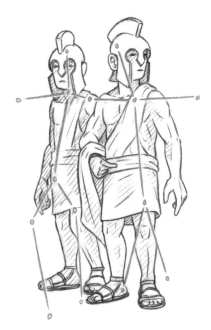

Gemini was the inspiration for the name of several NASA spacecraft in the 1960s. One of them, the Gemini S3, carried the first two American astronauts to ever travel into space together.

Gemini is most visible from January through May. During the winter and early spring, the Twins are high in the northern sky, but by summer they fade from view. To spot it, look for two big, bright stars close together—Castor is white and Pollux is gold. From there, you should be able to make out the two stick figures. If you have trouble locating them, you can use some of the other constellations to orient yourself. Orion's raised arm (remember, the arm that holds the bright red star Betelgeuse?) points toward Gemini. You can also follow the direction of the handle of the Big Dipper backward through its cup to locate the Twins.

The Southern Cross

If you live in a southern state like Florida or are traveling to the Southern Hemisphere, you'll be able to see the Southern Cross, named for its cross-like shape. Although it is the smallest of the eighty-eight named constellations, its outline makes it easy to find. Another clue to finding the Southern Cross is that it includes a very bright star. The star at the bottom of the cross, Acrux, is estimated to be 25,000 times brighter than the sun, a whole lot bigger, and several times hotter. It is only because Acrux is so much farther away from us—20 million times farther, to be exact!—that it looks so much smaller. (To understand just how far away Acrux is, consider this: It takes the sun's light just 8 minutes to reach the earth. The light from Acrux takes 321 years to get here.)

If you're in an area where you can see it, you can use the Southern Cross to navigate by imagining a line that extends four and a half times the distance from the star at the top of the cross, Gacrux, to the bottom star, Acrux. This line ends at the celestial south pole, an imaginary spot in space that hovers over the actual South Pole on earth. This might seem like a difficult and imprecise way to navigate, but it worked well for sailors who traveled thousands of miles across the southern oceans hundreds of years ago.

STARGAZING TIPS

Stars and their constellations shine their brightest when the sky is dark and clear. It also helps to have an unobstructed view. Trees and buildings can hide stars that are lower in the sky, but you can see far and wide in open fields, along the shores of large lakes, and from hilltops. The best places for stargazing are also far away from large cities, where light pollution makes it difficult to see all but a few of the brightest stars. In places like downtown Chicago or New York City, sometimes only thirty or forty stars are visible. But in remote locations like Grand Canyon National Park, thousands of stars fill the sky on clear nights.

If you can get your hands on some binoculars or get access to a telescope, the increased magnification will help you get an even better look at the stars, especially if you are fighting light pollution. Technology is another amazing stargazing tool. Free smartphone apps like SkyView, SkySafari, and Star Walk Kids use your camera to reveal the exact location of stars and constellations in the night sky. They'll also show you other celestial objects like planets, comets, and even satellites.

THE NORTH STAR TO FREEDOM

The stars in the night sky have guided mariners on long voyages, helped farmers plan their crop cycles, and enabled scientists and astronomers to calculate the age of our solar system. They also played a role in lighting the way during one of the darkest chapters in American history: the period before slavery was outlawed in the United States.

During this time, thousands of enslaved African Americans in the American South were able to find their way north to freedom via the Underground Railroad—the network of abolitionists who risked their lives by helping friends, family members, and strangers escape to safety. When you think of the Underground Railroad, you might have an image of an actual railway, connected by underground tunnels that freedom-seekers could travel through. In fact, most of the enslaved people who used the so-called railroad would have been traveling on foot, aboveground. They used the cover of night to shroud their whereabouts during the dangerous journey. That's where the North Star came into play. Most of the freedom-seekers were headed to northern states or to British North America, now known as Canada, and they used the North Star to orient themselves as they fled.

There were many conductors guiding freedom-seekers along the Underground Railroad, together with stationmasters who offered their homes as safe houses. The best-known conductor was Harriet Tubman, who led hundreds of people to freedom via the Underground Railroad and, later, was a scout and spy during the Civil War. Harriet had escaped slavery on the Eastern Shore of Maryland in 1849. She had a deep knowledge of the landscape of her home state, and she used that knowledge to ferry her charges to safety. Wading through marshes and moving through dense forest, she preferred to travel during winter, when nights were longer. Harriet would mimic an owl to warn freedom-seekers of danger or to let them know when it was safe to begin moving again. She knew the local plant life so well that she was able to tend to wounds and soothe babies using salves and potions made from wild plants, and to heal infections by using resin from sweetgum trees. She knew how to cross rivers to avoid being tracked by violent slave catchers. She knew how to wrap wounds in cobwebs and make slingshots out of oyster shells. She also knew how to wield a pistol, and she famously proclaimed that, despite the many perils involved in her journeys, she never lost a single passenger.

At first, she took her charges from Maryland to Philadelphia, following the same 120-mile path she had used to gain her own freedom. But in 1850, the passage of the Fugitive Slave Act made it legal for slave owners to travel into northern states and attempt to recapture their so-called property. For a time, Harriet moved to Canada, where slavery had been abolished in 1834. From there, she continued to return to Maryland to bravely lead others out of slavery. Her route to Canada was over 600 miles!

During the Civil War, Harriet put her woodsmanship skills to use as a scout and spy for the Union Army. Sneaking behind enemy lines to gather information, she used the intelligence she collected to free hundreds of enslaved men, women, and children. Resourceful, determined, and brave, she spent her life standing up for the right of human beings to be free. Harriet's skills as an explorer, naturalist, and freedom-bringer made her a hero to those enslaved, and a menace to those who would keep human beings bound as property.

WALK IN A STRAIGHT LINE THROUGH THE WOODS

You probably think walking in a straight line from one place to another isn't all that difficult, and most of the time it's not. After all, the hallways in your house and school are straight. The same goes for grocery store aisles and sidewalks. All those straight lines make getting around easier and faster in buildings, neighborhoods, and cities.

But the natural world doesn't work that way. It's full of twists, turns, and obstacles. Even most hiking trails don't go in a straight line for very long, because they have to follow the contours of mountains, go around lakeshores, or follow the meandering paths of creeks and rivers. In dense vegetation or environments without much topographical differentiation, navigation becomes even more difficult. In fact, scientific studies have shown that in places like thick forests, where the tree canopy blocks the view of the sky, and deserts, where everything looks the same, people without a compass or map to guide them often walk around in circles, even though they think they're traveling in a straight line. And when people are blindfolded and asked to walk in a straight line, they begin walking in circles almost immediately. (Try this with your friends in the backyard!)

Rather than walking around in circles and getting lost, there are ways to make sure you're walking in a straight line through woods or across a desert. Native Americans traveling across the wide-open grasslands of the Texas Panhandle used a navigational strategy that involved shooting arrows. In the morning, they'd get oriented according to the rising sun (remember, it rises in the east) and then shoot an arrow in the direction they wanted to travel. They'd then walk in a straight line to the arrow. Once they got there, they'd shoot it again. They could travel in a straight line for many miles, over the course of several days, using this technique. The following strategy is similar, but it takes advantage of features such as rocks, trees, and bushes that are already in place on the landscape.

- First, determine your intended line of travel.
- Find a natural landmark like a rock, stump, tree, or bush that lines up with the direction you want to travel. Start out with something that is fairly close to you.

- Next, find a second, more distant landmark that directly lines up with the first.
- Now walk to the first landmark and find a landmark that is directly in line with the second. Hopefully it will be a landmark that you couldn't see from the place where you started walking.
- Continue repeating this process to walk in a straight line.
- Once you feel like you've got the hang of it, try turning around and using the same technique to try to get back to the exact spot where you started.

WHAT TO DO IF YOU GET LOST IN THE WOODS

First off, never go out into the woods without telling your parents or another adult where you're going. Even if you're heading out with a friend, you should never break this rule! It applies to outdoorsmen and -women of any age, and there are lots of good reasons for it. If you twist your ankle while you're on the soccer field, your coach and any number of spectators would be able to help out. If the same thing happened in a remote spot, that would be a bigger problem, especially if nobody back home had any idea of your whereabouts. Same goes for getting lost—it's a lot easier to get found if the folks looking for you have a sense of where you were heading.

If you ever do find yourself lost in the woods, the number one rule is *don't panic!* You'll think more clearly if you stay calm. Remember the acronym STOP. This means stop, think, observe, and plan. If you have a phone with you, call your parents or 911. Even if you don't have service and can't make a call, leave your phone on low power mode (you can find it in your settings, under "battery"). Rescuers will still be able to find you by tracking your phone. Next, take a deep breath and don't move until you've had some time to calm down and think. If you need to, you can sing a favorite song or think about something you love to do for a few minutes. Don't get scared about bears, snakes, or other animals. They almost never hurt people. The same goes for getting in trouble. Don't worry about your parents getting mad at you for not being home on time. Instead, look at your surroundings and see if you recognize where you are or which direction you need to go to get back to safety.

Stay put if you still feel lost. Wandering around aimlessly will only make things worse. This is especially true if it's dark or about to get dark. Remember, there's nothing to fear about the dark.

Try shouting to see if anyone answers. If they do, shout back as loud as you can! It's also a good idea to carry a whistle in your backpack to make loud noises. Listen for people talking, dogs barking, or cars. Those noises could lead you toward safety.

If you still don't know how to get back to where you came from, or to a campground or other safe place where you might find help, you should wait for help to arrive. It's much easier for search parties to find you if you're not moving around. Look for a place where you can hunker down to stay warm and dry. Get under a big tree and put on all your extra clothes if it's cold. Cover yourself with the emergency space blanket from your exploration kit. It'll keep you warm, and its reflective material will make it easier for rescuers to spot you. While you're waiting, eat a snack and drink some water if you have them in your pack.

If it's dark and you have a flashlight or headlamp in your exploration kit, use it sparingly to save battery life, but keep it on if you hear or see rescuers looking for you. You might be scared, but don't run or hide if you see people. Shout and wave your arms! They're there to help you.

Remember that people who get lost and stay in one place are usually rescued in less than one day, and often within a few hours. You'll be found if you stay calm and wait for help.

MAKE A WALKING STICK

A few million years ago, our ancient ancestors began using sturdy sticks as digging tools, levers, and weapons. The same stick may have been used to dig tasty roots, to flip a rock in search of grubs and worms, or to stun a young porcupine by whapping it hard across the back of the skull. Certainly, these same tools were used as walking sticks for hunters and gatherers who traveled long distances in search of food and shelter. At some point, our ancestors started adding strips of animal hide to create comfortable handles on their sticks. And they began adorning their walking sticks with items like feathers, beads, and animal carvings. As time passed, walking sticks evolved into shepherd's crooks, canes, ornamental staffs for religious ceremonies, and tools like rakes and shovels. It's even fair to say that inventions ranging from canoe paddles to ski poles have a direct connection to those ancient walking sticks.

We've got many more tools and gadgets for collecting food nowadays, but a simple walking stick is a great thing to have on a hike. They provide support when you're walking long distances through rocky terrain, balance when wading across streams filled with slippery rocks, and a little extra lift from your arms when trudging up steep hills and mountains.

You can use any old ski pole for a walking stick, although today many serious hikers and mountain climbers use special collapsible trekking poles that can fold up and fit inside your backpack when you don't need them. But it's a lot more fun to make your own walking stick, just like our ancestors did. A good handmade wooden walking stick is light, strong, beautiful, and unique.

Choosing the Right Stick

The first thing you'll have to do is go locate the right material. Not just any stick will do. To make a sturdy, long-lasting walking stick, you'll need wood that is dense, hard, and strong. The best wood for your walking stick will come from hardwood trees like ironwood, beech, ash, maple, hickory, and oak trees. If possible, avoid species like willow, aspen, and cottonwood, which are soft and bendy. Some types of conifers, like Douglas fir, are pretty good choices for walking sticks, while others, like spruce trees, are weak and brittle. If you have a smartphone on you, you can use an app like iNaturalist or PlantSnap for tree identification; you can also check out a tree species field guide from your local library, or just download a few pages' worth of information from the internet and pack it along with you.

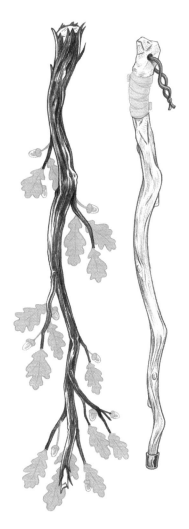

Next, you'll need to decide if you want to start with live wood that is still green, or else dead wood that is already dried out. If you're using a green stick, you'll need to let it dry in the sun or indoors until it's no longer heavy and springy. "Curing" green wood in such a way can take several weeks. It's worth the wait, as a properly cured piece of wood will make a strong walking stick that could last many years. But if you need something right away and can't wait, you might find a good piece of dead wood that's already lying out in the woods. Make sure it is strong and light, without any rotten sections or cracks. Test it for strength. If you can break it easily, it won't make a good walking stick.

The ideal walking stick is one that has a diameter of about 1½ inches, but choose a size that comfortably fits your grip. Don't worry too much if one end is a little thicker than the other—the thicker end will be your handle. The perfect length should measure from the ground to right between your elbow and your shoulder, but some people like them a little longer. Of course, you want a fairly straight stick, although it's okay if yours has some interesting bumps and knobs and isn't perfectly straight. That's what makes every handmade walking stick unique. And don't worry about any small branches, as these can be sawed away. Just make sure to pick a stick you like! While you might get lucky and find the perfect stick lying on the ground, you'll most likely need to cut down a small sapling (a young tree) or remove a branch from a tree. Once you've got your raw material, you're ready to start working.

What You'll Need

- Stick
- Handsaw
- Pocketknife
- Sandpaper (40 grit and 120 grit)
- Minwax Helmsman Spar Urethane or other oil-based polyurethane varnish
- Handle: 550 paracord (optional, for bonus steps)
- Base: 1-inch length of copper pipe, two-part epoxy glue, and Popsicle stick or Q-tips (optional, for bonus steps)

Building Steps

1. Use a handsaw to cut your stick to your desired length. A longer walking stick will accommodate your upcoming growth spurts.

2. Remove all the bark with your pocketknife. This is an important step because any moisture trapped under the bark could cause your stick to rot and weaken. Be careful carving the bark away, especially around knots and bumps on the stick where your blade might slip, and always carve away from your body. Get help from your parents if necessary.

3. If you are using green wood, cure your walking stick by drying it out indoors for at least several weeks. Skip this step if you are using strong, dry dead wood.

4. Sand your walking stick. Start with the coarse 40-grit sandpaper to remove any remaining chunks of bark or other rough spots. Use the finer 120-grit sandpaper to make your stick completely smooth and comfortable to handle.

5. Seal and protect your walking stick from moisture. Clear varnish retains the beauty of the wood's natural color. You can buy varnish that you spray on, or you can get the kind that is applied with a brush. Either way, use protective gloves and do this job outside. Following the directions on the container of varnish, apply one coat and allow it to fully dry before applying a second coat. This will add many years to the life of your walking stick.

6. Go out on a hike and test your new walking stick!

Make a Lanyard for the Handle

This step and the bonus steps that follow aren't necessary, but if you're inspired to go the extra mile, read on for ways to make your walking stick unique.

1. Carefully use a power drill to make a small hole through the end of the handle, then thread a length of paracord through the hole. You'll need a partner or parent to hold the walking stick while you're drilling the hole.
2. Tie the two ends of the paracord together to make a safety loop called a lanyard. Use a lighter or match to melt the ends of the paracord so it doesn't fray and unwind. Don't touch the paracord until it has cooled off.

Make a Sturdy Base

1. Go to a hardware or home and garden store and ask them to cut you a 1-inch length of copper pipe with a slightly smaller diameter than the bottom of your walking stick. (If your stick has a 1½-inch diameter, use 1¼-inch pipe.)
2. Whittle the end of your walking stick down a bit narrower until you can just barely get the piece of pipe fitted onto the bottom end, then use a hammer to gently tap it all the way onto the stick. Mix the two-part epoxy, then use a Popsicle stick or Q-tip to fill in any gaps between the copper pipe and the base of the walking stick with the epoxy. Allow it to dry and harden. The metal base will make the bottom of your walking stick more durable and protect it from cracking.

Decorate Your Walking Stick

- Use wraps of paracord or strips of leather for an even better grip.
- Try carving decorations into your finished walking stick. Add your initials, carvings of birds or other animals, or any other designs you like. Use a Sharpie to draw your decoration on your walking stick first, then use your pocketknife to start slowly and carefully carving out your design.
- Use glue, paracord, or sturdy string to attach colorful beads, yarn, ribbons, or items like feathers, animal bones, or seashells that catch your interest while you're out hiking around.

BECOME A BIKE MECHANIC

The area in which animals move around on a daily basis searching for shelter, food, water, or mates is called their home range. A chipmunk has a tiny home range not much bigger than the size of the average backyard. (You might even have a couple of chipmunks living in yours.) On the flip side, wolverines are constantly on the move, traveling as much as 20 miles a day through a huge home range consisting of hundreds of square miles of rugged wilderness.

You might be wondering what all this has to do with learning how to fix your bike. Well, you've got a home range, too. And a bicycle is a perfect tool for expanding and exploring it. On two wheels, you can cover a lot of ground much faster and more effi-

ciently than you can by walking. However, that's only true if you can rely on your bike to get you where you want to go.

The two things that are most likely to take your bike out of commission are a flat tire and the chain falling off the sprocket. If you know how to take care of these problems, you and your bike will be back in action in a few minutes.

Fix a Loose Bike Chain

Your bike chain wraps around the big front sprocket near the pedals and a small back sprocket, or gear, on the axle of the back tire. When you pedal, your feet are spinning the front sprocket. This moves the chain, which spins the back axle and powers the bike forward. Sometimes, though, your chain will become loose or get jammed and will fall off one or both of the sprockets, leaving you with a bike that won't go anywhere. Luckily, it's usually pretty easy to fix a loose chain, and most of the time you can get it back on the sprocket without any tools. Here's how.

1. Flip your bike over so it's standing upside down, on the handlebars and seat.
2. Unwind any kinks in the chain. If your bike has a chain guard, work from the side where you can reach the chain.
3. Loop the chain back around the rear sprocket.
4. Lay the chain over the top of the front sprocket so that the teeth on the sprocket engage with the holes in the chain. You probably won't be able to get it all the way back on yet, but don't worry about that.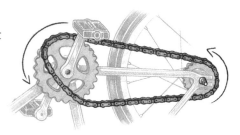
5. Slowly push a pedal forward to spin the front sprocket, and the chain should completely reattach itself as you move the pedals.

If your bike chain falls off a lot, it's probably loose, and you will need to move the rear wheel a little further back to take up the slack. Most bikes have a quick-release tab on the axle for removing and attaching the wheels, but for others you'll need a socket wrench to get the wheel off. Have a bike shop technician or your parents show you how the first time and you'll be able to do it yourself if it happens again.

Fix a Flat Tire

You are bound to have a flat tire sooner or later. Sometimes all you need to do is pump it back up and you're good to go. But if the tire doesn't hold air, you've got a hole in your inner tube. Fixing a flat is more complicated than tightening a loose chain, so you'll want to work in your driveway or garage with some help the first couple of times it happens. With a little experience, you'll be able to make tire repairs on the go, as long as you're carrying the necessary supplies. All this stuff will fit easily in your backpack, or you can get a small inexpensive pack called a saddlebag that attaches to your bike seat or frame.

Tools

- Patch kit, for repairing small holes in an inner tube
- Extra inner tube, in case the hole is too big to patch
- Tire lever, for popping the tire off the rim
- Mini-pump, for refilling your tires with air

Repair Steps

In order to fix or replace a punctured inner tube, you'll need to be able to take the flat tire off and put it back on. Quick-release axles make this simple and fast, but if your bike doesn't have them, you'll need a wrench. If your bike has hand brakes, you'll also need to squeeze the brakes and release the brake cable to get the tire off. To remove the rear tire, you must first remove the chain from the sprocket. Here's what to do next.

1. Use the tire lever to pry the tire off the rim so you can get to the inner tube.
2. Pull the inner tube out of the tire and closely inspect it for damage. Even tiny pinpricks can cause a flat.

3. If the hole is small, use your patch kit to fix it. If you can't find the hole or it's too big to repair, you'll need to use your replacement inner tube.

4. Pump a little air into the repaired or replaced tube and slide it back into the tire with the air valve facing out.

5. Push one of the tire beads, or edges, back onto the rim, and push the air valve on the inner tube through the valve hole in the rim.

6. Push the other tire bead onto the rim. Use the tire lever if necessary, but be careful not to pinch or damage the tube.

7. Put the tire back on the bike frame, and then reattach the chain and brake cable, if necessary.

8. Using your mini-pump, inflate the tire completely.

FOLLOW A GAME TRAIL

Most people walk at an average speed of about 3–4 miles per hour on flat ground. Of course, it's much slower if you're bushwhacking through an area of the woods where thick briar patches, steep embankments, and other natural barriers could slow you down or halt your progress altogether. Rather than giving up on your explorations, you can move through wild landscapes more efficiently by following the trails created by animals.

Compared to us humans, it seems that wild animals have only a few basic needs: food, water, shelter, and space to move around. These four basic things allow them to have the nutrition they need to stay healthy, be protected from bad weather and predators, hang

out with other members of their species, and find mates. The amount of space needed depends on the animal. Cottontail rabbits usually don't need to move very far to find these things. They can survive their entire lives in an area not much bigger than a football field. Other animals have to travel much farther. Some barren-ground caribou herds that live in Arctic tundra environments migrate more than 2,000 miles every year in search of the best food sources, safe places to rear their young, and areas where they can avoid deep snow. That's like walking from Washington, D.C., all the way to California! But no matter how far animals must travel to survive, what they all have in common is the ability to navigate across the landscape without using unnecessarily large amounts of energy.

Many animals move efficiently though their environment by making and using trails that follow the path of least resistance, or at least provide a way through, under, over, or around obstacles. We call these game trails, and following them can be a good way to get around in the woods when there isn't a hiking path. Animals usually cross streams at shallow points, for example, so following their trails is helpful when you need to get to the other side of a creek without getting too wet. If you're looking for a way to climb up or down a steep hill, work around a mucky swamp, or cut through thick, thorny brush, game trails are likely to show you the easiest route—after all, animals don't like struggling through difficult terrain much more than you do. Game trails are also great places to see wildlife. The game trails that are most common and big enough to accommodate a human are typically made by deer, simply because deer live in so many of the same places that we humans do. But in the right areas, game trails are just as likely to be used by elk, moose, bears, foxes, coyotes, raccoons, and even wild turkeys. All of these animals will readily use the same trails, though they'll exercise plenty of caution to avoid predators or humans that might be encountered along the way.

Fortunately, game trails are usually not too difficult to identify if you use a few tricks.

- Look for game trails where you'd expect to find them. This might sound obvious, but we don't always realize the power of trusting our own instincts! If you see a narrow gap through a patch of thick trees and think that animals could be drawn to that particular path, you might be right. In fact, animals probably made the gap, or at least widened it with their frequent passings. Once you start moving through these natural-seeming passageways, you might discover that you're on an animal path that will lead you through other obstacles that might not be so easy to figure out on your own.
- Look for animal tracks through the snow or mud and follow them. Even a single set of deer tracks through the snow in a field might eventually lead to more sets of deer tracks, which will eventually lead to well-worn trails used by many deer as they pass through difficult terrain.
- Look for game trails in the worst places. Animals are most likely to make trails in the places where trails would be most

helpful. There's little need for raccoons to follow a trail along the open shoreline of a lake, where they can pretty much walk wherever they want. But when that shoreline turns into a cattail marsh, the raccoons will follow narrow paths to allow them to get through quickly and easily.

- In dry, rocky areas, game trails can be harder to follow, but look for areas on the ground where the loose rocks have been pushed aside to expose a line of travel in the underlying dirt.
- If you lose a game trail that you're trying to follow, make sure to look out ahead of yourself as you try to get back on track. Staring straight down at the ground around your feet will cause you to miss important clues. Instead, you need to see the landscape from the perspective of an animal that's traveling through it. By looking ahead and choosing the path of least resistance, you're likely to end up right back on the game trail.

When you're following a game trail, make sure to ask yourself a few questions. What kinds of obstacles do the animals go straight through? What obstacles do they go around, and why? On steep hills, do game trails go straight up and down, or do they cut across the slope at easier angles? You can learn a lot about how to move more efficiently in the outdoors by considering how animals do it. But remember that sometimes game trails change directions for reasons known only to the animals that use them. In other cases, game trails will split up into smaller trails or else join a network of other large trails that go in all sorts of different directions. You might also come across a game trail only to find that it simply fades away altogether. These are the mysteries of game trails. The only way to solve the mysteries is to follow them.

CLIMB A TREE LIKE
A SQUIRREL

In the animal kingdom, tree climbing is a matter of survival for many species. Black bears are great tree climbers. When a mother black bear senses danger, her first instinct is to shoo her cubs up into a tree where they'll be safe. The bears will continue to climb trees for the rest of their lives. And in some regions, black bears prefer to den high off the ground in hollow trees rather than the caves and underground burrows where you'd expect to find them. African leopards will stash their kills high up in tree branches where aggressive lions and hyenas can't steal their food. Porcupines climb trees to feed on twigs, buds, and the nutritious inner layer of bark. But when it comes to climbing, tree squirrels have them all beat. That's because tree squirrels, which include pine squirrels, gray squirrels, and fox squirrels, are highly specialized climbers that spend most of their lives in trees, eating, sleeping, and avoiding predators. Their small, sharp claws provide a sure grip, and their long, bushy tails help them balance. They can scurry up a tree all the way to the tallest limb, jump several feet through the air to a neighboring tree, and even hang upside down by their back toes without falling.

There's little doubt that humans have always climbed trees as well. Around the world, hunters and gatherers have harvested bird eggs, insect larvae, wild honey, fruits, and many other edibles by climbing high above the ground into the branches of trees. Humans also climb trees in order to hide in waiting for prey species and to evade dangerous animals such as grizzly bears. And we climb trees just because it's fun! However, you should always take this activity seriously in order to avoid broken bones or other injuries. You're much heavier than a squirrel, so it takes much stronger tree limbs to support you. When you want to climb a tree, look for a healthy, mature live tree with plenty of sturdy branches at least as thick as your wrist. Avoid young saplings with thin, springy branches that won't support your weight. Also avoid trees with lots of dead branches, or trunks made of soft and rotten wood, or dead bark that is peeling away. These trees could be dead or dying. If you see any of these signs of weakness, look for another tree to climb.

There are dozens of species of trees that are good for climbing, and some that aren't. It's a big help if you are able to identify different species. Trees like poplars and willows have soft wood that bends easily, and species like spruce trees have weak, brittle wood. You'll be better off climbing trees with stronger wood that can support a lot of weight. Many of the most common types of hardwood deciduous trees (trees that shed their leaves in the fall), like maple, oak, sycamore, cherry, and apple, make great climbing trees, and they are found all over the country. Some coniferous trees (trees with needles), like Douglas fir and eastern white pine, are good for climbing, too.

TREE CLIMBING TIPS

If you're afraid of heights, tree climbing might seem a little scary. But with the right climbing techniques you'll be scrambling up, down, and around trees almost as well as a squirrel. As a bonus, climbing trees will make you physically tougher and mentally more in tune with your surroundings. You'll also develop better hand-eye coordination, flexibility, and physical strength. And high up in the branches, you'll get a bird's-eye view of the world below.

As you climb, keep these tips in mind:

- No matter the species, look for a tree with branches you can reach from the ground to start your climb. It might be tempting to use a ladder to reach the lowest branch, but save this move for when you have a lot of climbing experience and a grown-up to help you out.
- Look for sturdy branches that are evenly spaced all the way up the trunk, so that you can easily and safely move up and down, from one branch to the next.
- The crook of the branch (the spot where it joins the trunk) is where you'll find the best footrests and handholds.
- The higher or farther from the trunk you go, the thinner and weaker the branches will be. Stay near the trunk and only climb as high as you're comfortable with.
- Always maintain three points of contact. In order to greatly improve your balance and reduce the risk of slipping or falling, always have two hands and one foot (or two feet and one hand) in contact with the tree as you carefully climb.
- Don't let your guard down as you're descending. You can relax when you have two feet on the ground!

RIDE A WAVE LIKE A DOLPHIN

Did you know that dolphins love to surf the ocean's waves? The aquatic mammals are often seen riding the fast current generated by waves near the beach or even the waves created by big boats. And like us humans, they seem to be doing it just for the pure fun of it. Of course, dolphins live their whole lives in the water, and those flippers and powerful tails make them expert swimmers even in the biggest, roughest waves. Humans usually use surfboards or body boards to ride waves. But with a little practice, you can learn to position yourself in the water so that you can bodysurf like a dolphin. Once you get the hang of it, you'll understand why dolphins are such big fans of waves.

- Spot the right waves. For bodysurfing, look for waves about 2 or 3 feet tall. If they're much smaller, they won't have enough energy to carry you very far, and if they're a lot bigger, you'll have trouble controlling your ride. The right waves for bodysurfing should break (fall over and collapse in a spray of white-water) about 10 to 20 yards from shore. As you gain experience you'll get a feel for which waves are best for bodysurfing.

- Choose the right spot. When you're ready to give it a try, swim or wade out into the water to get in position. Look around at how the waves are behaving to get a sense of how far out you should go. You want to be waiting in a spot before the waves begin to rise to their crest at their tallest point. Turn to face shore, but watch behind you for the perfect wave to ride.
- Get into position. When the wave is swelling right behind you and about to crest, get into a swimming position and begin paddling with your arms and kicking hard with your legs.
- When the wave catches you and starts carrying you toward shore, you'll start picking up speed. Drop your head down, bring your arms forward, and give it one or two more strong kicks.
- Now bring your head and shoulders up, move your arms down to your sides, close to your body, and point your toes straight back. Your body is now your surfboard. Ride the wave to shore as far as you can!

Even if you're a good swimmer, you should go bodysurfing only when there's a grown-up paying close attention or else a nearby lifeguard on duty. Stay out of the water during storms and rough surf, and never go swimming when there are riptide or "rip current" warning signs on the beach. Riptides are strong currents that can pull you out away from the beach. Lastly, bodysurfing is fun only in places where the beach has a soft, sandy bottom—you don't want to get all banged up and scratched on rocks or coral!

PADDLE A CANOE

Paddling a canoe is a quiet, peaceful way to travel by water, providing access to hidden swimming holes, fishing spots, and campsites that you can't reach on foot. The oldest boat ever found was a wooden canoe believed to be around 10,000 years old. It was discovered in the Netherlands in 1955. More recently, in June 2021, an archaeologist spotted a sunken canoe resting on the bottom of Lake Mendota in Wisconsin. Later that year, researchers were able to extract the boat from the water. At first, they thought that the canoe might have been built by Boy Scouts in the 1950s, but a scientific process called carbon dating proved it was actually a dugout canoe made about 1,200 years ago by the Native Americans who lived in the area. In 2022, the same archaeologist discovered another dugout canoe in the same lake. This boat was 3,000 years old and is likely the oldest boat ever recovered in the Great Lakes region.

Dugout canoes are made by carving a large log into a long, narrow boat. This ancient design is still used in some parts of the world today. However, dugouts take a long time to build and are extremely heavy. Many Native American tribes developed other types of canoes that overcame these disadvantages by using lightweight materials like animal hides and birch bark. After Europeans reached North America, frontiersmen and fur trappers used these types of canoes to explore the New World.

Today, most canoes are made from lightweight aluminum or plastic composites. Modern canoes can be anywhere from 10 to over 20 feet long, and can hold from one to four or more people. The most popular length for recreational use is about 16 feet, which is the ideal size for a couple of paddlers hauling some camping or fishing gear.

If you know what you're doing, paddling a canoe is a fun and efficient way to travel across water. Experienced paddlers can cover many miles of water in a single day. But if you're new to canoeing, it'll take some time to learn how to steer and navigate safely. The best places to begin are ponds, small lakes, and shallow, slow-moving rivers.

Paddling Tips and Tricks

Before you begin, it's important to know that canoes will likely feel unstable or tippy to beginner paddlers. The number one rule of canoeing is to always wear a life jacket. Not only will it help keep you safe, it'll make the experience less scary since you know you'll stay afloat if something goes wrong and you flip over. Stay away from waters where you may encounter swift currents or large waves, and keep an eye out for hazards like submerged rocks and logs.

Never stand while paddling. Sit, or kneel, with your body centered in the canoe.

When paddling with a partner, known as tandem paddling, pay attention to who sits where. The canoe will float and steer better if the heavier paddler sits in the back, or stern, of the canoe with the lighter person at the front, or bow. Tandem paddlers must work as a team. The person in the front is mostly responsible for keeping the boat moving forward, while the person in the back is mostly responsible for steering. Solo paddlers must do both jobs.

There are many different motions, or strokes, you can make with your paddle to propel and steer the boat. Luckily, you only need to know a couple of basic strokes to get started.

The forward stroke is the most basic canoe stroke. It is used by the paddler in the front to move the boat forward. If you're right-handed, you'll probably find it easier to paddle on the right side of the canoe, but you can switch to the left side if your arms get tired after a while. Here's how to do it.

- To paddle on the right side, hold the grip end of the paddle handle with your left hand.
- With your right hand, hold the shaft just above the paddle blade. Your left hand should be at or above eye level with the paddle held in a vertical position over the water.
- Turn your torso slightly to the right, reach forward a little with your left hand, and lower the paddle blade into the water.
- Paddle by pushing with your left hand and pulling with your right hand.
- As you paddle, rotate your right shoulder from front to back so you're using the muscles in your torso along with your arms.

- At the very end of your paddling stroke, rotate the blade 90 degrees, or about a quarter turn, toward you before you lift the paddle out of the water.
- Reach forward with the paddle, and repeat the forward stroke.
- Reverse your hand positions for paddling on the left side of the canoe.

To steer a canoe, there are a few strokes that can be used.

- The draw stroke turns the canoe by reaching out in the direction you want to turn with the paddle and pulling, or drawing, the boat toward the paddle.
- At the very end of the basic forward stroke, make a pry stroke by resting the paddle under the water against the back of the canoe. Pull the paddle grip inward toward your chest. Push, or pry, the blade outward away from the canoe to make a turn.
- The J stroke is a variation of the pry stroke used on both sides of the canoe by the rear paddler to make minor adjustments to the direction of travel. The path of the paddle through the water resembles the letter *J*.

Remember that sometimes you'll need to switch your paddle from one side of the boat to the other to execute a turn. Learning how to steer a canoe takes some practice, so don't get frustrated if it takes a while to get the hang of it. As you're learning, avoid banging your paddle on the side, or gunwale, of the canoe. This makes a lot of noise that will scare away wildlife as you move along the water. Learn to canoe quietly, and you'll be amazed at how many birds and animals you can see as you creep along as quietly as a water snake.

MAKE A BATHYSCOPE

Almost three-fourths of the earth is covered by water. While much of that water is thousands of feet deep, there are still millions of shallow-water ecosystems—ponds, creeks, lagoons, sloughs, marshes, rivers, and more—that are just waiting to be explored. No matter where you live, you may be just a short walk away from an aquatic environment that is teeming with hidden life-forms such as fish, molluscs, crustaceans, and insect larvae, plus amphibians and reptiles like frogs and turtles that spend most of their lives in the water.

Organisms that live underwater are a lot different from the kinds you can find on land. Some have feet and long tails like a lizard but breathe through gills just like a fish. Others are ferocious predators that can attack and kill prey two or three times their own weight. Still others will live for a year or more underwater, breaking free of the water's surface and flying high into the sky for the second part of their lives. Observing these underwater mysteries might seem impossible unless you're a scuba diver, but there's actually a much easier way to accomplish that all on your own. The trick is to overcome the glare that happens when sunlight is reflected off the surface of water. Fishermen do this, at least a little bit, by wearing special sunglasses with polarized lenses that help block the glare. With these, you can better see fish, along with rocks, weed beds, and other pieces of habitat where fish like to hide. But an even better way to see underwater is to build a bathyscope. Think of this as having your own private glass-bottomed boat, but one that's small enough to carry around on your bike. Also known as aquascopes or underwater viewers, bathyscopes are easy to make yourself with just a few materials and tools you probably already have at home. With a little work, you'll get a crystal-clear view of aquatic environments.

What You'll Need

- Cylindrical container (a 1-quart yogurt tub or any other large cylindrical plastic container with a snap-on lid)
- Duct tape
- Heavy-duty plastic wrap (you can also use a piece of a large ziplock bag)
- Heavy-duty rubber band
- Utility knife, pocketknife, or multi-tool
- Scissors

Building Steps

1. First, make sure your container is clean and dry.
2. Remove the round bottom part of the container. To get started, use your knife blade to poke a hole through the side of the container, just above the bottom. Use this hole to start cut-

ting your way around the container with your scissors. Cut all the way around, so that you remove the bottom part of the container.

3. Use your knife and scissors to remove a circular cutout from the lid of the container. Leave just enough of the rim that you can still snap the lid back onto the container.

4. With the lid off, place the clear plastic wrap over the top of the container. Make sure you use more than enough to cover the opening, with plenty of extra material hanging over the edges.

5. Secure the plastic wrap with the rubber band, so that the plastic wrap is tight like a drum's covering. Snap the container's lid back on, over the plastic wrap.

6. Finally, wrap duct tape around the edges of the plastic wrap for an extra layer of waterproofing. Now you're ready to use your bathyscope.

How to Use a Bathyscope

Use your bathyscope wherever you can find shallow water. Tidal pools, golf course ponds, public beaches, and drainage ditches can all be great locations. Places that are around knee-deep are best, especially if the water is nice and clear. (Muddy water can be more frustrating, because you might only be able to see a couple of inches.) You can use your bathyscope by walking along the shore and peering into cool-looking places, but it's better if you can wade into the water and explore hard-to-reach spots. But stay away from deep water and fast currents, unless you're with a grown-up who's a strong swimmer.

CATCH A CRAYFISH, COUNT THE STARS

The secret to discovering the best stuff is to be super-stealthy. Pretend you're a blue heron quietly hunting its way through shallow water in search of prey. Move slowly, without making a bunch of waves. And be careful not to stir up mud on the bottom, which will reduce your underwater visibility. When you get to an area that you want to explore, push the end that is covered in plastic wrap into the water. Then put your eyes close to the open end and use the bathyscope like a telescope. If you're quiet and patient, you'll start to see movement along the bottom. In weedy freshwater ponds you might see insect larvae and tadpoles. In cold, clear streams you might see small trout or suckers hiding behind rocks. In a saltwater tidepool you might watch a hermit crab as it tries to break into a clam's shell in order to eat it. Pretty soon you'll get good at identifying the best places to see some good underwater action. You'll discover a whole new world that you never knew existed.

PLAN A HIKE

Research has proven that hiking leads to improved strength and endurance, reduces stress, and helps your memory and other brain functions. If you think hiking is something only grown-ups like to do, try planning a hike with some friends to see if that makes it more fun. You'll get to use your map-reading skills, test out the orienteering techniques on pages 22 and 35, and enjoy the feeling of charting your own path in the great outdoors.

Try attaching a goal or purpose to your hike, like hiking to a swimming hole on a hot summer day. Plan hiking routes on trails where there's something cool to see along the way. Some trails pass by unique rock formations, historic landmarks, or overlooks with picture-worthy views. You can also plan a hike to coincide with events that only happen during certain times of the year, like when wild raspberries ripen during late summer or when the leaves are changing colors in the fall. Try planning your hikes based on personal interests, too. If you love fishing, hiking along a creek can be a lot of fun. As you're walking, you can look for good fishing holes and stop to make a cast now and then. If you've always wanted to see a big waterfall or look inside a cave, a hike might be the perfect opportunity to check that off your adventure to-do list.

It's a great idea to kick off the planning process by chatting with your parents or an older sibling to make a plan. Get a trail map for the area near where you live, or where you'll be going on a camping trip or vacation. Trail maps can be purchased at sporting goods and outdoors stores like REI and Sportsman's Warehouse; the Trails Illustrated series of maps from National Geographic covers hiking trails throughout the entire United States. And if you happen to be visiting a state park or national park, you'll find free trail maps at the park headquarters.

You can also do some research online by typing "hiking trails near me" into your search bar. Your results should bring up a list of hikes with trail descriptions that include the distance and difficulty level as well as interesting sights and landmarks along the way. If you have a smartphone, download a hiking app such as onX, All-Trails, or Hiking Project. These apps allow you to search for trails and download maps onto your phone ahead of time, so you don't need a cellphone signal to use them out in the wilderness. You can also use them to plot distance and estimated hiking times for specific trails.

Once you have your maps, you can start to get serious about planning. You don't want to bite off more than you can chew, so limit your excursions to no more than a couple of miles at first. You don't want to come home cranky and exhausted after your first adventure. Better to build up endurance over time than be overly ambitious as a beginning or intermediate hiker.

When it comes to actually getting out on the trail, make sure you pack plenty of water and snacks so that you don't get thirsty or run out of energy. Wearing the right clothing and footwear is important, too. Check the weather forecast in the days and hours leading up to your hike, and prepare accordingly. Pack your rain jacket, a warm hoodie, or a brimmed hat and sunscreen. Whatever you do, leave your flip-flops and Crocs at home if you're going on a long hike. Instead, wear a pair of comfy socks and running shoes or hiking boots with good traction so you don't cut your feet or get a blister.

READING TRAIL MAPS

Whether you're using a mobile app, a traditional paper map, or both, there's a lot more that you can learn from a trail map than just the location of a path. You can study your map to find interesting sights and features that you might pass near along your hike. For instance, if you want to explore a creek or river, look for the blue lines on your map that mark the locations of moving water. Lakes and ponds will show up as blue spots on the map. You'll probably also notice little symbols on the map called icons. These icons identify the location of everything from picnic areas, campsites, marshes, and scenic overlooks to caves, waterfalls, and fishing spots. If you're unsure about what an icon means, look for a key, usually near the bottom of the map, that explains the meaning of the symbols. Hiking apps often allow you to add your own custom icons, pins, and waypoints so that you'll remember the locations of interesting things you passed along the way.

Of course, you can only learn so much by studying a trail map. They are great tools, but they can't predict when or where you'll find a loaded raspberry patch, an osprey's nest, or the perfect climbing tree. You have to get out there yourself and do some exploring to make those special kinds of discoveries.

SLEEP UNDER THE STARS

Sleeping under the stars with the sounds of nature all around can make you feel alive and strong. Many of us know that playing outdoors is good for your mind and body, but there are special benefits to sleeping outside that might surprise you. Sleeping outdoors can help strengthen your immune system, and it improves cognitive and physical development, which is a fancy way of saying it will make you healthier and smarter. And then there's the fact that no one can deny: Sleeping outside is just plain fun!

Most people think about camping when they think about sleeping outside, and if you've never camped, you might want to do some research to find a nearby campground where your family can go for the weekend. But you don't need to make a special trip to sleep outside. You can turn your own backyard, or that of a friend or relative, into a campsite that's right outside your house. You could even make a real adventure out of going into some nearby woods to sleep in a primitive shelter (see the building instructions that start on page 77) with a friend, sibling, or parent. At first it might seem intimidating, but as long as you have the right stuff with you, you might like sleeping under the stars more than in your own bedroom. Here's what you'll need for a backyard campout:

- **Tent.** A tent will keep you dry if it rains overnight, and it's fun to have your own private space to set up your bed. If you don't have a tent, you can sleep under an awning or porch roof if you've got one. Or, if the weather forecast is dry and warm, you can skip the tent and sleep right under the night sky (you can run inside if an unexpected rainstorm moves in).

- **Sleeping bag.** Make sure your sleeping bag is warm enough to keep you cozy at night when the temperatures drop.

- **Sleeping pad.** You'll need some kind of sleeping pad to use as a comfortable mini-mattress that will insulate you from the cold ground. Inflatable sleeping pads work well, or you can use a foam pad or an extra sleeping bag.

- **Pillow.** Sleeping without a pillow is a recipe for an achy neck in the morning. Use the pillow from your bedroom, an old couch pillow, a wadded-up puffy jacket, or an inflatable camp pillow.

- **Flashlight or headlamp.** Make sure to bring a light source with you so you can read a book, play a game, or investigate any weird sounds you hear at night.

- **Extras.** Binoculars or a telescope for identifying constellations, your dog for a sleeping buddy, a beanie to keep your head warm, snacks, a water bottle, and whatever else you think will make sleeping outside more fun.

CONSERVATIONIST IN CHIEF

Though he was born to one of New York City's wealthiest families and educated by private tutors, Theodore Roosevelt (1858–1919) suffered from a number of health challenges starting from early childhood. He had poor eyesight and severe asthma, along with other ailments. At the urging of his doctors, Roosevelt sought out fresh air to alleviate his difficulty breathing, and he came to see the outdoors as having a powerful healing effect. Bird-watching became a beloved pastime, with the sight of a rare species always causing him delight. He scoured the streets of Manhattan for signs of the natural world, from mice skittering in dark alleyways to the strange marine creatures on display at the local fish market. These and other sights would be carefully noted and sketched in his journals. Even after he was elevated to the office of president of the United States, Roosevelt retained a childlike enthusiasm at the sight of birds and other wildlife.

As a young man, Roosevelt developed a taste for adventure.

He became an avid hunter and traveled to remote, wild places to test his skills, adopting a philosophy that he would come to call the "strenuous life." Roosevelt became a tireless champion of an active, outdoor lifestyle, and he embraced a variety of physical pursuits, from weight-lifting and boxing to horseback riding and hiking.

As he was beginning a career in politics, tragedy struck with the death of his wife during childbirth and the loss of his mother, just a few hours apart. To distance himself from those painful memories, T.R. headed west in 1884. He took up ranching in the badlands of the Dakota Territory, raising cattle and pursuing adventure as a hunter. Although his neighbors initially scoffed at the idea of a well-to-do gentleman from New York starting a new life along the frontier, Roosevelt soon earned their respect. The years he spent in the West reignited his confidence and inspired in him great concern for the changes he saw firsthand. Railroads now crisscrossed the continent, a rapidly growing nation was gobbling up natural resources, and many wildlife species were in decline.

Returning to the East, Roosevelt once again pursued public service. While serving as vice president, he would unexpectedly assume the highest office in the land when President William McKinley was assassinated in 1901. Through this twist of fate, Roosevelt was able to bring his passion for conservation to the White House.

As president, he used the authority of his office to undertake an unprecedented campaign to protect the natural world. Roosevelt established the U.S. Forest Service and set aside more than 150 million acres as national forests. He created what would become the first national wildlife refuge at Pelican Island in Florida, and went on to designate another fifty-one such reserves during his term of office. Working with Congress, he expanded what would eventually become the National Park System and protected millions of acres of lands. While in office, he traveled across the country to view the United States' most impressive landscapes and bring attention to the cause of conservation.

Although his legacy is celebrated widely today, at the time Roosevelt's ambitious efforts to safeguard wild places earned him the resentment of some very powerful people. Some were against any restriction on their ability to profit from natural resources like timber, coal, and iron. Others believed that he had overstepped the powers of his office. But Roosevelt never wavered, and he always remained certain of the righteousness of his cause.

Near the end of Roosevelt's second term, his opponents in Congress passed a bill that would eventually prevent him from creating new forest reserves in Colorado, Idaho, Montana, Oregon, Washington, and Wyoming. Knowing he could not veto the legislation and that the Constitution only allowed ten days before he needed to sign it into law, Roosevelt asked his close ally and head of the U.S. Forest Service, Gifford Pinchot, to identify landscapes that he could conserve with his limited amount of time to do so. After working around the clock for those ten days, he proclaimed twenty-one new forest reserves and added land to eleven that already existed. In all, he protected more than 16 million new acres of American land just before signing the law stripping him of the power to ever do it again. The audacity of this last-minute announcement infuriated Roosevelt's opponents, but his gambit would stand the test of time. The areas Roosevelt protected became known as the "midnight forests," on account of the late nights worked by the president and his staff to accomplish their goals.

Throughout his life, Roosevelt spoke frequently of the need to use resources wisely and in a way that would allow us to pass them on to the next generation. His own experiences in nature had inspired him to a cause greater than himself, and he used the power of his office to protect the country's greatest and wildest landscapes.

—By Randall Williams

BUILD A CAMPFIRE

If you needed to build a fire to stay warm or cook your food, could you do it? In our homes we have gas and electric stoves, furnaces, and hot water heaters, but it hasn't always been that way. In fact, for most of human history, wood fires were the primary heat source for most people around the world. Many paleoanthropologists (scientists who study fossils, bones, and artifacts left behind by ancient humans) believe that our ancestors began using fire close to 1 million years ago—although the very first humans to benefit from fire didn't know how to build one themselves. Perhaps by eating the remains of charred animals killed by wildfires or lightning strikes, our ancestors learned that cooked meat tasted better and was easier to digest than the raw meat they normally consumed.

They may have taken advantage of these natural fires by carrying away smoldering embers and then adding fuel like dry wood or animal dung to maintain campfires for cooking meat and staying warm. However, many thousands of years passed before humans truly learned how to make fires on their own. Some of the earliest methods involved wooden hand and bow drills that generate friction and heat to create a smoldering ember. Fire could also be made by striking pieces of flint rock or pyrite (fool's gold) to create blazing hot sparks. Starting fires using these primitive tools was very difficult and required a lot of skill, but these techniques gave our ancestors a reliable source of heat and a way to cook food. Human-made fires also provided a light source on dark nights, protection from predators, a visual signal to communicate with others, and a place to gather and share stories.

Today, we have waterproof matches and butane lighters to make things easier. But even with these conveniences, getting a fire started and keeping it going out in the woods can still be difficult. Fire needs three things to start and keep burning: fuel (for a campfire, that's your firewood), heat, and oxygen. Sounds simple. But if a strong wind blows out all your matches, the fire won't start. If your firewood is too wet, it won't burn. And even dry wood can put out a fire—if you add too much too fast, the fire's supply of oxygen will be cut off and it will "suffocate" and die. Even if all you want to do is make a safe campfire to roast some hot dogs and marshmallows in the backyard firepit with your family or friends, you'll need to master some skills.

Collect Your Materials

The first step in making a campfire is collecting all the materials you'll need. The building blocks of any fire are tinder, kindling, and fuel wood. Tinder is easily lit material like newspaper, but natural materials like birch bark, old bird's nests, dry grass, and clumps of sticky pine sap called pitch all can be used as tinder. Kindling is made up of small, dry sticks no thicker than your finger that will get your bigger pieces of fuel wood burning. Look for dry fuel wood that snaps, cracks, and breaks easily. If it's bendy or crumbles, it won't burn well. You'll need thicker sticks or small logs that are 1–4 inches in diameter and 1–2 feet long. A good rule of thumb is to collect way more wood than you think you'll need. You don't want to be rummaging around for more wood while your fire is dying out.

If you don't have a saw or hatchet to cut your firewood, you can break long pieces into smaller ones by wedging one end between a tree trunk and a sturdy branch and pushing or pulling on the other end until the stick breaks.

Prepare Your Firepit

Unless you're building a fire in a metal or cement firepit in the backyard or at a campsite, you'll have to pick and prepare a good spot. If you're camping, pick an area near, but not too close to, your tent or shelter. Never build a fire inside any kind of shelter! That's a serious fire hazard, along with the potential for smoke inhalation.

If it's cold, you can build your fire in front of a boulder or build up a big pile of rocks right next to your fire to create a heat reflector that will help keep you warm. Next, clear away anything on the ground that could burn easily, like dead leaves, grass, and small sticks, until you have just bare dirt or sand. You'll also want to get rid of any low-hanging branches or nearby brush. Now use a trowel or shovel (or a homemade digging tool) to dig a firepit that's a few feet wide and at least a few inches deep. Set a ring of rocks around the edge of your firepit, then pile the dirt from the pit nearby. The pit will help to contain your fire to a small area, but as long as the fire is burning, you'll need to pay attention. If your fire escapes the pit and starts spreading, you'll need to quickly extinguish it. Throwing or shoveling dirt or sand onto a fire will smother its supply of oxygen and put out its flames. If possible, it's a smart idea to have a bucket of water or a garden hose nearby. (Oftentimes, there are local regulations that restrict open campfires in order to prevent wildfires. Work with a grown-up to make sure your fire plan is safe and legal.)

Starting Your Fire

Now you're ready to start the fire. You can use matches or a disposable butane lighter to light your tinder, but remember that these items will not work if they get soaking wet. There are other fun, interesting, and unexpected ways to start a fire, and it's worth experimenting with them. On bright sunny days, a magnifying glass can concentrate sunlight into a narrow beam that's hot enough to start a fire if the beam is focused on your tinder. You can also use steel wool and a 9-volt battery to start a fire. When the battery terminals touch a clump of fine steel wool, the electrical current from the battery will cause the steel wool to glow orange and get hot enough to ignite your tinder. Pretty cool, right? And did you know even the salty snacks in your backpack can be used to get a fire started? The oil in Fritos, Doritos, and potato chips makes them flammable. They light easily and work great as tinder.

For a more practical tip that'll help you get your fire started efficiently, try making your own tinder with cotton balls rubbed with a coating of petroleum jelly such as Vaseline. You can store them in a plastic sandwich bag in your backpack until you need them. (One of those plastic chewing tobacco "tins" is the perfect container for your treated cotton balls; just make sure that you don't put any tobacco into your mouth and start a bad habit.)

How to Build a Teepee Fire

1. First, gather all of your fire-making materials and make three separate piles: tinder, kindling, and firewood.
2. Lay a bundle of tinder that's a little bigger than a baseball in the center of your firepit.
3. Next use your kindling to form a small teepee above the tinder ball. Use the smallest pieces of kindling you have, leaving a small opening in the teepee so that you can light the tinder.
4. Add another layer to the teepee, using bigger pieces of kindling (about as thick as a pencil). Don't cover up the opening.

5. Now, gently lay several of your smaller, thinner pieces of fuel wood (about 1 inch thick) over your kindling teepee.

6. Light the tinder ball. The flames from the tinder should ignite the kindling, which gets the fuel wood burning.

7. If your fire sputters and fails to ignite the fuel wood, you may need to keep adding pieces of kindling to keep it going until the fuel wood catches fire.

8. Once the teepee is lit and burning well, carefully add more small pieces of fuel wood until you have a rip-roaring campfire with glowing orange coals.

9. Now you can carefully add bigger, thicker pieces of firewood one at a time. Lay them gently over the fire. Don't worry if the teepee collapses, but be careful not to add too much wood, or you may smother the fire and have to start over.

10. Enjoy your campfire, and try roasting some hot dogs and marshmallows.

Safety warning: Campfires are a useful survival tool and a great way to enjoy being out in nature with friends and family, but if they're not carefully monitored and controlled, they can be dangerous and destructive. Every year in the United States, millions of acres of land are burned by wildfires, and many of these fires are started by careless human beings. Make campfires with adult supervision. Pay attention to outdoor fire bans and avoid making campfires during hot, dry, windy conditions when the flames can easily spread. Keep water, dirt, or sand nearby to put out fires quickly, and make sure fires are fully extinguished before you leave the area. And never, ever build a campfire inside a tent or homemade shelter.

BECOME THE CAMP COOK

In the early to mid-1800s, Americans numbering in the hundreds of thousands used the Oregon Trail to travel across the western half of the continent. They started in the state of Missouri. From there, the settlers traveled west over the Great Plains and Rocky Mountains along a route that snaked through present-day Kansas, Nebraska, Wyoming, Idaho, and Oregon. Most of them hoped to find good farmland at the end of their route. Others hoped to strike it rich with gold prospecting, hunting and trapping, or starting a business. Traveling the Oregon Trail could take as long as five or six months. All that while, the settlers had to prepare their meals while camping on the trail. They had to eat very simple foods that were lightweight and that wouldn't rot in the heat. (Remember, they didn't have refrigerators or ice.) This meant a diet that was mostly dried beans, flour, cornmeal, and beef and pork that was packed in barrels of salty water (called brine) in order to keep it from spoiling.

Nowadays, shopping and storage options like convenience stores and coolers help us enjoy much better food while we're camping. But many of the skills used by travelers on the Oregon Trail are still relevant for modern-day campers. For one thing, you have to make do without all of the luxuries of your home kitchen. That means being resourceful and figuring out how to accomplish tasks using unusual things. For instance, did you know that there's a common water plant called scouring rush? It gets its name because it's often used by wilderness travelers to scrub their dishes after meals. You also have to learn how to manage a campfire and use it for cooking. That wasn't easy in the days of the Oregon Trail, and it's not always easy now.

Maybe you've already done some outdoor cooking. One of the most popular camp meals is a hot dog that's been skewered on a stick and roasted over the fire. Just put it on a bun, add ketchup, and you're done. That's about as simple as it gets, but you can't eat hot dogs for every meal. There are some other pretty cool, fun cooking techniques you can use to keep everyone at camp happy and well-fed.

Foil Packs

Foil pack cooking is perfect for making breakfast, dinner, and even dessert when you're camping. You don't need a stove, pots, pans, or cooking utensils. And when you're done eating, there are no dirty plates or bowls to wash. Best of all, you can get pretty creative with the dishes you choose to make.

When cooking foil packets for a group, you should let everyone have their own packet. Just be sure to use plenty of heavy-duty aluminum foil for each serving. Pull a couple of feet of foil off the roll and then fold it over on top of itself so you have a double-layered square of foil that won't tear or puncture easily. Push the square down a little in the middle to make a container so the food won't spill out. Put the food in and then fold the edges of foil up and over the top of the food so you have a good tight seal. That's it. You've made a cooking pot and a serving bowl all in one. All you have to do now is let it cook near some hot campfire coals. When it's done, let it cool off, then eat it right out of the foil pack.

Just like hot dogs for dinner, instant oatmeal is the easiest camp breakfast you can make. But for something a little heartier, try making breakfast bowls by mixing frozen hash browns, a scrambled egg or two, and a couple of slices of bacon in a foil pack. You should have breakfast ready after about 15 minutes of cooking time.

A great foil pack dinner idea is cooking a trout and a loaded baked potato for each person at camp. And instead of classic s'mores for dessert, make campfire banana boats.

First, poke a few holes in a potato with a fork, sprinkle it with salt, and wrap it in foil. Put it on the coals to cook. While the potato is cooking, place a 10–12-inch gutted trout on a foil square. Sprinkle it with salt and pepper, top it with a couple of pats of butter and lemon wedges, and wrap it up in foil. Next, grab a banana and remove one section of the peel from the concave side. Make a slice down the length of the exposed part of the banana and set it on a foil square. Add your favorite dessert toppings and then wrap the foil around it. If you need some ideas for toppings, try any combination of strawberries, Nutella, honey, marshmallows, peanut butter, chocolate chips, caramel sauce, chopped nuts, or coconut.

The potato will take about 45 minutes to cook, so put the trout on the coals after about 30 minutes, so that they're both done about the same time. Let the potato cool for about 10 minutes, and then carefully open up the foil pack—it will be hot inside! Slice the potato open and top it with butter, cheddar cheese, sour cream, bacon bits, or whatever else you like, then cover it back up with the foil for a couple of minutes so the toppings melt. Open the fish and the loaded potato, grab a fork, and dig in! While you're eating your dinner, put the banana boat near the campfire coals. It should only take 10 minutes or so for your dessert to warm up and melt the toppings.

Keep in mind, you're not limited to cooking food in foil packs directly on campfire coals. You can also use a grill grate over a campfire or use a metal firepit or propane grill at home.

Pie Irons

Cooking with campfire pie irons is another fun way to make breakfast, dinner, and dessert. Pie irons are also called sandwich presses, and if you're not familiar with them, they look like two small square or round cast iron pans, one sitting on top of the other. These two pieces are joined together with a hinge, and there are two long handles that allow you to open and close the press. If you've ever used an electric waffle maker at home, pie irons work the same way. To use them you put food in the bottom piece of the container and close the top over it. Then lock the handles together, so the pie iron stays shut, and stick it into a campfire to cook whatever is inside.

The long handles allow you to handle the pie iron without burning yourself.

If you like grilled cheese sandwiches at home, you'll like them even more cooked at camp with a pie iron. Generously grease the inside of both pieces of the pie iron with butter and put a couple of slices of cheese (and some ham if you want) between two pieces of bread. Close the pie iron around the sandwich, close the latch on the handles, and shove it into the fire. Flip the pie iron over after 3 minutes and cook for another couple of minutes. That's fast food! Of course, you'll have to let the pie iron cool for a bit before you open it and pop the sandwich out.

You can use the same technique to make pizza pockets with bread, sauce, mozzarella cheese, and your favorite pizza toppings. The same goes for tacos and quesadillas. At lunchtime, a warm, gooey pie-iron peanut butter and jelly sandwich is the best you'll ever eat. Cheesy tater tots are pretty darn good, too. For breakfast, try making a toad-in-the-hole with a slice of bread and an egg, or even French toast. Just remember, no matter what you're making you have to grease the inside of the pie iron with butter or cooking oil so the food doesn't stick.

There are plenty of other simple ways to make satisfying camp meals, too. It doesn't take much effort to heat up a pot of premade soup or stew on a campfire grill grate. Pasta with spaghetti sauce is pretty easy, too. Or you can try making a Frito pie you can eat with a spoon. Cook some ground meat with taco seasoning and put it into a single-serving-sized bag of Fritos topped with cheese and salsa. Whatever you cook, you'll find there's something about sharing a meal with friends and family in the great outdoors that makes food taste better.

SIX KNOTS TO KNOW

The use of string and rope has been a crucial component of human civilization for a very long time. Some of the oldest examples found at archaeological sites were used to fasten stone blades to wooden handles, or to stitch together clothing made from animal skins. These earliest forms of cordage were made from plant fibers, animal hides, and even tendons removed from the legs and backs of large mammals. Some peoples would use the long hairs from a horsetail in order to braid the bridle necessary to ride the horse.

Today, most of our strongest ropes and cords are manufactured using man-made materials derived from petroleum. Everything from wispy fishing line to the strongest mountaineering rope is made from oil that's been pumped up from deep beneath the earth's surface. Regardless of what your rope or cord is made from, you'll need to know how to tie good knots in order to put it to use.

In the outdoors, that might mean anything from setting up a fishing rig to building a shelter to keeping your canoe from floating away. There are hundreds of different knots, and many of them are pretty hard to tie. But you really don't need more than five or six to get yourself through most any adventure. If you can tie your shoelaces, you'll be able to master these knots with just a little bit of work. Once you do learn them, make sure to practice now and then with a piece of paracord or an old shoelace so that you don't forget.

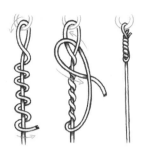

1. **Clinch knot.** This is the first knot that most fishermen learn. It is a strong and simple knot for tying hooks or lures to your fishing line.

2. **Blood knot.** A blood knot is used to splice two different pieces of fishing line together.

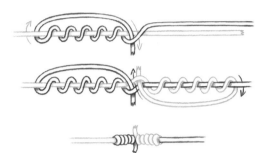

3. **Bowline.** Used for tying boats to docks, or in other situations when you need to create a secure loop that is easy and quick to get undone.

4. **Timber hitch.** A great way to tie a rock or log to a rope so that it can either be dragged or thrown up and over a wall or tree limb.

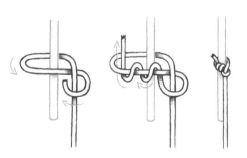

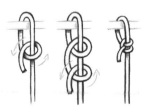

5. **Double half-hitch.** This simple knot is used for attaching rope to any kind of item or structure. It's easily adjustable and won't come undone when it's carrying a load.

6. **Clove hitch.** A quick-release, adjustable knot used to tie ropes to cylindrical objects. This is how cowboys and cowgirls often tie their horses to hitching posts. It's also good for anchoring tents and tarps to tree branches and lashing poles together. You can prevent the clove hitch from slipping when something pulls on it by adding a simple over-hand knot (the same knot you use during the first step of tying your shoes) near the end of the rope.

POOPING IN THE WOODS

Sometimes nature calls when there's no toilet around, so sooner or later you're going to have to go poop in the woods. Taking care of bodily functions in the great outdoors doesn't have to be embarrassing, scary, or gross, and it's really not a big deal if you know how to do it. The only thing worse is pretending that it'll never happen, and then being ill-prepared when it eventually does.

First, there are some rules you'll need to follow in order to keep yourself, others, and the natural environment clean and healthy. Just like at home, you must always wash your hands after going to the bathroom. That means bringing hand soap on camping trips and keeping a miniature bottle of hand sanitizer in your backpack. While you're at it, throw some biodegradable toilet paper in there, too. This type of toilet paper decomposes naturally without harming the environment.

When it's time to go, find a hidden, private spot at least 200 feet

from any lakes, creeks, or other water source, and the same distance from trails or campsites. That's two-thirds of the length of a football field, or just over twice the distance between home plate and first base on a baseball field. The reason behind this rule is that you don't want rain or flooding to carry fecal matter into water sources and habitat for humans and other species. Staying away from water and trails prevents the spread of bacteria, viruses, and other nasty germs. Look for a spot with soft soil: You'll have to dig a small toilet, called a cathole, about 8–12 inches deep, and you don't want to make the work any harder than it needs to be. On camping trips, bring a sturdy trowel or shovel for this job.

Now all you've gotta do is squat over the cathole and do your business. When you're done, wipe, toss the toilet paper in the hole, and bury everything with the dirt you dug up. This ensures your waste will break down and decompose without contaminating the surrounding environment.

You're probably thinking, "Hold on a minute! What if I'm on a hike, or out fishing or biking, and I don't have a shovel?" You still need to bury your waste. Be prepared to dig your hole with a stout stick or a flat rock if you get caught in an emergency pooping situation without a shovel. Or find a rock at least the size of a basketball that's partially sunk into the ground. Flip it over (this might take a little elbow grease) and then go number two in the depression where the bottom of the rock was resting in the ground. Flip the rock back over to cover up the evidence. That's all there is to it, so don't worry if you've gotta go and the nearest toilet is miles away.

BUILD THREE KINDS OF SHELTERS

For most of your life, you've probably slept inside your house in a cozy, comfortable bed. When we're tucked away in our houses, we don't need to worry if it's cold, raining, snowing, or windy outside. We just turn off the lights, hop under our bedcovers, and go to sleep. Even if you've done some tent camping, the temperature outside might have cooled off quite a bit during the night, but you probably had a sleeping bag to keep you warm. But what would you do if you had to spend the night outside without a tent or sleeping bag?

You would need to either find a natural shelter or build one yourself. In an emergency, that would mean looking for a spot where you would be shielded from wind and rain. You might have to tuck under a rocky overhang or beneath a big pine tree with thick, low-hanging branches. You would probably be uncomfortable and wouldn't get much sleep, but if you wrapped yourself up in the extra clothes and rain poncho you packed in your exploration kit (pages 4–7), you'd make it through the night. However, you'd be better off if you built a primitive shelter to protect yourself from the elements. You can do this using natural materials found and gathered nearby. In most wooded environments, nature provides all that you'd need to build a simple shelter that would keep you warm and dry through the night.

You should practice building these shelters before you actually get stuck out in the cold—it's a valuable skill to have, and it's a lot of fun, too. Shelters don't have to be just for emergencies! You may wind up building a special fort that's a secret hideout where you can hang out with your friends. It will take some time to get these set up, so you would want to start working at least a couple of hours before sunset. There's a really interesting book called *The Land of Feast and Famine,* about hunters and trappers in the Canadian wilderness back in the 1920s. When traveling in the winter, they would stop moving in the early afternoon. That would give them 5 or 6 hours to build a shelter and cut enough firewood to keep them alive for the night. That's a lot of work!

Before you start building, try to pick the best place to set up your shelter. Ideally, a shelter should be erected close to your building materials so you don't waste time carrying things a long way. Also look for a flat, dry, slightly elevated area, and avoid soggy ground or low-lying places like gullies or ravines where cold air collects at night and water pools when it rains. Also avoid cold, windy, exposed areas on the top of high ridges or mountains. Try to locate a building site that provides a natural windbreak, like in the shelter of a hill or a large tree. (Just remember not to build your shelter under dead trees, especially when it's windy or if they're leaning and ready to topple over. These are called "widowmakers," and there's always a small chance that a dead tree, or dead limb, could fall while you're underneath it. It's no fun to think about, but people have died this way.)

Lean-To

A lean-to is the simplest shelter you can build out in the woods. As the name suggests, it is a shelter that leans against an existing structure for support. A large boulder could work, or else the root wad or trunk of a fallen tree. The side of a cliff or steep bank will also work well as a supporting wall for your lean-to. You could even use two small trees as the foundation for your lean-to in a pinch. All you'll need are a bunch of long, sturdy sticks for building the roof and some other natural materials to cover your shelter.

1. First, find something strong enough to support your shelter. A boulder or thick tree trunk creates a protective wall, but if you can't find either of those, look for two trees that are about 6 to 8 feet apart and have branches sticking out about 4 or 5 feet from the ground. These branches will support the crossbeam that will hold up the roof of the lean-to.

2. Skip to step 4 if you're *not* using two trees. If you are, find a sturdy crossbeam at least as thick as your arm and a little longer than the distance between the trees. A dead stick is fine as long as it's strong, or you can cut a live one if you have a saw.

3. Wedge the crossbeam into place on top of the branches and against the trunk of both trees.

4. Collect sticks for the roof. They should be about 6 to 8 feet long and anywhere from 2 to 4 inches in diameter. If needed, use a saw to cut the sticks or break them into the right length using the method described on page 62. Remember, you'll need to collect enough sticks to completely cover an area big enough for you to lie down in.

5. Now, make a roof by laying the sticks at a 45-degree angle against the supporting wall or the crossbeam between the two trees.

6. Next, cover the roof with a thick layer of leaves, grass, or moss, filling in all the gaps between the sticks. Then

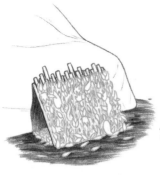

cover the first layer of roofing material with pine boughs, leafy branches, big strips of bark, or whatever else you can find to keep out water and trap heat. Go inside your shelter and look for any spots where light coming through reveals holes in your roof.

7. Line the floor of your lean-to with natural mattress material. A thick layer of dry leaves and pine boughs works very well, but use whatever dry material you can find. This will insulate you from the cold ground.

8. Bonus step: Add walls that cover the side and front openings, leaving just a small area open for a door.

A-Frame

The A-frame is a small triangular shelter that looks a little like a pup tent. Building an A-frame shelter requires many of the same materials and building steps as a lean-to. But when built properly, a simple A-frame design provides more protection and warmth than a lean-to when you're sleeping outside.

1. First, find a support pole that will hold up your shelter. You'll need a sturdy stick that is a few feet longer than your height.

2. Next, find a tree with a low limb that branches off the trunk; you can also use a tree with a trunk that splits a few feet from the ground, or even a thick, solid stump or rock that is about 3 or 4 feet tall. Place one end of your support pole in the crook of the branch and trunk, in between the split trunk, or on top of the stump, and place the other end on the ground.

3. Now, lay roofing sticks at a 45-degree angle along both sides of the support pole. You'll need longer sticks at the end by the tree trunk, and progressively shorter ones as you move toward the end of the pole that's lying on the ground.

4. When you're done creating the roof, you should have a triangular-shaped opening at the front of the A-frame. This will be your door.

5. Now it's time to add waterproofing and insulation materials to your A-frame. The best combination is one layer of pine boughs, then a layer of dry leaves or grass, then another layer of pine boughs or moss on top. Make sure you're not leaving any holes in your roof. You can even lay a few more sticks on top of everything to hold the materials in place.

6. Add a thick layer of mattress material to the floor of your A-frame. To make your shelter warmer and drier, stuff the door opening with leaves and pine boughs to block the wind.

7. Bonus step: Although it's not completely necessary, your A-frame will be much sturdier if you lash the two longest roofing poles at the door end of the A-frame to the main support pole with rope or paracord. Use the clove hitch or use wire loops to hold them together.

Teepee

Teepees are conical tent-like shelters that shed rain and withstand wind very well. Native Americans from the Great Plains historically used teepees made with long wooden poles and covered with bison hides. Their teepees were large enough for eight to ten people to sleep in but were designed to be easily set up, taken down, and moved from one spot to another. This allowed the tribes' nomadic hunters to follow the movement of the great buffalo herds that fed them and provided the materials for their clothing and shelter. You'll want to make a much smaller teepee that has just enough space for a couple of people; it'll be much easier to make one with the help of a partner or two.

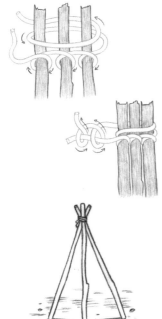

1. Start by gathering your materials. First you'll need to find at least 6–8 main support poles. You can either use strong dead sticks or cut live green poles. They should be 6–8 feet long and 3–4 inches in diameter. Another option is to use pieces of PVC pipe from your local hardware store. Make sure you have several feet of rope or paracord, too.

2. Now you'll need to make a tripod. Lay the three sturdiest poles on the ground alongside each other, making sure the ends line up closely. Lash these three poles together at a point about a foot from one end of the poles; make a loop around each individual pole, then a loop around all three. Secure the loop by tying a double half-hitch knot (see page 72) around all three poles.

3. Next, you'll have to stand up your tripod. Stand the three poles up in a vertical position. Crouch down and pull the ends on the ground out and away from the center of the tripod, until they're far enough apart that the tripod stands well on its own. Each pole should support the other, so that the tripod makes a sturdy foundation for the rest of the teepee materials.

4. Now you can add the remaining support poles by leaning them into the notches at the top of the tripod. Fill in the re-

CATCH A CRAYFISH, COUNT THE STARS

maining gaps with as many long, thinner sticks and branches as you can find. When you're finished, the teepee should look like a big cone made with long sticks. Remember to leave a small opening for a door.

5. Lay pine boughs, leafy branches, and big pieces of bark on the outside of the structure for insulation and waterproofing. If you have some extra rope, you can tie the branches to the support poles (see knots on pages 72–73) to make sure they stay in place. Add clumps of dead leaves and grass to fill in any holes.

6. Line the floor of your teepee with bedding material.

7. Bonus step: Use some thick pine boughs for a door to your teepee.

Experiment with all three types of shelters and see which one you like the best. Keep in mind that bigger isn't necessarily better. You might be tempted by the idea of building a really big shelter, but you'll have an easier time making a small structure sturdy and weatherproof. Try reinforcing your shelter with whatever materials you can find, natural or man-made. The Native Americans used animal hides to insulate their teepees, and fur trappers used sphagnum moss as waterproof roofing material and to fill in gaps in their log cabin walls. You might have an old plastic tarp in your garage that you can tie over your shelter to make a wind- and waterproof covering, and you'll really appreciate a wool blanket or a sleeping bag when it's chilly. What else can you do to improve your shelter? Use your imagination to come up with other ideas. Just don't leave any of the man-made materials behind in the woods.

MAKE A SNOW FORTRESS

Nature provides us humans with lots of building materials. Some of them are obvious. Wood and rocks, for instance, are easy to spot when they're used to make or decorate houses. Other natural materials are a little harder to identify. Did you know that all the concrete used to make our sidewalks, our schools, and the foundations of our homes comes from the same types of sand and gravel that you see every day when you're playing outside? Same goes for the asphalt used to make roads, which contains "fillers" of sand, gravel, and crushed rock. Other products of nature can be used as building material. Bamboo is one example. Snow and ice are others. Every year, in Finnish Lapland, a place called SnowVillage builds an entire restaurant out of ice. The restaurant stays open during the winter, and then melts back into the ground in the spring. It's called the Ice Restaurant.

In the far north of the Arctic, Inuit peoples have been building structures from hard-packed snow for perhaps thousands of years. These were not year-round dwellings, as it wasn't possible to keep them functioning and maintained during the spring and summer months. But in the winter, especially when temporary shelters were necessary while traveling across sea ice, igloos made from hard-packed snow were warm and comfortable refuges from the deadly conditions outside. You can use this ancient technique as an inspiration to design and build your own sturdy fortress.

First, you'll need at least 6 inches of snow on the ground, but more is better. Keep an eye on the weather forecast for big snowstorms moving into your area. Not just any snow will work for

building a fort, though. The dry, light, powdery snow that downhill skiers love is terrible for making forts. You want the kind of heavier, wetter snow that's good for packing snowballs or making a snow-man. It should hold together almost like mud or wet cement.

Once you have the right snow conditions, it's time to build your fort. You can do it on your own, but the job will be easier with a construction team made up of family and friends. Before you start, you'll need a mold or two for making the blocks that you'll use to build the walls of your fort. You can use buckets, plastic trash bins, or rectangular plastic totes. A small shovel will make filling your molds with snow faster and easier. You'll also need a spray bottle, but we'll get to that later.

Start by making the outline, or "fortprint," of your snow fort. You can make it rectangular, triangular, or even circular. Just don't make it too big. Ten feet wide is more than enough room for you and a couple of friends. Once you've decided on a design, stomp the outline into the snow where you want to build the walls.

Now you can begin putting up the walls. Fill the mold with snow and use your hands to pack it down. As you pack it down, you may need to keep adding more snow until the mold is full and you have a solid block. Now flip the mold over in the outline of the fort in order to place the block where you want it. You might need to bang the side of the mold or gently shake the mold in order to get the block of snow to come free. Now take your empty mold and fill it again, and repeat the process. Keep going until you've laid down the first layer of snow blocks all the way around the outline of your fort. Remember to leave a small gap in the wall for a doorway. Then start carefully adding more layers of blocks until your wall is about chest high. Once the wall of your fort is complete, pack any gaps or holes between the blocks with snow.

The last step in the construction of your fort is what will make it really sturdy. First, make sure the air temperature is below the freezing point of 32 degrees. Then grab your spray bottle and fill it with cold water. (If you want to make your fort really stand out, add your favorite color of food coloring to the bottle.) Now coat the entire surface of the fort with water. You may need to refill the bottle a few times, but when the water freezes into a layer of ice, it will harden and strengthen the walls. Now your fort will withstand a barrage of snowballs from your friends while you and your teammates mount a counterattack.

TAKE AN AWESOME
OUTDOOR PHOTOGRAPH

Photography has existed for 200 years, but the earliest outdoor photographers had it tough. Around 1826, a French photographer took the first landscape photo—and his photograph required an 8-hour exposure. That means the photographer had to make sure the camera didn't move for a whole 8 hours while the photo was taken. Nowadays, you could take thousands of digital photos in that amount of time. Some of the most amazing early outdoor photography was the work of a photographer named L. A. Huffman. In the late 1800s, he photographed Native Americans and hunters on the Great Plains of eastern Montana. He arrived just in time to capture a landscape and lifestyle that were quickly disappearing. Huffman's camera weighed 50 pounds, and he had to haul it on a horse. His photography studio was built from boards that he scavenged from an old broken-down boat.

Even today, taking a great outdoor photo isn't exactly easy. There's more to it than punching a button on a cellphone. How you compose, or frame, a picture can make the difference between a great photograph that ends up in a frame on your bedroom wall and a bunch of duds that you'll end up deleting.

The Rule of Thirds

When most people take a photograph, they center its subject right in the middle of the shot. They do this whether it's a mountain or a

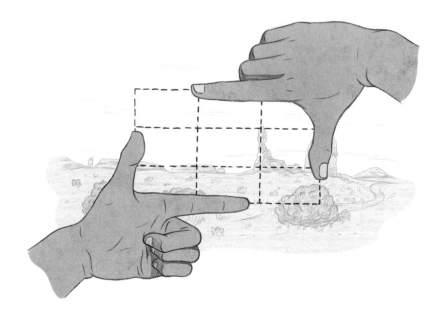

mouse. But there's a better way to set up a photo. Professional photographers often use what's called the rule of thirds to help them decide how to take a picture. Some cameras even have a rule-of-thirds grid setting.

The basic idea is to mentally divide your screen into a 3 × 3 grid, with nine squares. This way, the screen has three horizontal rows as well as three vertical rows. You can do a lot of experimenting with this grid, but the basic idea is to avoid placing the subject, or the specific thing you're photographing, in the center of the grid. You should also avoid placing the sky's horizon in the center. This visual trick leaves more open space in the rest of the frame. It forces the viewer to search for the subject and take in the details of the entire image. It also allows the photographer to include more of the surrounding scenery.

Of course, the rule of thirds isn't actually a rule. It's more than okay to do your own thing and break that rule. Maybe you want to take a portrait of your little brother or sister holding a fish they just caught. Or perhaps you're taking an extreme close-up of a beetle or a flower—that's called macro photography. If that's the case, do what makes the most sense for capturing your photograph. But keep the rule of thirds in mind, and experiment with taking a new style of outdoor photograph that might be your best image yet.

Here are some additional tips that'll help you ramp up your photography game.

- The best natural light for photography usually happens during the "golden hour," around sunrise in the morning or sunset in the evening. In the middle of the day, harsh, bright sunlight can wash out details and color and create shadows that might ruin a picture.
- If possible, take photos with the sun at your back, so that light is streaming directly toward your subject.
- Try taking photos from different angles. Climb a tree or lie on the ground. Placing the camera up high or down low can lead to some interesting results.
- Tell your photography subjects to take off their sunglasses before you take a picture. Bright eyes are better than dark glasses! Watch out for hats that cast dark shadows on people's faces, too.
- Capture the action as it happens. Be ready to snap a picture when things are moving fast.
- Slow down and keep an eye out for anything that grabs your attention. Maybe it's a reflection of a mountain on the water, or a chipmunk nibbling on an acorn. You never know what might end up making for a great photo.

II

COLLECTING AND FORAGING

This next section is all about scouring the landscape for treasure. The natural world is chock-full of amazing collectibles, from seashells to edible berries to the skeletons of wild creatures. These things can be used to decorate your home or bedroom, or even to feed your family. Once you learn what you're looking for, every outdoor adventure will turn into an opportunity to score some of nature's bounty.

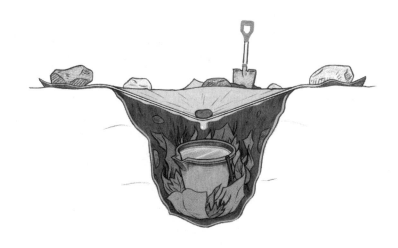

MAKE YOUR OWN DRINKING WATER

If you've ever been tempted to drink directly from a creek, lake, or pond, don't do it—even if the water is crystal clear. Unless it's an emergency and truly a matter of life or death, you should purify natural surface water before drinking it. There are exceptions to this rule, such as underground springs, freshly collected rainwater, and glacial ice melt. But most natural water sources can contain bacteria, parasites, and other germs that will give you a bad stomachache or worse. Ever heard of the intestinal infection called giardiasis? You may have heard it called by its nickname, "beaver fever." It's a nasty bug that causes fever, vomiting, and bloody diarrhea. When beavers and other animals poop in the water, they contaminate it with microscopic parasites, and drinking that water without purifying it can lead to a bad cause of giardiasis.

The water that pours out of your faucet, on the other hand, has been purified before it gets to your house. Water sourced from deep underground wells is naturally filtered through many layers of soil, sand, and rock to remove microscopic contaminants. Water that comes from treatment plants passes through human-made filtration systems and is disinfected with chemicals like chlorine.

The good news is that you can mimic the processes that make your tap water safe to drink, even when you're out in nature. Some people use small water purification tablets that kill germs when they dissolve in water, but the chemicals they contain can leave a weird flavor behind. Here are three other water purification options, starting with the simplest.

- Heat water that you've collected from a stream, lake, or creek in a pot over a campfire or a camping stove. Let the water boil for several minutes. The heat will kill all the germs that are living in the water.
- Use a small, portable water filter such as a LifeStraw filter that attaches directly to your water bottle.
- Use ultraviolet, or UV, light to kill aquatic germs. Leaving a clear water bottle out in direct sunlight for several hours will do the trick, but it's much faster to use a Steripen, which is a small battery-powered device that emits UV light. All you need to do is dip the Steripen into your water bottle and swirl it around for 90 seconds, and your water is purified.

For a fun do-it-yourself project that involves vaporizing water to remove germs, you can also build your own solar still. The distilled water you can buy at a store is made through a similar process—

water is boiled, turned into steam, and then cooled to condense back into purified, liquid form. Distilled water is often used in hospitals and other medical facilities to clean and sterilize equipment, but you can drink it, too. Solar stills use the heat of the sun to turn liquid water into water vapor. After the vapor cools and condenses back into liquid, it becomes pure and germ-free. As a bonus, solar distillation also gets rid of contaminants like harmful chemicals and salt. Solar stills can even turn salty ocean water into fresh drinking water, which is great to know if you're ever stuck on a remote island.

The method works best on warm, sunny days. Don't wait for an emergency before you try making one. Do a test experiment first, to make sure you understand the process. And be sure to build your solar still early in the morning so that it has plenty of time to work.

Materials

- Several fist-sized rocks or objects of a similar weight
- A sheet of thick, clear plastic that's at least 4 feet by 4 feet
- A shovel or other digging tool (a sturdy stick or flat rock will work in an emergency)
- A cooking pot, large bowl, water bottle, bucket, or any container that's big enough to collect a quart or more of water

Building Steps

1. Start out by digging a round pit that's at least 2 feet deep and 3 feet wide. Look for a spot with moist, soft soil or sand. In the center of the pit, dig a small depression to keep your water collection container from tipping over. If the soil is dry, pour a

bunch of unfiltered water into it. Any natural water source will do, including a pond, creek, lake, the ocean, or even a mud puddle. You can also add green leaves, grass, and plants to the bottom of the distillation pit—the water inside these plants will evaporate and turn into vapor, adding more water to your supply. If the soil is already very moist, you can skip that part of this step.

2. Now you're ready to make clean drinking water. Place your water container in the small depression in the center of the pit. Then cover the hole with the sheet of plastic. Weigh down the edge of the plastic sheet with enough rocks to make sure it stays in place. Next, put one rock in the center of the plastic sheet and carefully push the rock down so it hangs just above the water container. The plastic sheet should sag downward, but don't let it touch the bottom of the pit.

3. All you need to do now is wait. As the moisture in the pit heats up, it will turn into vapor, leaving any contaminants behind in the soil. The water vapor will then rise, cool, and condense back into purified liquid on the bottom of the plastic sheet before dripping into the collection container. Under ideal conditions, a solar still can produce more than a quart of drinking water per day—about half the amount of water a person needs to drink in a day, depending on their size, the weather, and their exertion. On really hot, sunny days, you can check your solar still after several hours, but if it's cooler or cloudy you should wait all day, or even two days. Remove the rocks from the edge and top of the plastic sheet and carefully lift the sheet away from the pit. You should find a container of clean, purified drinking water.

WATER "WITCHING"—FACT OR FICTION?

When you think of water in the natural world, you're probably thinking of flowing streams, rivers, oceans, and lakes. But there's another source of water out in nature that isn't visible to the naked eye, and it lies beneath your feet. It's called groundwater, and it's found beneath the surface of the earth, often in underground rock formations known as aquifers. Some groundwater sources are just a few feet below the surface, while others flow through layers of rock thousands of feet underground. One of the world's most famous underground aquifers is the Ogallala Aquifer. (Pronounced "oh-ga-lah-lah," it covers 174,000 square miles and lies beneath portions of eight different states. About a third of the groundwater used to water crops in the United States comes from the Ogallala Aquifer.)

Groundwater is used as a source of irrigation for farming, and many communities rely on it for their water needs. It's a valuable resource, especially in arid environments—which is why across history, the ability to find underground sources of water was sometimes thought of as a kind of magic. Modern hydrologists locate groundwater through the use of sophisticated tools known as seismoelectric survey instruments. They can also find underground water by looking for telltale signs of underground hydration on the landscape. Helpful clues might be water-loving plants such as willow trees or cottonwoods that aren't near obvious sources of surface water. The sight of seeps or springs bubbling up from underground is another clue. There are also thousands of water dowsers or so-called water witches who believe they can find underground water by using a mixture of intuition, observation, and a forked tree branch called a dowsing or divining rod.

Evidence of divining rods goes back thousands of years across various cultures. The exact tools and methods have varied over time, though most dowsers believe in using a branch cut from a live tree or metal contraptions made from wire. The instruments supposedly respond to the presence of water by tipping or swinging toward a particular spot on the ground. Dowsers believe this may have something to do with electromagnetic currents flowing through the groundwater. Some water witches claim that the pull of the water is so strong it makes their arms shake!

Most likely, water witching is a form of "pseudoscience," meaning it seems scientific but it's really pretty much bunk. In controlled tests, water witches are no more accurate than people just making a simple guess. But that doesn't stop folks from believing! Either way, it's harmless fun. So if you'd like to give it a try, go for it. Make your rod by cutting a small Y-shaped branch from a live tree. Hold on to the stick at the forked end, with a hand on each branch of the fork, and walk around the area where you want to do your water witching. If the rod detects water, the butt end of the stick will tip toward the ground.

You probably don't want to spend hours digging up holes to test your theory. Instead, try using your divining rod in your backyard and see if you can detect your water line. Don't dig it up, or you could cause some serious plumbing problems! Just have an adult who knows the property confirm or deny your water witching suspicions. Who knows, maybe you'll prove the scientists wrong and demonstrate that dowsing is an actual skill.

FORAGE FOR WILD FOODS

Before the invention of agriculture, most humans lived a nomadic existence. Traveling in small bands made up of extended families, hunter-gatherers would walk hundreds of miles over the course of the year as they moved from campsite to campsite in search of food sources. Looking for food took up lots and lots of time. In fact, until the transition to farming shifted their focus to tending crops, searching for food was probably the main thing that people did. Many of them hunted and fished. They stalked big game with spears or bows, they clubbed birds and small animals, and they netted fish. But foraging (looking for wild food) was one of the most important skills employed by hunter-gatherers. They foraged for wild nuts, fruit, mushrooms, roots, and other edibles. No doubt, the ability to find such foods often meant the difference between life and death.

Nowadays, most people who forage aren't required to do it. For most of us, we can always eat other things that come from the store. However, foraging remains a very important part of life for many people who love to be out in nature and who think it's important to know how to take care of yourself in the wild. Foraging is a fun and rewarding pastime. And, just as important, it's a way to find some of the best-tasting food that you'll ever eat.

RULES AND SAFETY TIPS FOR FORAGING

Here are some basic rules to follow as you become an expert forager.

- **Never eat a plant or mushroom that you can't identify.** There are many poisonous plants and fungi out there—some that could give you a terrible stomachache, and others that could do even worse. If you find a new food that you *think* you've identified, make sure a knowledgeable adult can confirm (or help you do the research) before you put it in your mouth.
- **Own up to mistakes.** If you've eaten something you shouldn't have, let an adult know as soon as possible.
- **Don't overeat any plant or mushroom the first time you try it.** Especially with mushrooms, start with a very small amount, like a forkful or two—your digestive system may need time to adjust to new food sources.
- **Check the calendar.** Berries grow in summer, and nuts are ready for harvesting in the fall. Certain kinds of mushrooms can be found from spring to fall, or even winter in some places. Plan and schedule your expeditions accordingly!
- **Search near water sources, and during wet years.** Water is necessary for all forms of life, including plants. Plant and fungi food sources tend to grow

plentifully near sources of hydration like ponds, streams, and rivers. And unless you live in the Pacific Northwest, where rain is a way of life and mushrooms grow year-round, you'll have better luck mushroom hunting during a year with lots of rain during the spring and summer.

- **Be like a bear.** Even if you're not out on a berry-picking outing, keep an eye out for potential food sources. Bears, as well as birds and squirrels, are opportunistic foragers. That means they're always paying attention and staying alert for an opportunity to score some grub—even if they're not hungry at that particular moment. Act like they do to increase your chances of foraging success.
- **Shop the sidewalk.** You don't have to be in the woods or mountains to forage. Fruits, berries, and nuts can be found all over most cities and suburban neighborhoods. Often, these foods are hanging right over the sidewalks. Raspberries, apples, rose hips, mulberries, figs, walnuts, beech nuts, and many other edibles are just sitting there while most people walk right by. Be on the lookout and you'll be able to harvest these treasures—as long as you can beat the squirrels to them.

A Few Options for Beginning Foragers

There are thousands of edible plants and fungi in North America. So getting to know what's edible in your neighborhood (or near your campground) can be a really big project. But here are four berries and a couple of mushrooms that you can start looking for right away. They're easy to recognize and common across North America. Because there are some poisonous berries and poisonous mushrooms out there, you should never eat foraged food without having it identified by a knowledgeable adult. For more rules on safe foraging, turn back to the sidebar on pages 97–98.

Hunting for mushrooms might not sound as enticing as foraging for wild berries that taste sweet and refreshing. But finding a tasty mycological specimen hiding behind a rotten stump might turn you into a convert. "Mycology" is the official term for the study of fungi, a type of life-form that also includes the mold on old bread and even the stuff that causes athlete's foot. That might sound gross, but mushrooms have lots of incredibly cool properties. They communicate with each other by exchanging electrical pulses through an underground network called mycelium, and some mushrooms can soak up environmental pollution, healing damaged soil and laying the groundwork for a thriving ecosystem. But the best mushrooms out there are the ones you can bring home to eat. There are edible mushrooms that you can find in the wild that are extremely hard to find anywhere else—not even the fanciest grocery stores. Learn how to find and identify some of these special varieties and you'll be in for a treat.

Raspberries and blackberries. These bramble berries may look smaller than what you're used to seeing at the grocery store, but the wild ones are generally much better to eat. You won't believe how they explode with flavor. Look for them on low-lying, usually thorny bushes. When ripe, the berries will be pink or black. Watch out for the thorns while gathering them, to avoid getting pricked! The leaves of bramble berries are wide at the base, then taper to a narrow point, and they're jagged along the edges. You're most likely to find them at the edges of woodlots, field edges, fencerows, abandoned lots, or other "disturbed" areas where human activities have stirred up the ground or cleared away old trees. Such locations often create a good place for wild shrubs and bushes to start growing. If you're lucky, you'll find bramble berries there as well.

Blueberries and huckleberries. Look for these tasty berries in the cooler climates of the northern United States and Canada. Young blueberry plants will look like small shrubs, but tall bushes of certain blueberry varieties can grow to be 6 feet tall or more. Blueberry bushes don't have thorns, and their small, oval leaves are pointed at the ends. Huckleberries are related to blueberries but have a delicious flavor of their own. In some areas, huckleberry picking is such a competitive sport that people closely guard the location of their huckleberry spots. If you find a good one, be careful whom you tell! If you find a bush that's just loaded with berries, lay a blanket or a tarp under the bush and whack or shake the branches. Ripe berries will fall right onto your blanket, and you can carefully lift up the blanket and funnel your berries into a bucket. And if your berry-picking adventure brings you into bear country, you should be extra "bear aware." In addition to being delicious in your pancakes, berries are beloved by birds, bees, deer, foxes, skunks, raccoons, opossums, and bears. Stay alert, make plenty of noise, and never run away from a bear.

Morels. These weird-looking, brain-like mushrooms are a real treasure for foragers when they turn up in the spring. Morels grow all across southern Canada and the United States (except for Hawaii), though they're a little harder to find in drier areas such as the Southwest. They come in yellow, gold, brown, or black, and they look more stretched-out and pointy than the classic mushroom you might be picturing in your mind. But the main way to identify them is to look out for their wrinkles and folds. They do have look-alikes called false morels, but a trained eye can easily tell them apart. False morels look like lumpy, squashed cousins to real morels. They're shaped more like a cabbage than a cone, and the cap isn't fused to the stem in the same way as a morel. Eating a bite of a false morel isn't likely to kill someone, but it can make you very sick to your stomach or worse, especially in larger quantities. It's a good idea to go online and look at photos of morels and false morels so that you're not worried about confusing them.

Chanterelles. This orange, yellow, tan, or red mushroom is a fun one to spot in late summer or early fall. Like morels, they are widely distributed in the United States. Look for them near older trees, especially after wet summers with lots of rain. Chanterelles are shaped like trumpets, and they have wavy edges and "false gills." This means their gills look wrinkled, and a bit like they're melting

MUSHROOMS AND SAFETY

Any mushroom hunter needs to be aware that poisonous mushrooms are not just something out of cartoons and fairy tales. There are hundreds of types of poisonous mushrooms in North America alone. Some of these are so poisonous that they can be lethal, even when ingested in small quantities. Others will just give you a bad stomachache. Either way, the risk is not worth taking! That's why we're only talking here about two very easy-to-identify mushrooms. And it's why, no matter what you're foraging, you should never, ever take a bite of any food (particularly a mushroom) before a knowledgeable adult can confirm that it's safe. There's a very real risk of getting sick or worse from eating improperly identified mushrooms. (Make sure to identify every mushroom you pick, too—poisonous "look-alikes" can grow right near their safe-to-eat counterparts.)

into each other. Overall, the mushroom looks smooth under the cap and on the stem. This is important, because chanterelles have a sort of a look-alike called a jack-o'-lantern. Jack-o'-lanterns have true, defined gills. Their caps also look different—rounder and without the chanterelle's wavy edges. Look these up online to see how different they are. Jack-o'-lanterns can cause severe intestinal issues and other problems, so it's important to know the difference.

Once you've gotten your morels or chanterelles home or to your campsite and had them positively identified, they should be cooked for ease of digestion and flavor. Try them sauteed in oil and butter, with a bit of chopped-up garlic. And remember, a little goes a long way.

If you get excited about foraging and want to learn more, there are loads of great books and apps that can educate you on the subject. Many areas have local mycology clubs as well. Joining up with a mycology club is a great way to learn about mushrooms and go on cool field trips where you can master the skill of identifying a wide variety of wild mushrooms.

SACAGAWEA SURVIVES

Imagine a world with no grocery or clothing stores, no cars, roads, or buildings. Imagine everything you possess has to be made or acquired from the land around you or traded from another people who also have to forge their way. Tribal people in what is now America have lived close to the land for thousands of years. They have long understood the intricacies of living off the land—where to fish, where to hunt, where to pick berries, and how to sustain themselves through careful attention to the land and the animals. They know which plants offer the most nutrition and where to gather seeds, nuts, and protein-rich roots. They learned to grow crops and nurture the land that provided for them.

Now imagine being removed from your people and the lands that are familiar.

One day a powerful enemy raiding party attacks your home place, fights and kills your beloved relatives, and steals you away on horseback to a land you have not seen before, a place you have only heard about in stories. Maybe you are as young as nine years old or as old as twelve. You travel for days with an enemy who does not speak your language. You understand that you are in danger, and in order to survive, you must pay attention to everything—every rock, every hill, every tree. You remember the changing ecoscape so that you can feed and clothe yourself when you escape. You cross streams and rivers. You cross vast country where you might hear a giant herd of buffalo rumble in the distance. You travel so far that everything becomes foreign and strange, and when you come at last to enemy territory you are sold or gambled away to a man who is not only different but entirely alien. You have never seen a white man before, and now white men are everywhere among the tribal people in this unfamiliar land. Now a white man named Charbonneau claims to own you.

In this new landscape you rely on the skills and lifeways you were taught by your people, the Lemhi Shoshone. You are well prepared. You know how to snare small animals, how to skin, butcher, and preserve deer, elk, buffalo, and antelope. You know how to tan hides and make clothing and moccasins for yourself and others. You know how to build lodges and make travois (frames dragged by horses) to carry heavy things over long distances. And although women among your people were not required to hunt and fish, you learned these skills, as all women in your tribe have for centuries, because it is essential to your people's survival to pay attention and to learn. You know how to weave baskets, how to carve and fire-harden cooking bowls and digging sticks, and how to make scraping tools from antlers and bones. You always know where to find nuts and seeds and roots. You know how to build a fire quickly with a handmade wood drill and dry grass, how to dress warmly, and how to care for yourself and others when wind whips snow to powder at 20 degrees below zero. Through careful attention you know how to care for a baby in the harshest of conditions. If you had to, you could make your own bows and arrows to kill a buffalo, eat well for many days, and make a lodge from its hide. But more importantly, through your own wit and ingenuity, you know how to stay safe when you are a lone woman surrounded by enemy men.

In the years you live among the Mandan and Hidatsa tribes you learn many skills from these people and the many different tribes who pass through to trade, as well as the French fur trappers and traders scattered throughout the villages. You witness the making of bull boats, round frames of willow saplings with single buffalo hides stretched over each frame. In these boats, women fearlessly navigate the rivers no matter how high the waves. The knowledge you gain from them will one day help you when you encounter unexpected winds as you travel on the river with the Lewis and Clark expedition. In your years with Charbonneau, you see whole villages left decimated in the wake of the smallpox epidemic. You reside among the Hidatsa people at Metaharta, one of several Mandan and Hidatsa villages on the upper Missouri, near the Knife River confluence. On certain nights you believe you hear voices from the lost villages as wind gutters beneath the high bluffs.

Now imagine one day that representatives from a powerful army come upriver and offer the chance to return to your people. The men have been chartered by President Thomas Jefferson, whose name you do not know, to map and claim territory in the northwestern part of the United States. Their journey will come to be known as the Lewis and Clark expedition. The expedition hires your captor, Charbonneau, as an interpreter, but these men will later come to find out how little help he can offer. Now you must travel with thirty white men and one other enslaved person. You and your baby will be held up as symbols of peace to any hostile tribes. Again you will cross difficult and treacherous terrain and waters where you know you will encounter grizzlies and rattlers, possibly stampeding buffalo, and enemy tribes. In high wind-whipped waves, you will retrieve important equipment that washes overboard while the man who enslaves you whimpers and cries. In the company of foreign men who long for women, you may have to hide to nurse your baby and to bathe, but perhaps you meet no one more dangerous than your captor, Charbonneau. You must travel beside an army who will rename and claim to discover the land tribal people have always occupied. You will act as their interpreter and guide. These white men seek a Northwest Passage that Indigenous people know does not exist.

History will remember you as Sacajawea or Sacagawea but will not record the date of your death. Nontribal and tribal historians, your descendants and relations, will continue to tell stories of your life until you become both myth and memory.

—By Debra Magpie Earling

FIND A CUP OF TEA IN YOUR GARDEN

Did you know that you can probably walk to your local park or a patch of woods right now and find the ingredients for a cup of tea? Brewed across many cultures and for thousands of years, tea is simply an infusion of plants, soaked in boiling water in order to release their flavor and, sometimes, their health benefits. Most caffeinated teas are made by brewing the fermented leaves of the *Camellia sinensis* plant—from the same family of shrubs that produces the lovely-smelling camellia flower. That particular plant changed the course of history many times over. Ever heard of the Boston Tea Party, an event that was partly responsible for inciting the American Revolution? That had to do with the American colonists' anger about paying unfair taxes on a variety of important items, including tea. As an act of protest, American colonists boarded merchant ships in Boston Harbor in the year 1773. They dumped an entire shipment of tea into the harbor, destroying it all.

Tea can be made from countless other types of plants and fruits, from the bark of the cinnamon tree to the root of a dandelion to the flower of the jasmine vine. Some of these teas are made by drying parts of the plant in order to concentrate their flavor, but many can be made by simply picking their leaves, flowers, or roots and steeping them in hot water.

If you plant peppermint in your garden, you'll soon find that you're very rich in peppermint leaves, which make fantastic tea. This hardy herb is very good at growing . . . and growing . . . and growing some more. One great way to deal with a mint surplus is by making mint tea for your family after dinner—mint is great for digestion, and steeping fresh mint leaves in water is a beloved tradition in Middle Eastern and North African cultures, where the concoction is sweetened in the pot and sipped throughout the day.

Do you have a rosebush or two in your garden? If you leave the wilted flowers on the plant instead of pruning them, you might not get as many lush blossoms the next time around—but you'll allow the plants to produce oval-shaped fruits, with seeds inside, that ripen in late summer or fall. The fruit, which is called a rose hip, grows red, pink, or orange and can be used in syrups, jams, and teas. To use rose hips for tea, simply pour hot water over them.

Some flowers can be brewed into tea as well—jasmine, chrysanthemum, and chamomile all make for nice floral brews. The flavor will be more intense if you take the time to dry the flowers on a sunny windowsill or counter, but you can use fresh flowers, too.

Once you figure out what kind of tea-making potential your area holds, you might find yourself getting into the habit of offering up cups of tea to guests when they visit—this is considered a sign of hospitality and welcome in many cultures. In fact, in some places it would be considered rude not to offer a guest a cup of tea.

FLIP A ROCK

Scientists estimate that the world has around 10 quintillion insects. A quintillion is a billion billions. Or, put another way, there are 1,250,000,000 insects for every human being on earth. Keep in mind, that doesn't even count all the spiders, which are actually arachnids. If you want to get an idea of how many spiders are out there, consider this: If you weighed all the bugs that get eaten by spiders every year, those bugs would weigh more than all the humans on earth. Yet most people go through their day without ever stopping to appreciate how much life is out there, hiding in plain view. One of the easiest ways to start learning about all of these life-forms is as simple as can be: Take a few seconds now and then to flip over a rock or rotten log. You won't believe what you can find under there. There's likely to be a lot more than just insects and spiders. Many small creatures try to avoid getting eaten by larger ones by staying out of sight beneath rocks—and plenty of hungry creatures crawl into those places searching for something to eat. Others prefer the dark, moist habitats and cooler underground temperatures found beneath rocks and logs. Worms, crickets, beetles, grubs, millipedes, centipedes, pill bugs, spiders, slugs, and even creatures like salamanders and toads can be found under rocks and old rotting logs. You really never know what you might find when you flip one over. (You might encounter something that bites or stings, so use some caution and common sense when flipping rocks. Don't grab anything unless you know it's safe to handle it.)

Rocks and logs resting in places with moist soil are the best ones to flip over. If you see lots of moss and rotten wood and leaves around, all the better. These are the kinds of places where insects and other subterranean critters like to find food and shelter. Look for rocks that are resting on or just barely under the surface of the ground. If a rock is buried so deeply that it's impossible to flip over with your hands, then it's not a good place for critters to hide.

Don't forget to check out rocks in aquatic environments, too. You'll find cool life-forms in some freshwater lakes and ponds, but saltwater tidal pools are one of the most interesting places to go on a rock-flipping excursion. Over periods of thousands of years, the steady pounding of ocean waves and currents erodes areas near shore, leaving behind holes and depressions in the shoreline. These holes form small saltwater ponds and pools that are constantly getting resupplied with water from waves and tides.

A wide variety of ocean-dwellers are found in tidal pools. Some are permanent residents. Others can become temporarily stranded in the pools during low-tide periods. The creatures you might find there include molluscs such as clams, mussels, and periwinkles; echinoderms such as starfish, sea urchins, and sea cucumbers; and crustaceans such as shrimp and crabs. Various species of small fish and corals also inhabit tidal pools. You might be able to locate some of these life-forms without flipping over rocks, but many shallow tidal pool inhabitants are vulnerable to predators like herons, gulls, raccoons, and otters. Flipping over a rock will expose their hiding spots and allow you to examine them closely.

An aquarium or bait net is a handy tool for catching tidal pool creatures. Bring along a small plastic bucket and fill it halfway with water to create a place to temporarily store your catch while you look them over. Handle them gently and carefully, and when you're done, pour them all back into the tidal pool—in many places, harvesting certain creatures from tide pools is against the law.

Try keeping a running tally of how many different life-forms you find underneath rocks. After you flip over a rock, whether on land or underwater, always carefully return it back to its original position so critters can continue using it as a hiding spot.

BUILD A BUG HOTEL

Once you've experimented with locating insects and other bugs, you can advance your skills by learning how to capture and temporarily keep them for observation. You probably won't have to search far and wide. One researcher at the Smithsonian National Museum of Natural History in Washington, DC, a guy named Gary Hevel, collected more than four thousand different insect species, just in his own backyard! That's only a small fraction of the million species of insects that have been officially identified by scientists around the

world. And Gary Hevel's collection of bugs didn't count all of the non-insects that might have been living in his yard, such as millipedes, centipedes, and pill bugs.

It is possible to catch some insects by hand, but make sure to handle them very gently. To catch flying insects and fast-moving ground-dwellers, you'll need a butterfly net. Bring along a small food storage container with a snap-on lid for transporting bugs while you're out in the field. But when you get back home, you'll want a better place to temporarily house your bugs. A clear glass container, such as a quart-sized canning jar, is perfect.

Before you add your guests, you'll need to properly set up your bug hotel. Put a thin layer of soil, pebbles, or sand on the bottom of the jar. Then add some vegetation like a small leafy branch, some grass, or a patch of moss. A rock or piece of bark will give bugs a place to hide, and a stick or two will encourage them to climb around. Every now and then sprinkle a couple of teaspoons of water into the jar so your bugs stay hydrated.

Insects need plenty of oxygen too, so your bug hotel needs to be well ventilated. Mason jars have a two-piece metal lid with a flat circular top and a round ring that screws onto the jar. Punch several ventilation holes through the flat top with a hole punch tool or a hammer and nail. Or you can cover the opening of the jar with a piece of cheesecloth material and use the metal ring to screw it down over the top. That'll let in plenty of air.

Now you're ready to check in your hotel guests. Rule number one is don't overcrowd them in a small space. Put only a few bugs in the jar at a time. Also be aware that some insects make better hotel guests than others. Ants, beetles, crickets, and grasshoppers are tough little critters, so they tend to do well during short periods of captivity. Butterflies and some moths, on the other hand, are pretty fragile, and their wings get damaged easily, so you may want to leave them outside. Caterpillars are a different story, though. This immature life stage of moths and butterflies is an ideal specimen for a bug hotel. Some of the coolest large insects you can get your hands on are walking sticks and praying mantises. And of course lightning bugs, also known as fireflies, put on an impressive light show at night.

You may end up with a strange bug that you don't recognize. If you're unsure what you're looking at, try using the Picture Insect app. All you need to do is snap a photo of any insect, and the app will analyze the image and help you identify the species. There's always the chance that you might discover a new species of insect. Every year, thousands of previously unknown insects are identified. In 2016, a two-year-old girl in Kentucky named Sylvie was with her mother watering the garden when they found a new species of insect called a treehopper. That species of treehopper is now named after Sylvie.

Finally, remember that even though the vast majority of bugs are completely harmless, some can deliver a painful, venomous bite or sting. Never mess with black widow and brown recluse spiders, fire ants, bees, wasps, or scorpions. Look these bugs up so that you know what they look like, and if you see them, steer clear. As long as you give them plenty of space, they won't bother you.

THE SILENT SPRING

The writer and marine biologist Rachel Carson had already written several books about the ocean when she received an alarming letter from a friend. The friend, who lived on a stretch of the shoreline of Massachusetts, had seen a plane flying over the town, spraying for mosquitoes. The next morning, Carson's friend found three dead birds by her front door. Three more perished near the birdbath the following day. Finally, a robin dropped from a branch just as she was walking by. After that, she and her husband stopped looking for bird corpses.

The plane had been spraying DDT (dichlorodiphenyltrichloroethane), a chemical meant to kill off mosquitoes to control outbreaks of malaria. The potion was very effective. During World War II, use of the chemical had almost eradicated cases of malaria and typhus in American soldiers. It was also used to control populations of tree-loving spongy moths and invasive fire ants. But it was obvious to both Carson and her friend that the chemical was killing off the birds and fish that depended on the bodies of water it polluted. For eons, Mother Nature had regulated the balance between hungry insects and plant life on its own. Now, in their quest to control nature, human beings had created a monster.

Rachel Carson got to work on what would become her most famous book, *Silent Spring*. The book was published in 1962. In it, she warned of a future without birdsong, without birds to herald the arrival of spring. The title had a double meaning—the "silent spring" was also a deadened tributary of water that held no fish. "It is ironic to think that man might determine his own future by something so seemingly trivial as the choice of an insect spray," she wrote. "How could intelligent beings seek to control a few unwanted species by a method that contaminated the entire environment and brought the threat of disease and death even to their own kind? Yet this is precisely what we have done." Carson talked about other pesticides as well, and how after their use these chemicals would travel through an ecosystem, creating damage far beyond their intended goal. Eventually, they would work their way up the food chain and poison both children and adults, she wrote.

The information in her book was already known to many scientists. But it took a brave voice to get the attention of the general public. After the publication of *Silent Spring*, chemical companies attempted to discredit Carson and her work. But no book before or since has had a greater impact on global environmental policies. *Silent Spring* gave rise to the environmental movement. An entire governmental agency, the Environmental

Protection Agency, was established in 1970 as a result of Carson's groundbreaking work. The use of DDT was banned in the United States in 1972, and in 1980, sixteen years after her death, Carson was awarded the Presidential Medal of Freedom for her contributions to her nation and to the health of the planet.

MAKE A KICK NET

Just like the rocks found on land and inside tidal pools, rocks at the bottom of streams and rivers support an abundance of fascinating life-forms. Many flying insects, including mayflies, caddisflies, stoneflies, and dragonflies, begin their lives as immature nymphs and larvae that live around and under rocks in streams. After spending a year or more living underwater, they swim to the surface and emerge as winged adult insects. Crustaceans like crayfish and freshwater shrimp, along with aquatic beetles, worms, and snails, are permanent residents of the rocks, gravel, sand, and mud on stream bottoms. And small fish like bullheads, sculpins, madtom catfish, and many species of minnow search for food under rocks while hiding from larger predatory fish that might eat them for dinner.

The problem for anyone who is interested in observing these underwater life-forms is that they can be very difficult to catch if you're just using your hands. Many of the creatures that dwell beneath rocks in moving water are fast swimmers. The moment you move their protective rock, they swim downstream. Even slower swimmers are aided by the current, which helps them vanish from sight in a hurry. If you want to catch them, you'll need a special piece of equipment used by scientists to collect small life-forms that live in moving water. This piece of equipment is called a kick net. The name comes from the way it's used. If you kick around on the bottom of a stream or river, the net will catch the critters that get stirred up. Of course, you don't need to be a professional scientist to make or use a kick net. Here's how to get started.

Materials

- Two straight, sturdy sticks 1 or 2 inches thick and about 3 feet long
- A rectangular piece of wire or plastic window screen that measures 2 by 3 feet (easily found at any hardware store)
- Staples and a heavy-duty staple gun (you can also use the kind of staples that can be tapped in using a small hammer)

Building Steps

1. Lay the screen on the ground with long sides on the top and bottom.
2. Place a stick on the edge of the shorter side of the screen. One end of each stick should line up with the top of the screen and the other end should extend about a foot past the bottom for handles.
3. Wrap the edge of the screen around each stick. It's best to give the stick a couple of wraps of screen, so it's solidly held in place.
4. Staple the screen to the sticks so your kick net doesn't fall apart.

That's it. You're done building your kick net. The only other thing you'll need is an observation container to temporarily store your catches, and a friend to help you use your net. A plastic dishwashing tub works great as an observation container, but you can use a standard 5-gallon bucket or a large plastic container from your kitchen cupboard if that's all you have.

How to Use a Kick Net

Catching small stream-dwellers with a kick net is as simple as building one. First, find an area along a stream where it is easy to wade in and out. Look for a spot near shore with lots of gravel and rocks on the bottom. Avoid areas with swift current that could knock you over or deep, soft mud. When the water is warm enough to go swimming, you can "wet-wade" in shorts, but wear a pair of old sneakers so your toes don't get banged up on rocks. When the water is too cold to wet-wade, you'll need a pair of hip boots or chest waders to stay dry and warm.

Kick-netting is easier to do with a partner, so here's how to do it with one netter and one kicker.

- Before you start, add an inch or two of water to your observation container.
- The netter wades into the stream ankle- to knee-deep and faces upstream, into the current, while the kicker wades in about 5–10 feet directly upstream from the netter and faces downstream, toward the netter.
- The netter holds the net by the handles and dips it into the water until it touches the bottom of the stream. Then the kicker shuffles around, aggressively kicking up all the nearby rocks and gravel around their feet.
- The netter should wait a minute or so for the current to carry all the bottom-dwellers that have been dislodged by the kicker into the screen. Then the netter carefully lifts the net out of the water with a scooping motion, so nothing falls out.
- Lastly, the netter and the kicker need to get out of the water to put all the critters trapped on the screen into the observation container. Turn the net carefully upside down over the container and tap it to knock your sample organisms into the container.

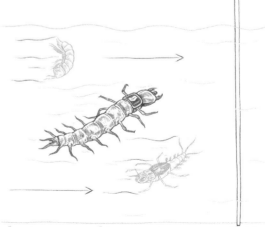

Once you've transferred your bottom-dwellers, wait a minute or two for things to settle down. Pretty soon you'll start to notice creatures crawling and swimming around in your observation container. You'll probably be surprised by the amount of life that's hidden on the streambed. What do you see? Chances are good that you've caught a ton of tiny bugs and maybe some big ones, too. There are probably also some squirmy worms and little fish. There might even be some unusual creatures that you don't recognize. It's not a bad idea to bring along a magnifying glass to get a closer look at all the weird stuff you've never seen before. Take pictures of your finds so you can research and identify them later. Check the library for books like *A Guide to Common Freshwater Invertebrates of North America*. Another great resource for identifying aquatic bugs and other macroinvertebrates is the PocketMacros app. The Picture Fish app is tops for fish identification.

Once you get the hang of your kick net, keep in mind that it can be a handy tool for when you go fishing. Anglers use kick nets all the time to catch fishing bait or to find out what sorts of foods the bigger fish are eating. That way, you can pick out a fly or an artificial lure that resembles real-life fish food. What other uses can you find for your kick net?

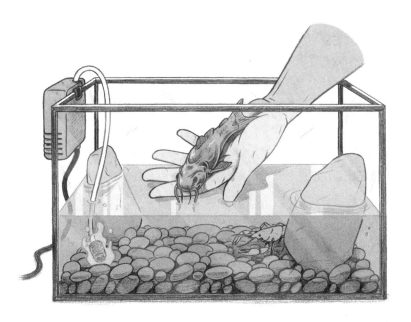

STOCK AN AQUARIUM

If you've ever visited an aquarium in a big city, you've already gotten a glimpse at the fascinating assortment of creatures that live in underwater worlds. The variety of fish alone is astounding. From one exhibit to the next, you can see a multitude of tropical fish species in every color of the rainbow, armor-plated sturgeon that were around when dinosaurs roamed the earth, and even giant whale sharks over 30 feet long that survive by eating tiny microscopic organisms called plankton. At one of the world's largest aquariums, in Atlanta, Georgia, visitors can view over 1 million aquatic organisms, including 500 different species of fish from sixty different types of habitat around the world. Most people won't ever have the chance to see all those amazing underwater life-forms out in the wild, but aquariums give us the unique opportunity to observe an alien environment full of a diverse array of interesting, unfamiliar creatures that are normally hidden from human eyes.

You can get a small taste of these wonders if your family has a home aquarium, or even if you have a single betta or goldfish in your bedroom. But there's only so much you can learn by observing fish purchased from a pet store. If you're really interested in learning more about wild fish, amphibians, crustaceans, and other creatures, try stocking your own aquarium with them. Chances are good there is an aquatic environment near where you live. It doesn't have to be a big lake or river. In fact, it's often easier to catch aquarium specimens in small shallow bodies of water than in big deep ones. Just seek out any small pond, creek, or swamp that holds water throughout the year and you're sure to find something interesting.

When fishing for food, you'll always be hoping to catch the biggest fish you can. But things are different when it comes to catching specimens for an aquarium. Large fish that are captured in the wild can be difficult to keep alive at home, since they get very stressed when they're confined in small spaces. Small fish are more abundant, easier to catch, and make better aquarium residents. You might look for minnows, creek chubs, bullhead catfish, and any of the many species of sunfish like bluegills or rock bass. You'll make your aquarium even more interesting by adding crayfish, damselfly and dragonfly larvae, aquatic beetles, and snails. Some amphibians can be kept in aquariums, too. Green frogs and leopard frogs are common in much of the United States, and their small size makes them good candidates. You can bring some species of wild turtles home, but most are too big for aquariums, and there are some species that you're not allowed to catch.

It's a good idea to make sure you're following the rules before you put anything from the wild into your aquarium. Every state has what's called a fish and game agency, which makes rules and regulations about keeping fish that might be used for bait, food, or pets. They create similar sets of rules about amphibians and reptiles. For certain species, there may be a limit for the number you can keep and also a size limit for how small or big it needs to be. There may also be closed seasons, or parts of the year when you're not allowed to keep certain species at all. You can learn what you can and can't do by calling or visiting the local branch of your fish and game agency. Fish and game agency websites are also good places to find the information you need.

After you've checked the rules, you'll want to set up your aquarium before you go out and catch anything. When it comes to aquariums, bigger is better. Wild fish are used to going wherever they want, so you don't want to overcrowd a bunch of wild fish in a small goldfish bowl where they'll feel confined and stressed. A 10-gallon aquarium is big enough to keep a few small fish and a couple of other critters.

Fish breathe by absorbing oxygen in the water through their gills, so you'll need to attach an aerator to the aquarium to make sure the water stays highly oxygenated. When a fish or other aquatic creature dies in a bucket or aquarium, it's usually because the water ran out of oxygen. You can find inexpensive electric or battery-powered aerators at pet stores or in the fishing department at sporting goods stores.

The next step is creating a natural aquatic habitat inside your tank. Place your tank in a cool place out of direct sunlight. Then add a layer of clean gravel or sand and place a couple of nice-sized rocks on the bottom before you fill the tank with water. Amphibians like frogs or salamanders need a place to climb out of the water now and then, so make sure one of the rocks sticks out of the water a little bit. If you use tap water to fill your fish tank, you'll need to treat it first with a water conditioner that neutralizes common tap water chemicals such as ammonia and chlorine that are harmful to fish. You can usually find a water conditioner, such as AquaSafe, at any pet store. Otherwise, a good choice would be to fill your tank using the same water source as where you'll be looking for aquarium residents.

Now you're ready to capture some live specimens. Depending on what you're after, you can use several of the different types of equipment discussed in this book, including kick nets (page 116), fishing poles (page 154), and minnow and crayfish traps (pages 162 and 193). Handheld bait nets and butterfly nets work well, too. You can even use your hands by cupping them together beneath the creature and gently lifting it up. If you're fishing, try small hooks and small pieces of bait to attract small fish. Use pliers to smash down the sharp barb that faces the opposite direction of the point of the hook. A barbless hook is easy and safe to remove from the mouth of small fish.

Look for fish in areas where there are underwater rocks and weeds. It's always a good idea to check shallow water areas that are close to deeper water. A lot of fish like to hang around those areas, known as drop-offs. Areas around docks and where creeks enter or exit a pond are also places where small fish, amphibians, and aquatic bugs gather to feed and hide from larger predatory fish. Remember, though, it's not a numbers game. You need to catch only a couple for your aquarium. Try to minimize the amount of time any aquatic animal that breathes through gills is kept out of the water. After you catch something, get it into a small bucket of water quickly so you can transport it home and transfer your catch into the aquarium. If you're interested in seeing the fish and other creatures in your aquarium eat, wait a few hours for them to calm down before you feed them. Most fish and amphibians will eat small worms or insects. If you have small minnows the size of your pinky finger, you might try goldfish flakes or breadcrumbs.

Lastly, remember that all wild creatures are highly adapted to survive and thrive in their natural environment. In most cases, it's okay to temporarily keep insects, crustaceans, amphibians, or fish in a comfortable enclosure that closely mimics their habitat in the wild. But don't insist on turning them into permanent pets. The well-being of any wild creature in your care is a big responsibility. It's up to you to keep them safe and healthy. After a day or two of observation, you'll need to release them back to the same exact place you found them. Then go out and catch something new to put in your aquarium.

FIND AN ANTLER

The first thing you should know about antlers is that they are not the same thing as the horns found on animals such as bison, cows, sheep, and goats. Horns are made up of an outer sheath of keratin, the same material found in your own hair or fingernails, and that sheath surrounds a bony spur. Both males and females grow horns; females' horns are usually smaller. And most horns increase in size slowly throughout the animal's life. A horned animal will keep the same set of horns for their entire life. Their horns do not shed, or fall off. The only exception to this rule is the American pronghorn, which sheds the outer sheath of its horns every year.

Antlers, on the other hand, are extremely hard, strong bones that grow out of two protrusions called pedicles on top of the animal's skull. While horns have a single point, antlers usually split into multiple pointy branches called tines. Antlers are only found on members of the deer family. This group of animals, known as cervids, includes elk, moose, whitetail deer, mule deer, and caribou.

Scientists used to believe that the main purpose of antlers was for defense against predators like wolves. In most deer species, only the males (they're called bucks, bulls, or stags, depending on the species) grow antlers. Sometimes deer do try to fend off predators with their antlers, but male deer grow antlers primarily to attract females (does, cows, or hinds). During the fall breeding season, also called the rut, older male deer with bigger antlers get more attention from female deer. Antlers also serve as a visual display of strength against competing males during the rut, and sometimes rival males fight for dominance by clashing and locking antlers.

The primary difference between horns and antlers is that antlered animals grow a brand-new, and usually bigger, set of antlers every year. In fact, antlers are one of the fastest-growing animal tissues on the planet. Deer begin growing their antlers in the spring, and during the summer, they can grow by an inch or more each day. A bull moose can grow a set of antlers over 6 feet wide and weighing 80 pounds in as little as 100 days. That's the equivalent of growing the same amount of bone found in four adult human skeletons in just over three months! By late summer or early fall, the antlers stop growing. They're surrounded by a layer of velvety tissue that supplies blood to the antlers' bony core, and that velvet begins to dry up and fall off. Deer will rub their antlers against trees and bushes to help scrape the dried velvet away. The animals then shed their antlers in the winter, a few months after the fall breeding season has ended. The following spring, the process starts all over again.

Normally, shed antlers will slowly decompose on the ground or get nibbled up by rodents such as mice, squirrels, and porcupines, which are hungry for the minerals the antlers contain. Sometimes larger animals like coyotes, bears, and wolverines will gnaw or eat shed antlers. But not all antlers end up rotting away on the forest floor or lining the stomachs of wild animals, and that's where you come in. Found antlers can be used as simple, striking decorations for your home, wherever they are displayed. They also come in handy for arts and crafts projects. Antlers can be used to make knife handles, door and cabinet knobs, belt buckles, napkin holders, coat hangers, jewelry, checker pieces, and even chandeliers. They make great chew toys for dogs, too.

Looking for antlers is called shed hunting, and the best time for shed hunting is late winter or early spring. Many folks in the mountainous regions of the American West love to shed hunt for elk antlers. They're often sold in pet stores as chew toys, so they can be worth a lot of money—around $20 a pound. A hefty elk antler can weigh as much as 20 pounds, so that would be a $400 find!

No matter where you live, there's a good chance that a whitetail deer antler is just waiting for you to find it. Whitetail deer are the most common antlered animals in the United States, occupying every state but Alaska, Hawaii, Nevada, and California. They also live across the southern half of Canada and almost the entirety of Mexico. The trick is to search in places where whitetails spend their time during the winter shedding season. At that time of year, deer are focused on staying warm, finding food, and conserving energy. They spend a lot of time on slopes and hills that face south and west—these spots get the most sun, which means less snow and more food for deer. During the antler shedding season, deer also conserve energy by spending a lot of time lying down in bedding areas where they rest and sleep. Bedding areas are often located in areas of thick brush, tall grass, or groves of pine trees that block cold winter winds. You'll know you're in a good bedding area if you see a lot of deer-sized oval depressions either melted in the snow or pressed down into the grass. Make sure to check for shed antlers along well-used deer trails as well. If you want to maximize your chances of finding an antler, make it a team activity. A group of friends searching the woods together will always find more antlers than a solo shed hunter.

Once in a while you'll get lucky and find a big antler lying out in the open just waiting for you to scoop it up. But antlers often rest on the ground for months or even years. Over time they get covered up by dead branches, leaves, and grass. Luckily, these antlers eventually turn white, just like old bones. That white color will stick out when everything else on the ground is brown or green. Fresh antlers can be light tan or dark brown, and they usually have ivory-colored tips. These antlers, especially smaller ones, can be easy to miss because they look a lot like sticks.

The key to finding shed antlers is to cover a lot of ground without moving too fast. Walk a few yards and thoroughly scan the ground all around you, and then move a little ways and look around again. Look for curved tines and sharp points, and keep in mind you probably won't see an entire antler. There might just be one antler tine barely sticking out of the grass, so even if you are pretty sure it's just a stick, go check it out. Remember, deer have two antlers. If you find one, there's likely to be another nearby. Try walking in ever growing circles around the spot where you found a single antler and you just might locate its partner. Bringing home a matched set of antlers from the same deer is one of the greatest achievements in shed hunting.

DISSECT AN OWL PELLET

There are over 200 species of owls in the world. In North America, one of the largest is the great horned owl, which gets its name from the feathers on top of its head that look like two sharp horns. These impressive birds have a wingspan over 4 feet wide and razor-sharp talons up to 3 inches long. In contrast, northern saw-whet owls stand only 7 inches tall, which is about the size of a robin. The barred owl is a medium-sized owl that is commonly found throughout the eastern United States, parts of the western United States, and much of Canada. Barred owls are well-known for their recognizable hooting call—it sort of sounds like they're saying, "Who cooks for you? Who cooks for you, all?" Their call can be heard from very far away, so listen for it if you're out in the woods early in the morning or around sunset. These low-light periods are good times to listen for owl calls, because many owls are either crepuscular predators (active around dawn or dusk) or nocturnal predators (active in the dark of night). This makes owls different from hawks and eagles, which are diurnal predators and scavengers (active during the day).

Most owls hunt by sitting in a tree, patiently waiting for their prey to appear. Their eyes are very large, and their heads can swivel in an almost complete circle. This enables them to clearly see small prey in any direction, even far away on the darkest nights, since they also have extremely good night vision. Many owls also hunt by sound. Their feathers and concave, dish-shaped faces funnel barely audible noises toward their keen ears. Some owls have such good hearing that they can detect the sound of a mouse walking through the grass a hundred feet away.

Owls eat up prey like small birds, mice, voles, rabbits, frogs, and lizards by swallowing them whole. However, they're unable to completely digest the entire animal, so within several hours of swallowing their meal, they regurgitate, or cough up, a wad of stuff like teeth, bones, hair, and feathers. This oblong wad of nondigestible materials is called an owl pellet. The pellets are usually 1 to 2 inches long and grayish in color. Ornithologists (scientists who study birds and bird behavior) dissect them in order to find out what the owls have been eating.

You can do your own research on owls by finding and dissecting owl pellets. Your best chance is to look under the branches of trees where owls rest, or roost, during the day. It's common to see roosted owls up in trees when driving through farm country or other rural areas. With some owl species, it might be hard to see them in their roosts because they prefer to spend their time in nests built in coniferous trees like pine, spruce, and fir. They might nest in hollow cavities found high up in large hardwood trees, or even inside old barns. But you can find any of these owl hideouts by looking at the ground. The birds often leave behind white liquidy sprays of owl poop on the ground that are easy to identify. Look around in these areas and you're likely to find some owl pellets as well.

Owl pellets can be confused with the poop of animals like raccoons and coyotes, which you shouldn't pick up. One way to tell the difference is that owl pellets don't smell bad. But to stay on the safe side, keep your hands clean and germ-free by wearing disposable gloves when you're collecting and handling owl pellets. Store any pellets you find in a plastic ziplock bag until you can sterilize them at home. To do that, wrap them in tin foil and bake them in the oven for 40 minutes at 325 degrees. This will kill any germs in the pellet. If you live in an urban area where owls don't live or if you have trouble finding owl pellets on our own, you can also order owl pellet kits online. These pellets have already been sterilized, so they are safe to handle right out of the box.

Your science experiment begins with the dissection of the owl pellet. Place it on a piece of cardboard or construction paper and use a couple of toothpicks or a pair of tweezers to gently pull the pellet apart. You'll almost certainly find the remains of small rodents, like mice. Pick the bones very gently and carefully out of the hair with a toothpick. Many should be completely intact and unbroken.

You should find lots of long, skinny bones that might be leg or rib bones. You'll also find small spinal vertebrae that look like jagged little cubes. Hopefully you'll find a skull or two, which makes it easier to identify what kind of prey animal you're seeing. Try to verify what the owl has been eating by putting all the pieces of the skeleton puzzle back together. Try downloading a free online owl pellet bone chart to help you identify what species of small rodent the bones belonged to. Is there anything else interesting inside the pellet? A magnifying glass will help you identify what you're looking at. How many different creatures are in the pellet? Maybe you'll find the tiny claws and teeth of a shrew, the beak and feathers of a small bird, or even the exoskeleton of a big cricket.

PREPARE AN ANIMAL SKULL FOR DISPLAY

Humans have always used animal bones as tools. Native Americans would turn shoulder blades, or scapulas, into garden hoes. Ancient hunters in Siberia sharpened spear points from the shin bones of various animals, and Native Hawaiians crafted fishing hooks from bird bones. In the Arctic, hunters even used whale bones to build the walls of their houses. But beyond these practical purposes, humans have also used bones for decorative and spiritual purposes. Some of the oldest known forms of artwork are carvings made by ancient people who etched the figures of animals and humans into chunks of bone. Some of the earliest examples of jewelry were crafted from animal bones and teeth. The ancient Egyptians decorated their homes with bone sculptures, and Native American tribes of the Great Plains used buffalo skulls to perform important rituals. For thousands of years, Inuit peoples have adorned their clothing, hunting weapons, and boats with bone and ivory figurines and charms representing important people and animals.

Among many cultures, animal skulls are particularly prized for display. When hunters of the High Arctic region were successful in killing a polar bear, they might show their respect for the animal by placing its skull in a spot where the bear's spirit could see that the hunter who took its life was a good person. You've probably seen deer skulls on the walls of homes, restaurants, and other places where people tend to gather. Hunters often refer to preserved skulls (and antlers, horns, and hides) as trophies. That's not a bad way to think of them, but they're much more than a prize to be claimed. Skulls can serve as memorials that remind us of the places we've been and the experiences we've had, often with friends or family. They can act as totems, or symbols, that honor the beauty of the natural world. And, last but not least, they're also incredibly cool-looking and awe-inspiring.

You can make a skull mount out of just about any animal. It doesn't matter if it's a wild turkey, a beaver, or a big whitetail buck, and it's pretty simple to prepare and preserve a skull for display, though it does take a little work and time. Of course, you might be wondering how you'd even get your hands on the skull of a wild animal in the first place. The answer to that question is pretty easy if you or someone you know is a hunter or trapper. But spend enough time outside and you can still get yourself an animal skull, even if you don't know any hunters. Far more animals die from encounters with predators, starvation, exposure, sicknesses, and vehicle collisions than from crossing paths with hunters. So it's not at all uncommon to stumble across what hunters call a "deadhead" when you're out in the woods. The term usually refers to the antlered skull of a male deer, but a deadhead could really be the skull of any animal.

If you're lucky, taking a deadhead home can often be as simple as grabbing it off the ground. When an animal dies, it usually doesn't take long for scavengers like coyotes and crows to find it and take advantage of a free meal. Fortunately for you, they tend to do a pretty good job of picking the bones clean and separating the skull from the rest of the skeleton. If it's clean, dry, and free of bad odors, you

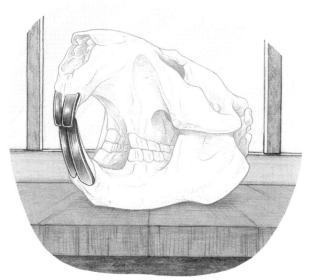

can display the skull at home right away. Just remember that collecting animal bones is prohibited in national parks and may require a permit on public land in some states, so be sure to check the rules at your local fish and game office.

Otherwise, the first step in preparing a skull with hide, muscle, and other tissue attached to the bone is getting rid of all that stuff. This can be a little gross if you're working with a skull covered in stinky, rotten flesh. A good solution is to transport it home in a plastic garbage bag, remove it from the bag, and then bury it in the backyard for a few weeks to allow small subterranean critters and the natural decomposition process to remove all the nasty stuff for you.

The head from a recently dead animal that was hunted or trapped won't stink, but you will, however, have to remove it from the body. This requires cutting through the muscle at the top of the animal's neck and separating the base of the skull from the top of the spine. Next, you'll need to remove as much hide and flesh from the skull as you can. None of this is too difficult on birds and small mammals, but you may need some adult help if you don't have a lot of experience skinning animals or handling knives. Small knives are better for this sort of job. A very sharp paring knife or pocketknife would be perfect (see pages 218–221). On larger animals like deer with thick, tough hides, you may also need a small flathead screwdriver to pry stubborn parts of the hide away from the bone.

Once the head has been skinned, use your knife to cut away the eyes and most of the flesh, fat, and sinew on the skull. You don't need to worry about getting everything. Remember to work very carefully and slowly with your knife so you don't cut yourself. And don't forget about the brain inside the skull! Make a small loop or hook on the end of a piece of coat hanger wire, stick it into the opening of the brain cavity at the base of the skull, and swirl it around aggressively. Then use a hose to spray all the scrambled-up pieces of brain out of the skull.

You'll notice the lower jaw is still attached to the skull. For herbivores (plant-eaters) like deer, you would normally cut this bone free from the skull and discard it at this point, since their lower jaws aren't very interesting and it's extra work to get them clean. But that's not the case with all animals. Some have super-cool lower jaws. Beavers and muskrats have long, curved incisors. Wild pigs have sharp tusks. Predators like bobcats and bears have sharp fangs. For those animals with an impressive set of teeth, it's worth making the lower jaw part of your display.

Now it's time to thoroughly clean the skull by getting rid of all the remaining pieces of tissue on the skull that you couldn't remove with a knife. At this point, taxidermists who get paid to preserve skulls for hunters often place skulls inside large containers that house a colony of dermestid beetles. These flesh-eating beetles will consume every last scrap of remaining soft tissue in a month or two. Believe it or not, you're probably within an easy drive of someone who could add your skull to their beetle tank. The service is offered by many taxidermists. Just call around to taxidermists in your area and ask about finding a beetle cleaning service. If you skip this cleaning step, the skull will end up rotting and stinking up your house later, so it's a must, whether you hire it out or do it yourself.

To do the job at home, you can simmer the skull in a pot of hot water until all the remaining meat and gristle have fallen off the bone. This quick and easy process will also kill any nasty germs living on the skull. If possible, take the job outside, using a single-burner propane camping stove or the side burner on your outdoor grill so you don't make a mess inside. Use a pot big enough to completely cover the skull in water. Tie one end of a thick piece of string or wire to the handle of the pot and the other end through the eye socket so the skull is suspended above the bottom of the pot. This gives you a way to lift the skull out of the hot water and keeps it away from direct heat so it doesn't burn.

Next, fill the pot with water and add a few squirts of dishwashing soap. The soap will help clean and degrease the skull. Turn the heat on your burner to low. You only want the water to barely reach a slow simmer, with just a few small bubbles popping up here and there. If the water gets too hot and starts boiling like crazy, the skull may fall apart. Check frequently to make sure the water isn't getting too hot.

Take a look at the skull after about 2 hours, and every 30 minutes after that. Eventually the soft tissue will fall off the skull and you'll be left with mostly bare bone. At this point, take the skull out. Use the string or wire that's tied to the skull to lift it out of the hot water. Be careful—it will be hot. Set the skull on the ground and let it cool off for 30 minutes before handling. If you kept the lower jaw, pull it free from the skull. Remove any pieces of meat or cartilage that are still clinging to the skull and jaw bones, paying careful attention to all the little nooks and crannies. Use your fingers (wear disposable rubber gloves), a knife, or pliers to scrape, pick, and peel away anything that isn't bone, especially in the nasal and brain cavities.

The next step is preserving the skull by treating it with hydrogen peroxide—its disinfecting properties will kill the bacteria that could make your skull decompose and get stinky, and it is also an oxidizing agent that will whiten the bone. You probably have a bottle of liquid hydrogen peroxide from the pharmacy for disinfecting cuts and scrapes at home. This stuff will eventually whiten a skull, but it's too weak to really do the job quickly and properly. A better choice for treating skulls is the more powerful hydrogen peroxide cream used in beauty salons for dyeing hair. Look online for a 32-ounce bottle of 40V (volume) cream peroxide developer. It should cost about $10, and it's enough to treat several large skulls. If you can't get the beauty salon cream, you can make your own weaker version by mixing equal parts liquid hydrogen peroxide and baking soda into a gel the consistency of paint.

Place the skull outside on a big piece of scrap cardboard. Carefully pour a few ounces of the cream or solution into a small plastic container or bowl. Now paint the skull with a ½- to 1-inch-wide paintbrush or a silicone brush that's used for dabbing meat with BBQ sauce. Leave a thick layer of the substance on the skull, making sure to get some in all the cracks, divots, and holes, including inside eye sockets, the nasal cavity, and the brain cavity. Be aware that hydrogen peroxide is weakly acidic and can cause irritation or mild burning to exposed skin. Fortunately, it's very simple to avoid this by wearing a pair of disposable dishwashing gloves while you're painting the skull.

Leave the skull in a spot where it will stay dry for a couple of days, then wash off the peroxide treatment under the faucet or with a hose. The skull will now be completely preserved, a bright, pure white color, and ready for display.

If you choose to keep the lower jaw, you can use clear epoxy or silicone adhesive to reattach it to the skull. Lots of people choose to permanently mount their skulls on a wall, and there are many simple mounting brackets you can make or buy for that purpose. But you can also display skulls on a bookshelf, windowsill, desk, or wherever else you'd like. And don't forget you can preserve and display other animal bones using the same exact process, too.

GO ROCKHOUNDING

Geologists are scientists who specialize in studying the rocks, minerals, and other materials that make up our home planet. There are many kinds of geologists. Some search for precious metals, gemstones, and other valuable resources like crude oil. Others research the movement of glaciers, mountains, and the continents. Geologists called volcanologists even climb into active volcanoes to study their behavior!

One thing all geologists have in common is they know a lot about rocks. Over 95 percent of the earth's outer layer, or crust, is made of rock. But you don't need to be a professional geologist to appreciate how interesting rocks can be. Rockhounds are just regular people who like to study and collect rocks and minerals as a hobby. In fact, if you've ever picked up a rock that caught your eye, you're already becoming a rockhound.

Rockhounding can be done just about anywhere and anytime. There's almost certainly a place to do it within an easy walk or bike ride from your home, or even in your backyard. The first thing you need to know about rockhounding is that there are three basic types of rock: igneous, sedimentary, and metamorphic. Igneous rock is formed when hot, molten lava cools and solidifies. Obsidian and basalt are two common examples of igneous rock. They are both black. Sedimentary rocks like coal, sandstone, and shale are formed by layers of sediment and organic matter that have slowly hardened into rock. Finally, metamorphic rocks are created when igneous or sedimentary rocks change into a completely new type of rock when they are exposed to the intense pressure and heat that occurs far beneath the earth's surface. Quartzite is an example of a hard metamorphic rock that used to be soft, crumbly sandstone. The marble used for sculptures and kitchen counters started out as a sedimentary rock called limestone.

Of course, there are dozens of other igneous, sedimentary, and metamorphic rocks you might find. Rockhounds also pick up minerals and crystals like quartz, mica, and pyrite. That last one, pyrite, is known as fool's gold. Because it looks like gold, it tricks a lot of beginner rockhounds into thinking they've found something valuable. The reality is that you'll probably never find rocks worth a

bunch of cash. However, you'll almost certainly find beautiful and unique specimens that you'll want to display at home. And if you put in some time and effort, you just might unearth what's called a semiprecious gemstone.

Agates are one of the most sought-after examples of a semiprecious gemstone. Agate is a type of chalcedony, and chalcedony is a type of quartz, and quartz is the most common mineral on earth. This is like saying a monarch is a type of butterfly, and a butterfly is a type of insect, and insects are the most common animal on earth. And just like butterflies, agates come in many shapes, sizes, and colors. Some are totally translucent like glass and will glow when you hold them up to a light. Others have vibrant hues and stripes that look like someone spilled paint on them. These special gemstones are widely distributed across the planet but are most common in places with a history of volcanic activity. Volcanoes play a crucial role in creating agates. The most common way these gems are formed is when mineral-rich water flows into the cracks and crevices of volcanic rock. Over millions of years, the minerals harden into agates. Places that have been disturbed by heavy machinery are good spots to look for agates, because the machines often dig them up. A place where a road was built through a hill or along a mountainside might be good. The shorelines of oceans and lakes are also good places to look. And anytime you're in a spot with petrified wood (pages 145–147), keep your eyes open for agates. These two things are often found together.

Rockhounding is all about surprises, but not every rock can be found everywhere. To begin your rockhounding career, do a simple internet search to find out what rocks and gemstones are available in your area. There are also a lot of great guidebooks that are specific to certain states and regions of the country. Local rockhounding clubs are a good resource, too, and might even offer field trips for aspiring rockhounds. And of course there are phone apps that can help identify a rock based on a photo and where you found it.

The best thing about rockhounding is that it's something you can do while you're enjoying other activities like hiking, fishing, or camping. You might even stumble across a cool rock on your school playground or in a friend's backyard. Just remember to always keep an eye out. You don't want to miss anything exciting that might be hiding right under your foot.

FINDING ANCIENT ARROWHEADS

Once you train yourself to look for fossils and rocks, there's a good chance you'll encounter artifacts as well. An artifact is something made by a human that has historical or cultural significance. Artifacts take many forms. Paintings in museums are artifacts. An old log cabin might be considered an artifact. A bone that an Ice Age hunter scratched with a stone knife while butchering an animal 20,000 years ago is definitely an artifact.

Among the most common artifacts found by rockhounds and fossil hunters are Native American arrowheads. Because they're made of stone, these artifacts can lie on the ground for thousands and thousands of years without changing. Many of them look as good as new, even though they're incredibly old. When you find one of these arrowheads, you're gonna feel a strong desire to put it in your pocket and bring it home!

Before you do that, you need to consider who owns the land where you found it. If you're on any sort of tribal, native, or government-owned land, you're not allowed to take artifacts home with you. In places such as reservations, national parks, and national forests, the artifacts are the property of the governing body or Native American tribe. If they get removed at all, they'd end up in the possession of a museum where archaeologists could study them and members of the public could see them.

It's different if you find an old arrowhead on private land. In that case, decisions about the artifact are up to whoever owns the land. For instance, if you found an arrowhead while working in your grandpa's garden, it would be the legal prop-

CLOVIS POINT ARROWHEAD

erty of your grandpa. There's nothing wrong with picking up and admiring, or even collecting, an arrowhead that you found on private land. Here's how to do it properly. First, you should try to take a photo of it *in situ*, which is a term archaeologists use for "in place." Get a few different shots from different angles and distances (up close, far away). You'll also want to document the location with a GPS device or by making a Google Maps pin on a phone. If you don't have a camera or a phone, that's okay; just mark the area where you found the arrowhead with an obvious pile of rocks or sticks. Now it's okay to pick up the arrowhead; if you decide to leave it in place, consider that the next rainstorm might rebury it.

Next, call your nearest local museum (ask for a curator) or local university anthropology department (ask for an archaeologist). Or you can find a curator or archaeologist on the internet and email them. Tell them what you found and send them your photos. They'll be able to tell you more about it, and you'll also learn a thing or two about being an archaeologist.

FIND A FOSSIL

When you think of fossils, you might envision something like a massive *T. rex* skeleton displayed in a museum. It's true that dinosaurs did leave behind a lot of amazing specimens. But fossils, which are the remains of past life preserved as impressions in rock, can also be small. A fossil might show details of leaves, twigs, insects, or fish.

For a fossil to form, the hard tissue of a creature or plant must leave behind an imprint in muddy sediment. Eventually, the mud surrounding the imprint becomes rock, and a fossil forms in the shape of the plant or animal. Technically, a fossil has to be at least 10,000 years old for a paleontologist—that's someone who studies fossils to learn about past life on earth—to regard it as a true fossil. However, most fossils are much, much older than that. Like millions of years old. It is not uncommon for fossil hunters to find fossils from sea creatures that were alive 400 million years ago. That's long before the time when dinosaurs

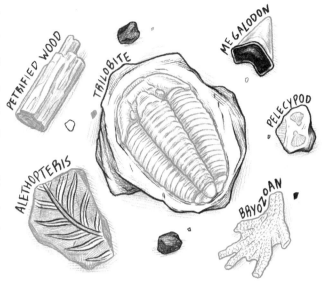

were alive. There are even fossils of jellyfish and mushrooms, though these are rare finds. In fact, there have only been ten mushroom fossils discovered in the entire world! Fossil hunters also search for things that might surprise you even more. There are fossils from microscopic bacteria, called stromatolites; fossilized animal tracks, called ichnites; and even pieces of fossilized poop—these are called coprolites.

Many experts agree that petrified wood is the most common type of fossil on earth. If you're interested in fossil hunting, petrified wood is a great place to start. Some fossils require fossil hunters to excavate tons of dirt and rock as they search. But a lot of petrified wood is just lying around on the ground, where you can find it without digging at all.

Although you can find petrified wood almost anywhere, some areas have higher concentrations of it than others. In Arizona, there's an entire forest of petrified trees that were alive 200 million years ago—it's called the Petrified Forest National Park. While you might not live in an area with that much petrified wood, you almost certainly live within a few hours' drive of a place where you can find some. In fact, every state in the United States has petrified wood. Go to Google and type in "find petrified wood in [your area]." You can be as specific as "find petrified wood in Brewster County, Texas," or as broad as "find petrified wood in New England." You might be surprised by how close you live to the remains of trees that were once eaten by dinosaurs.

When you're in the right area, one of the best ways to find petrified wood is to search along the banks of streams and rivers. River currents constantly erode the earth surrounding them, exposing pieces of petrified wood that have been buried for millions of years. But you must have a keen eye and a lot of patience to find a piece of petrified wood among all the river rocks, since at first glance they look pretty similar. Luckily, you can distinguish petrified wood from other rocks by paying close attention. Look for what is called a wood grain, which will appear as many lines or stripes formed by the wood fibers that grow inside trees.

Most pieces of petrified wood are smaller than your hand. And just like your fingerprint, no two pieces of petrified wood look the same. Colorwise, they can be blue, red, brown, green, black, pink, or white. For texture, some pieces that have been shaped by river currents are smooth and rounded like an egg, while others found in dry environments can be rough, jagged, or sharp.

When you do find some, hold it in your hand and think about what the world looked like when that tree was living. Were there dinosaurs that ate its leaves? Did it grow in a place that used to be a rainforest but is now a desert? Then consider what that fossil has seen in the millions of years that it sat there waiting for you to pick it up.

Holding something that is millions of years old is a powerful feeling. The only way to replicate that feeling is to find another fossil. If you look hard enough, you may come across other wonders like fossilized leaves or seashells. Amateur fossil hunters have even found mammoth teeth and dinosaur eggs! Playing in the dirt can lead to some amazing discoveries.

HUNT FOR BEACH TREASURES

When you think of treasure and the sea, you might be thinking of shipwrecks deep in the ocean or pirate chests full of gold on tropical islands. Those would be nice to find, no question about that. But there's lots of treasure that washes ashore on any regular beach near you, and it's mostly free for the taking. Because ocean tides regularly deposit new layers of natural and human-made debris on shore, you can return to the same spot on a different day and find something new. Hunting for beach treasures isn't just a seaside pursuit, either—lakes that are large enough to produce waves (from the action of the wind, rather than the tides) can also provide lots of interesting beachcombing opportunities.

Have you ever tried the old trick of picking up a conch shell and holding its open end to your ear? People say that you can hear the sea, but what you're really hearing is ambient noise from the environment (wind, voices, footsteps) moving through the shell's distinctively shaped chambers. Depending on where you are, you might find shells from many different kinds of molluscs, including clams, cockles, conches, cowries, mussels, and oysters, washed up on shore. If these shells aren't collected by a beachcomber, they will likely degrade as they're pounded by wind and waves. Over time, they will become part of the sand you see on the beach. Sometimes you'll find shells that still contain some of the soft tissue of whatever used to live inside of the shell. You'll probably know when this happens because you'll smell it! If you want to keep a smelly shell, just pour some rock salt inside and let the shell sit in the sun, then wash it out. That should do the trick. Some beaches have rules about collecting seashells, so check out the regulations where you're at.

There are lots of things to find while you're beachcombing besides seashells. Rocky beaches might not feel as nice on your feet when you're going barefoot, but they are great places for rockhounding. Pick up interesting-looking rocks and add them to your collection (pages 139–142) before they turn to sand in a few million years.

Another really cool thing is driftwood. That's a term for wood that has been washed onto a beach by the wind and waves. If it's in the water long enough, driftwood becomes polished and smooth. A nice specimen will make a great centerpiece for a dining table. Smaller pieces can be displayed on shelves. If your driftwood is stinky, soak it in a mixture of 2 teaspoons of bleach per gallon of water for a few hours, then dry it on a baking sheet in the sun or placed in an oven set to 110 degrees. If it's in the oven, check it every hour or so until it's light and dry. If you want to use a piece of driftwood as an extra piece of habitat in an aquarium, skip the bleaching process because it might harm the creatures in your aquarium. Instead, just boil the driftwood in plain water for an hour or two to remove tannins (a type of acid that's naturally present in wood and is reactive with water) so they don't leach out and turn your aquarium water brown. And here's an interesting thing about driftwood that you can tell your friends: Less than 200 years ago, there were Inuit hunters in the Canadian High Arctic who had never seen trees. When driftwood from faraway forests washed up on the ocean beaches of the islands where they lived, they assumed that the wood must have come from some form of seaweed that grew in the depths of the ocean.

No matter what beach you explore, you're probably gonna find some things that didn't come from nature. Trash in the oceans is a huge and very serious problem for the environment, but you can do your part by picking up the trash that you see. Throw away the gross stuff, but keep an eye out for trash you can repurpose. Pieces of old rope can always come in handy, and you might luck out and find a perfectly usable fishing pole, canoe paddle, or who knows what. Sea glass is a form of trash that's been turned into treasure. Over time, broken shards of glass are rounded and smoothed by the action of the waves and sand. Collect as much as you like—you can use it in all kinds of crafts. And while bottle caps will never become a thing of beauty, they can be added to wind chimes (page 266) or used to create a nifty fish-scaling tool (page 182). Pay careful attention when walking the beach, and you're certain to find something that is either useful or beautiful.

THE FATHER OF BIODIVERSITY

When the evolutionary biologist Edward O. Wilson (1929–2021) was seven years old, a pinfish nudged the young boy's bait as he was fishing off a dock. Wilson yanked on his fishing pole, and the pinfish sprang out of the water and flew straight into his face. Pinfish have sharp spines along the dorsal fin on their backs, and one of those spines stabbed him in the eye.

Wilson lost sight in the damaged eye. But over time, he learned that his working eye, the left eye, was very good at perceiving short-range detail. That's how he became interested in ants. He was still in high school when he discovered the first colony of imported fire ants in the United States. Later on in his career as a myrmecologist (a scientist who studies ants), he would make the groundbreaking discovery that the ants were communicating with one another through the use of pheromones. These chemicals, released by ants and other creatures, including humans, are a silent mode of communication designed to provoke specific reactions from other members of the species. Ant societies, it turned out, were a lot more complex than they seemed.

While he loved studying ant colonies up close, Wilson was deeply interested in what lessons we could draw from the animal kingdom. Although he continued to study insects, he eventually came to be known as the "father of biodiversity." Biodiversity is a measure of the variety of life-forms in an environment. Wilson believed that the biodiversity of our planet was essential to the survival of all life on earth.

One easy way to understand this concept is by thinking about mosquitoes. There's probably not a human being on this planet who likes being stung by mosquitoes. But mosquitoes and their larvae are a key source of food for birds, amphibians, arachnids, and fish, as well as for other insects like dragonflies and damselflies. So if you ever thought it might be nice to just get rid of mosquitoes, you'd have to think about all the other life-forms that would potentially become extinct as a result. As Wilson pointed out, because of their place in the food chain, mosquitoes are actually a whole lot more important than we are. "If all mankind were to disappear, the world would regenerate back to the rich state of equilibrium that existed ten thousand years ago," he wrote in his book *The Diversity of Life*. "If insects were to vanish, the environment would collapse into chaos." That was just one of many books Wilson wrote throughout his long and varied career, including a couple that were written or adapted for younger readers: *Letters to a Young Scientist* and *Naturalist: A Graphic Adaptation*.

As he learned more and more about the importance of biodiversity, Wilson became a passionate conservationist. Toward the end of his life, he was working on a project to catalog every single species on the planet into what he called an encyclopedia of life. There are around 1.4 million named species of plants, animals, insects, and algae on earth to date, and scientists theorize that there are millions remaining to be cataloged. That's lots of work left to be done for enterprising naturalists.

III

FISHING, HUNTING, AND WILDLIFE

R eady to try your hand at the ancestral practices of hunting and fishing? There's no better feeling in the world than sitting down with your family to a plate of fish or meat that you caught with your own two hands. This section will teach you how. Even if you're not old enough to hunt yet, you can still practice by stalking animals, building a wildlife-viewing blind, and crafting the hunting and fishing tools that will be necessary for your adventures. These are some of the toughest outdoor skills to master. They're also some of the most important. Master them, and you can become one with the wild.

BUILD A HOMEMADE FISHING POLE

If you want to catch something good for you and your family to eat, fishing is the surest way to get it done. Pretty much no matter where you go, there are rivers, creeks, and lakes where tasty fish abound. You're allowed to keep many different kinds of these fish as long as you follow some simple rules that are set out by your state or province. Depending on where you live, you might be allowed to harvest fish using a wide variety of techniques, including nets, spears, and even your bare hands. However, the most common way for recreational anglers to catch fish is by using a fishing pole. This method is generally legal for every kind of fish you can imagine, across all fifty states and the entirety of Canada.

In its simplest form, a fishing pole is nothing more than a stick with a length of line tied to the end of the pole, with a baited hook or artificial lure tied to the end of the line. It's a design that's been used for thousands of years in places ranging from ancient China to medieval Europe. The oldest fishing poles were made from long lengths of springy wood or bamboo. Animal sinew, plant fibers, silk, and even strands of hair from a horse's tail were woven into slender lengths of fishing line. Today, you're more likely to encounter lines made out of plastics, and rods made from other synthetic (man-made) materials like fiberglass and graphite. There are wispy ultralight rods designed for catching small trout and sunfish, and heavy rods built to battle giant blue marlin and sharks weighing hundreds of pounds. There are short rods for ice fishing, and really long rods for fishing along ocean beaches. There are also fishing reels in almost as many sizes and shapes. A reel is a device meant to store fishing line at the base of a rod, and to retrieve that line after you cast or when you're fighting a fish. But you don't actually need a reel or even a special fishing pole to catch a few fish and have some fun. Instead, you can get by with the same basic system that was used thousands of years ago: a pole with a fixed length of fishing line tied to the tip, and no reel.

This simple setup is still used by anglers all over the world today. ("Angling" is just another word for fishing, FYI!) The Japanese method of fishing known as *tenkara* uses just a rod, a short length of line, and a tiny artificial fly to catch small trout out of mountain creeks. In the oceans, tuna fishermen sometimes use a similar device—although much more heavy-duty—to haul tuna weighing hundreds of pounds out of the waves and into a boat. And right now, somewhere out there, there's a kid just like you using a homemade bamboo cane pole to catch catfish out of a pond or muddy river.

Building your fishing pole requires only a few materials and is very simple to do. Here's what you'll need and how to make one.

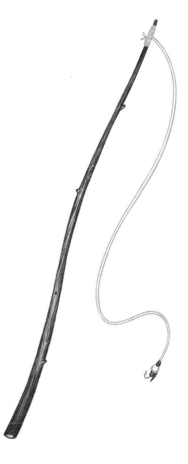

- **Select a limb for a fishing pole.** Dry wood is brittle and weak, so select a live limb that has some bend to it. The type of wood you use isn't super-important, but live willow branches and bamboo canes are two great choices. Look for a long, slender, springy branch with a gradual taper from roughly 1 inch in diameter at the thick end down to about ⅜ inch at the tip. It should be between 6 and 10 feet long. Shorter is good for small creeks that are only a few feet wide, and longer is good for ponds or rivers where you may need to reach deeper water away from shore to catch fish.

- **Test and cut the limb.** Grab the tip and bend the upper half of the pole a bit. If the limb cracks or breaks, look for a new one. If it seems strong enough to handle the pull of a small fish, cut the limb where the bottom of the handle will be with a small handsaw. Then use the saw or a pocketknife to remove any small branches where they are attached to the pole.

- **Cut a groove for your line.** Use a pocketknife to cut a thin, shallow groove around the circumference of the limb about 1 inch from the tip. Don't cut into the wood too far! The groove should be just deep enough that your thumbnail catches in it when you run it across.

- **Pick your line.** Fishing lines are rated according to their pound test, or breaking strength in pounds. You'll need a length of 8-lb. test monofilament fishing line that's 1–2 feet longer than your pole.

- **Finish your setup.** To attach the line to the pole, wrap one end of the line around the groove on the tip a couple of times and then tie it off using a couple of overhand knots stacked on top of each other. (That's the same knot you use during the first step of tying your shoes.)

Now you're ready to start thinking about where you'll fish, and what bait or lures you'll need to catch what you're after.

STUDY YOUR LOCAL FISHING RULES

There are rules that fishermen need to follow in order to make sure the fish in our waters stay healthy and abundant. That's a good thing, because if everyone went out and caught whatever they wanted whenever they wanted, many lakes and rivers would be empty of fish. Millions of people go fishing every year in the United States, and the fishing stays good from one year to the next. That's because we have great fishing rules! Most of these rules are created and enforced by your particular state or province. But in a few certain places, such as national parks or national wildlife refuges, there might be some additional rules created by the federal government that you'll need to pay attention to as well. All of the rules (many anglers call them "regs," which is short for "regulations") can be found online or in printed booklets that are given away for free in small sporting goods stores or at the sporting goods counters in big stores like Walmart.

It varies from place to place, but you generally need a fishing license once you turn fifteen or sixteen years old. Younger kids usually do not need a license, but they still need to follow the fishing rules in order to help keep fish populations healthy. For example, there are often limits to the number and size of fish you may or may not be allowed to keep. There may also be times of year when you're not allowed to keep certain species of fish. And you may not be allowed to keep some species of fish at all. Sometimes the rules in one lake are different from the rules in another lake that is only a few miles away! All of these different regulations can be very complex and sometimes a little confusing, but luckily the agencies that create and manage fishing regulations have employees whose job is to help you understand the rules. If you're really confused, you can always call the agency's local office or go with a grown-up to visit the office yourself.

If you're lucky, you might discover that your state has special waters near your home where only kids are allowed to fish. Your state fish and game agency also probably has learn-to-fish days for kids. At these events, all the fishing equipment is provided free of charge, and there are instructors who will help you learn how to tie knots, choose the right bait, cast, and maybe even clean a fish so you can eat it for dinner.

GATHER YOUR OWN FISHING BAIT

At the end of a really great fishing day, you might have a sore arm from pulling in so many fish. Other days, you can spend hours on the water without getting a single nibble. Those days when you don't get a bite on the end of your line can still be fun, but you're probably hoping to have more action-packed days than boring ones. The difference between the two kinds of days often comes down to what you're using as a lure or bait. "Lure" is a term that's generally used for artificial baits, such as fake worms or fake minnows made from plastic. "Bait" is a term that's generally used for natural things that fish like to eat, such as bugs, worms, or minnows. These types of baits can be used either dead or alive.

While every fishing situation is different, here's a fishing secret for you to keep in mind: Usually, you'll catch more fish using bait than lures—especially if you're a new angler who's just getting started out. Here's why. Fish feed by using a variety of senses to locate their prey. Species like bass and trout find food primarily by sight. But they also have a sensory organ called a lateral line that can detect subtle vibrations in the water created by the movement of nearby prey. Catfish, on the other hand, have extremely poor eyesight. They often rely on their whiskers, or barbels, to help them feel, smell, and taste for food that might be hiding in the rocks and mud. Considering all of the special tricks fish have for finding their food, it makes sense that you want to use a bait that they'll be able to locate in multiple ways and recognize as something good to eat.

Another benefit of fishing with live bait is that it's super simple and easy. When you are using an artificial lure, it's necessary to cast and retrieve it over and over again, keeping it moving so that it looks alive. The natural movement and scent of a lively worm or minnow will attract fish from a distance, so all you need to do is cast it out and let it sit until a fish finds it. You can buy all kinds of different live bait at tackle shops, sporting goods stores, and even from automated vending machines in some places. Or you can save a little money, learn a new skill, and be more self-reliant by gathering your own bait. Catching bait is just as much fun as catching fish! Keep reading to learn how to get your hands on some of the most effective kinds of live bait that can be found.

Earthworms

Worms are one of the most popular live bait choices, and for good reason. There aren't many kinds of freshwater fish, big or small, that will turn down a chance to eat a juicy earthworm. Catfish and trout love big, fat nightcrawlers, and sunfish and yellow perch can't resist a wriggly garden worm. Worms are also one of the easiest types of bait to collect.

Smaller pink and red "garden" worms are usually just 2 or 3 inches long. They prefer cool, dark, moist, loose soil, so don't waste your time looking for them in dry dirt, rocks, or sand. If you have an in-ground garden or a compost pile, you'll usually find worms there just by digging with a small hand shovel. Check the moist soil under mulch, bushes, leaf litter, and piles of grass clippings in your yard as well. In a pinch, you can sometimes dig up some worms in the moist earth right alongside creeks or ponds where you may already be fishing.

Nightcrawlers are large earthworms that can grow to over 6 inches long. They can be used whole for big fish or pinched into pieces for smaller fish. You'll occasionally find them while you're digging around for garden worms, but you don't actually need to dig for them. If you keep an eye on the weather and time things right, catching nightcrawlers can be as simple as gathering them up right off the ground.

Nightcrawlers prefer living in the soil under grassy areas like your backyard or a playground. But on warm spring nights when it's raining, nightcrawlers emerge from the ground in order to reproduce. When the right weather conditions line up for this breeding frenzy, you'll need to get outside an hour or two after sunset.

This is your chance to collect dozens in short order, but only if you know about a couple of the tricks.

The first thing to know is how nightcrawlers got their name—nightcrawlers avoid sunlight at all costs, because it will dry them up and kill them! They don't have eyes, but the sensors on their skin are so sensitive to bright yellow or white light that they'll scoot backward down their holes the instant they detect light. But you'll need a light source, ideally a headlamp, to see in the darkness. The solution is to use a headlamp with a red light setting, which won't trigger the sensors on nightcrawlers' skin.

A nightcrawler's other defense against getting caught is being able to sense slight vibrations on the ground caused by any approaching predators. So you need to walk with very soft steps in order to sneak close enough to a nightcrawler to grab it. There's an art to grabbing them the right way, too. If you can see that a nightcrawler is completely out of its hole, then you can just scoop it up and toss it in a bucket. But you'll need to be more careful if the worm is only partially exposed. Firmly but gently pinch the nightcrawler as close to its hole as you can and wait a few seconds. If you yank on the crawler too hard or fast, it will break in half. If you're patient, you'll feel its muscles relax and you can slowly slide the rest of it out of the hole.

Store your worms inside a small styrofoam cooler or bucket with a snap-on lid in a bedding mixture of moist soil and damp newspaper clippings. Warm temperatures will kill worms in a hurry, but they'll stay alive for several weeks or more if you keep them in a refrigerator. You may need to moisten their bedding occasionally, and you can feed them a sprinkle of breadcrumbs now and then.

Minnows

Earthworms are a great all-purpose fishing bait, but at times live minnows and other types of small baitfish can be even better. Many species of fish are *piscivorous,* meaning they prefer to eat smaller fish. Golden shiners, emerald shiners, and fathead minnows that are 2–3 inches long make great bait for crappie, walleye, and chain pickerel. Larger creek chubs, suckers, and other small fish are also commonly used as bait for largemouth and smallmouth bass, big catfish, and northern pike.

The minnows that are sold at tackle shops are caught in large traps by the hundreds, and you can use the same technique to catch them. The only difference is you'll be using a smaller trap that can be purchased online or at sporting goods stores for less than $20. A dozen minnows can cost $5 at a tackle shop, so getting a minnow trap will pay for itself pretty quickly. Some minnow traps are made out of nylon screen material, but get a more durable one made out of lightweight metal wire. They're tube-shaped, with inward-facing funnels that have small openings at each end. The funnels guide the minnows into the trap, but they have a hard time finding their way back out through the small openings.

There are a couple of things you'll need to do to set up your trap. First off, you'll need some bait to lure the tiny fish into the trap. A small can of cat food with a few holes poked into it works very well. It's also smart to add a glow stick to the inside of the trap. This step isn't necessary, but at night the light will attract tiny insect larvae, which in turn attract the baitfish that eat them. Lastly, tie a length of paracord or rope to the trap so you can secure it to something onshore before you put it in the water.

It's important to set your trap in a place where you're likely to come back and find it full of minnows. You'll get the best results in water that's at least a foot or two deep, with plenty of hiding places for small minnows. Find a creek or pond near where you live and look for a spot near shore with plenty of rocks, aquatic weeds, submerged logs, docks, or other underwater places where minnows might try to take shelter from predators. Normally, you'll know you're in the right place if you can see the minnows swimming around. In some places, though, the water might be too muddy to see clearly. If you are setting your minnow trap in a river or creek where there's enough current to move the trap around, put a couple of rocks in the trap to help weigh it down.

You can set your trap early in the morning and check it in the evening, or set it in the evening and leave it overnight. (Most states require that you write your name and phone number on any traps that are left in place, so check your local fishing regulations.) The key is to give the trap a long "soak" in the water for at least several hours. When it's time to check your trap, bring a bucket filled halfway with water so you have somewhere to put your catch. Gently pull the trap out of the water using the rope you attached to it. If you didn't catch anything, you may want to set your trap in a different location. But if there are a bunch of minnows in the trap, carefully open the latch and dump them into the bucket of water. Reset your trap in the same spot if you want more minnows for bait.

If you're not going to use the minnows right away, you'll have to transfer them to a place where you can keep them alive until your next fishing trip. Minnows will die in less than a day unless they're kept in well-oxygenated water in a cool, shaded place. You shouldn't overcrowd them in a small container, either. A 5-gallon bucket, a clean 10-gallon plastic trash can, or a big styrofoam cooler will hold several dozen minnows. Fill the container about three-quarters of the way with bottled distilled water—or, if possible, water from where you caught them. Don't use tap water, which has chemicals in it that are harmful to small fish. Once you get home, keep the water oxygenated with an inexpensive plug-in aerator from the pet store. Feed the fish occasionally with a small sprinkle of goldfish flakes or breadcrumbs.

There are other ways to catch minnows and baitfish, too. In freshwater, you can catch larger baitfish like creek chubs and suckers with a rod and reel and a small hook baited with a piece of worm. Saltwater baitfish like pinfish and small croakers can be caught the same way, on hooks baited with small pieces of shrimp or squid. Saltwater fishermen also use cast nets that are thrown into the water. It takes some practice to learn how to throw a cast net, but you can catch an entire school of baitfish in one toss if you know what you're doing. In ponds and creeks that don't have too many rocks and branches in the water, beach seines are a very effective way of catching minnows. You'll need a partner to properly use a beach seine. But since it's so much fun, you shouldn't have a hard time finding a helper.

Besides worms and minnows, there are many other kinds of live bait you can gather yourself. Crickets and grasshoppers are good bait for sunfish and trout. You can use a kick net (page 116) to collect hellgrammites out of streams. They're the larval stage of Dobson flies and one of the best baits for smallmouth bass and many other species—but watch out for their sharp pincers! Leeches and crayfish (page 193) can be trapped, and all kinds of fish love to eat them. If you're fishing on a sandy beach at the ocean, you can dig up a type of small crustacean known as sand fleas or mole crabs that live right where the waves hit the beach. These are great bait for whiting, pompano, and surf perch. Slightly larger crustaceans can be used to catch striped bass, redfish, and many other types of larger fish.

STOCK AND ORGANIZE A BASIC TACKLE BOX

Whether you're fishing with a homemade pole or a store-bought version, you'll be heading out onto the water with a whole bunch of pieces of small fishing equipment like hooks, bobbers, and sinkers. In the old days, fishermen either stored this stuff in heavy metal tackle boxes or tucked it into bulky fishing vests. Today, you can choose from many different types of specialized and lightweight tackle bags and boxes. All you really need, though, is some sort of container

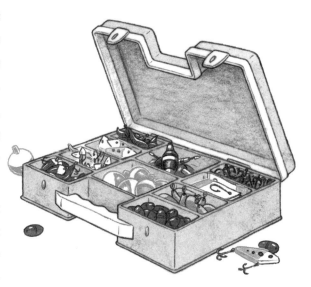

that will hold a basic selection of tackle and that you can stuff in your backpack or hang over the handlebars of your bike. As you get more interested in fishing tackle and different ways of catching fish, you will eventually get to a point where you are ready for what's called a rod and reel combo. That's a standard fishing rod paired with a reel. Such a setup will let you use the sorts of lures described below, and it'll allow you to cast both lures and bait much farther away from shore and into deeper water.

The simplest solution for hauling your fishing tackle is a plastic box with divided compartments. They're inexpensive, durable, and come in a bunch of sizes and configurations. You can find these semitransparent plastic boxes at hardware stores, home and garden stores, tackle shops, sporting goods stores, and places like Target and Walmart. Look for the Plano brand of boxes, which are high-quality and inexpensive. A box that's about the length and width of a sheet of paper should be small enough to fit in your backpack and big enough to hold all the necessary fishing tackle. You may want to get one that comes with extra dividers, so you can separate the main compartments into smaller compartments. Then you can organize your different types of tackle however you like.

Basic Fishing Tackle Selection

Start out by filling your box with a good selection of all the necessities. Once you've got the basics covered, you'll be prepared to catch a variety of different game fish wherever you go fishing. You may choose to add some new pieces of tackle as you gain experience, and you might even end up needing a second box eventually, but here's what you need to get started.

Hooks. Fishing hooks come in a huge range of sizes categorized by numbering systems. The systems are kind of tricky. Smaller-sized hooks are categorized by a number, although a larger number means a smaller hook. So a #10 hook is smaller than a #9, and so on. For freshwater species like bluegills and trout, a #6 or #8 hook is usually a pretty good choice. But having a supply of hooks ranging from #1 to #8 will prepare you for most freshwater situations. In case you're wondering, this system goes all the way down in size to the 20s, which are very small hooks!

For hooks larger than a #1, the system switches to a two-number system. From there, hook sizes look like this: #1/0, #2/0, #3/0, etc. But with these numbers, the hooks get bigger as the numbers get bigger. Halibut fishermen often use 12/0 or 16/0 hooks, which are larger than a baby's hand.

Lures. Fishing lures are artificial imitations of things like minnows, leeches, crayfish, shrimp, or squid. There are hundreds of different kinds of lures in every size, shape, and color imaginable. You definitely don't need all of them, but it's nice to have at least a small assortment to experiment with. The four main categories of lures are spoons, spinners, jigs, and plugs. You'll want a few of each in different sizes and colors.

Spoons are just what they sound like: spoon-shaped lures made from shiny metal. They are the most versatile and durable type of fishing lure—just about every predatory fish will eat a flashy silver- or gold-colored spoon. All you need to do is cast them out, let them sink a little, and reel them in. Fish mistake a moving spoon's wobbling, fluttering action for a struggling minnow.

Spinners have an oval or teardrop-shaped blade that spins around a weighted metal body when the lure is reeled in. Like spoons, spinners are very easy to use. Just cast them out and reel them in fast enough to make the spinner blade turn continuously.

Fish can feel the vibration *and* see the flash of the spinning blade from a distance. Along with silver and gold, try spinners in bright fluorescent colors. When it comes to fishing lure colors, there's a rhyme that many fishermen regard as fact: If it ain't chartreuse, it ain't no use.

Jigs are another versatile lure. They are made from a single bare hook attached to a heavy roundish head. The heads are usually made from lead or tungsten. The jig's hook can be used to hold live bait such as leeches, worms, or minnows. Usually, though, jigs are paired with worm-like rubber bodies called grubs. Many styles of rubber grubs have tails that twist and paddle back and forth when pulled through the water. Other jigs might have flashy synthetic materials attached to the hooks, or even bits of animal hair and feathers that mimic crayfish or shrimp. In all their different sizes and colors, jigs can imitate almost anything a fish might eat. White, black, pink, purple, and chartreuse are good jig colors—think back to all of the vibrant fish colors you might see in an aquarium or when using your bathyscope! To fish with a jig, cast it out and let it sink to the bottom, then retrieve it by reeling slowly and moving your rod tip in an up-and-down "jigging" motion.

Plugs are lures that look just like minnows and small fish. Most plugs have a clear plastic lip that makes them dive down into the water and wobble like a swimming baitfish as you reel them in. Others float and make a disturbance on the water's surface. Many plugs also have noisy rattles that attract fish from a distance. Plugs aren't a great choice for small fish, but it's a good idea to keep a couple in your tackle box for bigger predators. Try color combinations of silver and blue, gold and black, or white and red that look like real baitfish.

Sinkers. It can be tough to catch anything if you aren't fishing at the right depth. Sinkers are used to get your bait on the bottom or down into deeper water. The weight of the sinker also allows you to cast light baits farther. Just like hooks, there are many sizes and shapes of sinkers but you can get by with just a couple. Start with a selection of removable split-shot sinkers weighing ⅛, ¼, and ½ ounce. Reusable split-shot weights are very convenient and versatile because you can pinch as many as you need onto your line to get your bait to the right depth and then easily remove them. In very deep water or fast current, you may need to use heavy egg-shaped or pyramid-shaped sinkers instead of split shot. Traditionally, sinkers were all made from lead. Lead is cheap, heavy, and easy to work with. However, sinkers made from alternative nontoxic metals are available, and in some places regulations require their use. They don't work as well as lead sinkers, but more and more anglers think that the environmental benefits of non-lead sinkers make up for any inconvenience.

Bobbers. Sometimes fish feed near or on the surface, so you need to use a bobber, or float, to prevent your bait from sinking to the bottom. Bobbers also provide a visual clue to let you know when you're getting a bite. When a fish grabs your bait, the bobber will bounce and twitch on the surface or get pulled completely under the water. Get a couple of sizes of the cheap, round red-and-white plastic bobbers and some more sensitive and durable stick bobbers made out of balsa wood. Both styles allow you to easily adjust the depth of your bait by sliding the bobber up or down your line.

Swivels. Snap swivels are small metal clips that can be opened and closed. Tie one onto the end of your fishing line using a clinch knot (page 72) when you're fishing with artificial lures so that you can switch lures without having to tie a new knot. Always keep a few in your tackle box.

Tape measure. In many places, there are rules against keeping fish under, and sometimes over, a certain length. You can make sure you don't break those rules if you have a small spring-loaded flexible tape measure. They only cost a couple of bucks, and you'll be able to record the length of any monster fish you catch.

Stringer. If you're keeping fish to eat, you'll need somewhere to put them while you're fishing and a way to carry them home when you're done. A cooler filled with ice is the best option. It will keep fish cold and fresh. But if that's not an option, you'll want a stringer. That's an angler's term for any sort of rope or similar device that can be used to hold your fish. Rope stringers are inexpensive and simple to use. Run the sharp metal end through the gills and out the mouth of the first fish you catch. Then pass that metal end through the ring on the other end of the stringer. Now your fish is secure. Toss the fish in the water and tie the stringer to a rock or tree on the bank so the fish can't swim away. Add more fish to the stringer by sliding the sharp end through the gills and out the mouth. You can also find stringers made of lightweight chain with clips that can be hooked to a fish's jaw. These are easy to use but more expensive and cumbersome to carry than a simple rope stringer.

Tools. If you're going to eat the fish you catch, you'll need a knife to clean them (page 218). A knife also comes in handy for cutting fishing line and chopping up pieces of bait. A small, folding jack-knife will fit inside your tackle box. You'll also want a small pair of needle-nose pliers for removing stubborn hooks from fish, especially those species with sharp teeth like northern pike or bluefish. Or, even better, get yourself a good multi-tool that can serve the purpose of both a knife and pliers.

Besides your rod and reel and your tackle box, there are a few other things you may want to carry with you on fishing trips. Sometimes fish bite better after sunset. If you're going to be doing some night fishing, you'll need a headlamp. Sometimes, even if you've done everything right, the fish you hook will get away before you can grab them or drag them ashore. You'll lose a lot fewer fish if you have a landing net. Most experienced fishermen wear polarized sunglasses that reduce glare and allow them to see fish in the water. Polarized or not, sunglasses of some kind should be considered mandatory safety equipment since they'll protect your eyes from sharp hooks and bright sun.

A GRAND ADVENTURER

At the outbreak of the Civil War in early 1861, the explorer and adventurer John Wesley Powell (1834–1902) joined the Union Army. He was a schoolteacher at the time, but Powell's primary passion had always been investigating the natural world as an amateur field scientist. During summers, he would engage in rambling explorations all by himself along the waterways of the Midwest. He liked to collect interesting specimens and write down his observations about nature.

Throughout his childhood, Powell's family had moved westward across the young nation's most productive farm country. They went from upstate New York to Ohio. They then went on to Wisconsin and eventually settled in Illinois. Although he wasn't the eldest child, he was responsible for much of the hard work required to keep the family farm going. Those experiences, as well as his love for exploring the nearby fields and woods, created a lifelong interest in the outdoors. Inspired by the mentorship of a local, self-taught naturalist, Powell became committed to expanding his knowledge of the natural world, and he left home at the age of sixteen to pursue a life of books and learning. At that time, for someone from a rural background, anything beyond a basic education could be attained only through an unusual amount of perseverance and dedication.

Once in the Union Army, those characteristics, as well as his unusually inquisitive mind, allowed Powell to rise through the ranks with distinction. At the Battle of Shiloh in Tennessee, he lost his lower right arm after being shot. But Powell continued his military service until the end of hostilities in 1865. He had been promoted all the way to a major. Emerging from the conflict as one of countless disabled veterans spread across the country, he took great pride in the sacrifice that he had made in the fight against slavery. Later in life, as Powell's fame grew, the missing limb only added to his legend.

After returning home, Powell resumed his career as an educator. Despite his lack of a university degree, he found employment teaching science at various colleges throughout Illinois. His imagination, however, was preoccupied by curiosity about the expansive Western frontier. In 1867 and 1868, Powell led a group of his students and other amateur scientists on field trips to the Rocky Mountains, where they studied the geography of the region, drew maps, and learned about the cultures of the Native Americans living there.

In 1869, Powell set off on a western expedition to explore the last unmapped part of the country. The trip would forever change his life. Composed of ten men divided among four small boats, Powell's daring party set off from present-day Green River, Wyoming. From there, they descended the rapids of the Green and Colorado Rivers into a landscape shrouded in mystery. As they drifted downriver on the Colorado River, their small boats were hemmed in by towering cliff walls stretching thousands of feet toward the sky. Three months later, after newspapers across the country speculated that the expedition had been lost to the perilous waters of the Colorado, Powell and his men emerged nearly 1,000 miles downstream—the first American explorers to have witnessed the wonders of the Grand Canyon in an unbroken stretch from end to end.

Two years later, Powell repeated the feat, this time with funding from the federal government to survey and map the surrounding region, known as the Colorado Plateau. He was fascinated by the question of how the remarkable canyonlands of the Southwest were formed. Scholars had only recently come to appreciate how very small changes caused by natural processes, when taking place over enormous periods of time, could result in monumental transformations. Powell marveled at the different layers of rock, known as strata, stretching along the canyon walls. He understood that these features could be read like a book for insight on how the Colorado River and the geology of the region had developed over millennia. A published account of his adventures navigating the Grand Canyon thrilled readers and became a classic tale of adventure. Powell became a great promoter of government-supported science. He encouraged Congress and the American people to support public funding for research. After relocating to Washington, D.C., Powell headed up various agencies devoted to creating and compiling knowledge. He served as the director of the U.S. Geological Survey from 1881 to 1894. As a result of his involvement in policymaking, Powell also found himself at the heart of a passionate debate concerning the future of the American West.

Powell's vision for the future of the West was rooted in his observation of the natural world. He was among the first to recognize that the region's defining feature was its dry and arid climate. The West's finite water resources, he believed, called for limits on development and farming in order to preserve the landscape. But Powell's concerns about these environmental constraints were at odds with Americans who wanted to see the West fully developed and settled. Many people came to dislike Powell because of his beliefs.

At a time when most Americans were certain they could fully tame the so-called wild frontier, Powell maintained a deep respect for the power of nature. That might be surprising given that his nickname was "the Conqueror of the Grand Canyon." But even though John Wesley Powell was brave enough to explore the wilderness, he was also a careful observer of his surroundings and never lost sight of the bigger picture. He was a realist who tried to understand the world on its own terms. Powell achieved all he did because he balanced a taste for adventure with a curiosity for knowledge. These two complementary traits would help any naturalist lead a rewarding life filled with new experiences and opportunities for learning.

—By Randall Williams

CATCH A MESS OF PANFISH

The biggest fish ever caught with a rod and reel was an incredible 17-foot-long, 3,400-pound great white shark. It was landed by a charter boat captain named Frank Mundus in 1986 in the Atlantic Ocean off the coast of Montauk, New York. Mundus's nickname was "Monster Man," and for good reason. Catching that big shark was the equivalent of pulling in a pickup truck with a mouth full of razor-sharp 6-inch teeth! While that was a truly remarkable haul, bigger isn't necessarily always better, especially if you like eating the fish you catch.

Some of the tastiest fish in the water rarely measure longer than a 12-inch ruler. These smaller fish are called panfish, and besides being very good to eat, they're also a ton of fun to catch.

What exactly are panfish, though? They aren't one particular kind of fish, but rather a large group of different species of relatively small fish. American fishermen have been using the term "panfish" for a couple of hundred years to describe just about any freshwater fish that can fit inside a frying pan. In fact, there's no better choice for a fish fry. Even though they're small, most of these species are extremely popular among fishermen of all ages and experience levels because they are found in plentiful numbers throughout North America. Panfish species you're most likely to encounter include rock bass, white bass, bullhead catfish, white and black crappie, yellow perch, bluegills, pumpkinseeds, and many other members of the sunfish family.

With so many species to choose from, you can be sure to come across some type of panfish regardless of where you live. They can be found in a variety of aquatic environments, from small ponds on golf courses and parks to large lakes, reservoirs, and rivers. You can do some advance scouting by visiting your state's fish and game agency website. These websites will often publish reports that outline the availability and abundance of catchable fish species in local waters. If you can't find any information online about a particular body of water, don't be afraid to just give it

a try. Part of the fun of fishing is unlocking the mystery of what's lurking below the surface of the water.

Despite their small size, it can be pretty easy to catch enough panfish to feed your whole family if you're fishing the right spot at the right time. Here are some tips to help you fill up a stringer with a mess of panfish.

- Panfish can be caught year-round. In the northern states and across Canada, you can even catch them through the ice in the winter. But the best time of year to catch sunfish like bluegills and pumpkinseeds is in the spring, when sunfish gather in shallow, warm water near shore to dig nests where they lay eggs. To spot their nests, look for pale circles a couple of feet wide on the bottom that are much lighter in color than the surrounding area. These circles are made by the fish as they clear away muck, silt, and algae from the lake's bottom. Place a bait or small lure near the nests and the aggressive sunfish are likely to bite it.

- During the hot summer months, panfish are likely to hang out in shallow water during the early morning and late evening hours. In the middle of the day, look for them in deeper water.
- Panfish like to hang out near underwater structures that offer them protection from bigger fish and a place to hunt for small minnows and aquatic insects. Suitable structures can include rocks, weeds, lily pads, and dock pilings.
- Many species of panfish, especially crappie and yellow perch, travel in large schools. Where you catch one, you'll usually find more.
- Garden worms and crickets are top baits for sunfish, while small minnows work better for crappie and perch.
- Panfish have fairly small mouths, so use #6–10 bait hooks and $\frac{1}{16}$–$\frac{1}{8}$-ounce jigs for the best results. Small marabou crappie jigs and soft plastic twister tails work well for all species of panfish.
- Suspend your bait or jig below a bobber, so that it's suspended about a foot off the bottom. This gives the bait good "action," meaning it will move around like something that's alive. The bobber will also help you detect the soft bite of panfish.
- Panfish are often grouped together by size. If all you are catching are very tiny fish, look elsewhere for a school of bigger fish.
- Most panfish have sharp spines on their dorsal fin and gill plates. Handle them carefully by folding their dorsal fins down against their backs. You can also grip them firmly by the lower lip, since they don't have sharp teeth.

CATCH A CRAYFISH, COUNT THE STARS

CLEAN A FISH

Fish that are purchased from a grocery store have already been cleaned, and they're usually cut up and ready to eat. That's not the case with fish you've caught yourself. Before you can cook and eat your catch, you'll need to remove the fish's guts, gills, and scales. In some cases, you'll also want to get rid of the skin. That probably sounds like a messy job—and sometimes it is—but people have been handling fish guts for a lot longer than they've been going to grocery stores! The best tool for cleaning fish is a fillet knife. These knives have long, thin blades that are bendy. They're perfect for dealing with small fish. The Rapala Finlander is inexpensive and a great size for kids' hands. Cutting up a fish with a knife might seem intimidating if you've never done it, but it's actually not very difficult. Follow the instructions below and you'll soon master the basic method.

Before you clean your fish, you need to quickly and humanely kill it. Do this by hitting the fish with a sharp, forceful blow to the top of the head above the eyes. Use a sturdy stick, the handle of a big screwdriver, or even a rock.

Gut a Fish

Gutting a fish is a very simple way to clean any fish that will be cooked whole. Here's how to do it.

- If you're gutting a small fish, you can hold it in your hand with the belly side up and tail toward your body. For larger fish,

you'll need to place it on a sturdy surface. It's a good idea to use a cutting board if you have one.

- First, insert the point of the knife into the anal vent (the small hole on the belly where waste is expelled) and then cut the belly open up to the gills. Don't cut too deep. Slice through the thin belly meat, but not into the guts.

- Grab the guts and pull them from the anal vent toward the gills to remove them. They should come loose pretty easily on small fish, but you may need to cut them free near the gills on bigger fish.

- Next, remove the gills by yanking them out of small fish, or use kitchen shears (scissors) to snip the gills out of large fish.

- You'll see a dark reddish-black blood line running along the length of the spine inside the gut cavity. Use your thumb or a spoon to scrape it away.

- Fish can be cooked whole with the head on, or you can cut the head off by severing the spine with shears or your knife.

- Lastly, give the fish a rinse in cold water.

Fillet a Fish

Many people prefer to eat boneless fish fillets rather than having to pick the bones out of whole fish. To turn your fish into fillets, you'll need to do some knife work. Filleting is a little more difficult than gutting, but it does separate the flesh from all those pesky fish bones.

- Place the fish on a cutting board, with its back facing toward you and its belly facing away.

- Make a cut across the side of the fish. This cut should pass just outside the gill plate and around the pectoral fin (the fin behind the fish's head). Cut only through the skin and meat of the fish. Don't cut so deep that you cut through the spine.

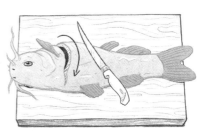

- Beginning where your last cut ended, make another cut from the cut below the head all the way down to the tail. This time you're cutting along the length of the fish, right along the spine. Keep your knife parallel to the cutting board, and run the side of your knife blade along the spine. Again, don't cut through the backbone.

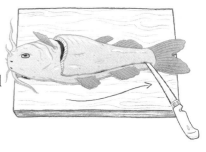

- Next, starting from the tail end of the fish, use careful cuts to pull and peel the fillet away from the bones. The final cut will be when you reach the head and slice the fillet away from the fish's skeleton.

- Flip the fish over and repeat the process.

- The rib bones will still be attached to the meat of the fillet. Make a shallow cut under the rib bones to slice them away.

Lastly, catfish and many other species of fish have tough, thick, chewy skin that you'll need to remove before cooking. Place the fillet skin side down on a cutting board with the tail end facing you. Hold 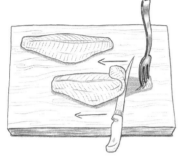 the tail end down tightly on the cutting board with the tines of a fork. Then, just in front of the fork, use your fillet knife to cut through the flesh. You want to cut down to the skin, but not through it. Next, turn the blade parallel to the surface of the cutting board between the skin and the meat. Push the knife away from you, working from the tail forward, to cut the skin free from the fillet.

SCALE A FISH WITH BOTTLE CAPS

Most fish have a layer of scales on the surface of their skin that protects them from injuries, much like a knight's suit of armor. If you get rid of those scales, you can eat the skin of many species of fish, and it's surprisingly good. For example, crispy panfish, trout, and salmon skin is a delicious treat that's like eating a fish-flavored potato chip.

You can use a knife to scale a fish, but the hard scales will quickly dull a knife blade. In a pinch, you can use a spoon, but it's not the most effective tool for this task. You *could* spend some money on a fish scaling tool from a tackle shop. But why not have some fun building a scaling tool of your own that works just as well? You probably already have the few materials you need lying around your house.

Here's what you'll need to make a bottle cap fish scaler, how to build it, and how to use it.

What You'll Need

- Two metal bottle caps with small sharp points around their edges—the kind that are used on glass bottles.
- A sturdy piece of wood about 8 inches long. The perfect piece would be a chunk of hardwood measuring 8 inches long, 1 inch wide, and ½ inch thick. You could also use a wooden dowel that's about 1 inch in diameter (a piece of broom handle would be good), but it's a little bit more difficult to fasten the bottle caps to a round surface than a flat surface.
- Two short, thin wood screws. If your handle is ½ inch thick, look for screws about ⅜ inch long.
- An electric or hand-powered drill with a bit that's slightly thinner than your screws.
- A screwdriver or bit driver that matches the head of your screws.

Building Steps

1. Start by placing the bottle caps on a piece of scrap wood that's okay to get scratched up, and use your drill bit or a hammer to punch holes through the centers of the bottle caps.

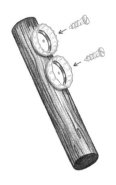

2. Place the bottle caps near the end of your piece of wood, and mark where the mounting holes should be. Drill two pilot holes into the wood. The pilot holes will keep the wood from splitting when you drive the screws into place. Make sure these pilot holes go to a depth that matches the length of your screws.

3. Drive the screws through the bottle caps and into the wood, tightening them firmly. If your piece of wood is round, you may need an extra set of hands to hold it still while you drill. You might also want to use some sandpaper or a pocketknife to make a flat place on the round dowel for the bottle caps to sit against. That'll help the tool be extra sturdy.

4. Now you're ready to scale some fish. Scaling is much easier if you do it before you gut or fillet your fish. To use the bottle cap scaler, just scrape the scales off the skin from the tail to the gill plate with the bottle caps. It won't work if you go in a head-to-tail direction. You have to move your scaler against the grain of the scales, which means from the tail toward the head.

Scaling is kind of a messy job, so work outside if possible. Scales will be popping off and flying all over the place! A great way to contain the mess is to scale your fish in the sink, with the fish slightly submerged in water as you scale. This prevents the scales from flying off, and makes cleanup much easier.

DISCOVER WHAT A FISH HAS BEEN EATING

It might sound weird, but you can learn a lot by cutting open a fish's stomach. As you're cleaning your catch, look for the large, pale sack inside the gut cavity—that's the stomach. You'll be able to tell right away if it's bulging and looks full. By pressing your finger against it, you'll be able to feel the food inside. To examine the contents, slice one end of the stomach with a knife and then give it a gentle squeeze to push out whatever is inside. Sometimes all you'll see is a lump of unidentifiable slimy goo, but fish are cold-blooded and their digestive system works pretty slowly. Quite often you'll find whole insects, crustaceans, or minnows. A good trick is to squeeze the stomach contents into a shallow bowl of water. This helps everything separate and you can see what's inside much more clearly.

See if you can identify what your fish has been eating. It's a great window into the secrets of aquatic environments, and it'll also give you a much better idea of what bait or lure to use. Fish often concentrate on whatever food source is most available at any given time. For example, if thousands of grasshoppers are jumping around in a field right next to the river you're fishing, chances are good that on a windy day a lot of them will get blown into the river, where they'll become fish food.

Fish are also opportunistic predators that will take advantage of unusual food sources. A trout that was eating grasshoppers might also consume a field mouse that fell into the river. Other fish are known to eat frogs, baby ducks, lizards, snakes, and even smaller members of their own species. So whenever you're cleaning fish, it's worth taking a couple of extra minutes to investigate what they've been eating. What you find in their stomach could help you catch more fish or could be a completely unexpected surprise. You never know what you might discover!

GIG A FROG

You might not think of frogs as food, but people all around the world eat them. In France and some parts of Italy, frog legs are considered a delicacy, while here in the United States you'll find them right alongside chicken wings and fried fish on the menus of many southern restaurants. As a matter of fact, if you like chicken and fish, you'll probably love deep-fried frog legs.

There are over a hundred species of frogs in North America. Most of them are much smaller than the palm of your hand. But not the bullfrog. These hefty amphibians are the largest species of frog in North America. Bullfrogs with bodies measuring 8 inches in length and back legs that are just as long are plentiful east of the Rocky Mountains, and they've also been introduced to western states including California, Arizona, Montana, and Colorado. The amphibians live in ponds, lakes, rivers, marshes, and swamps, spending most of their time in shallow, warm water near the shoreline. Look for them in areas with lots of aquatic vegetation like algae, reeds, and lily pads. They use this cover to hide from predators like herons and snapping turtles. Bullfrogs are voracious predators themselves. They eat worms, insects, mice, and anything else they can swallow, including smaller frogs. But don't worry—their teeth aren't sharp.

Before you go hunting for bullfrogs, remember to check your state's fishing regulations for open season dates and to find out how many you're allowed to keep. For safety's sake, always go with a partner or group, and don't wade in over your knees. You can start by hunting for frogs during the day to gain some confidence and experience. But the best time to find them is after the sun goes down. These nocturnal amphibians are most active on warm summer nights, when you'll hear their deep, booming mating calls that sound like "Jug o' rum! Jug o' rum!"

When you're hunting bullfrogs at night, you can't get by without a bright, powerful headlamp to help you spot them. Don't forget to bring some kind of sack or bag with a drawstring to hold the frogs until you get home. If you're quick, you can occasionally catch a bullfrog with your hands, but they're very fast and slippery. So the most effective way to hunt for frogs is with a multi-pronged spear called a gig. You can buy frog gigs or make your own (see the project on pages 190–192).

When you're gigging bullfrogs, you'll need to carefully scan the surface of the water along the shore with your headlamp. Sometimes bullfrogs will be out of the water, on a riverbank, or sitting on top of a lily pad, where they will be very easy to spot, but more often, only their eyes and nose will be barely sticking out of the water. Like many other animals, however, bullfrogs have a thin membrane called the tapetum lucidum over their eyes, an adaptation that helps them see in the dark. In the light of your headlamp, this adaptation also produces "eyeshine"—a bright green glow that will reveal even the most well-hidden frog. Also look for the bullfrog's white or yellow throat patch, which shows up brightly in the beam of a flashlight during the frogs' breeding season.

Once you've spotted a frog, you must be stealthy. Move very slowly toward it. If you rush or splash around, the frog will get spooked and vanish. Don't be tempted to throw your spear at the frog, either. It's a tiny target, so work your way to within a few feet of it, aim for the back of the frog's head, and thrust your spear quickly and forcefully. You'll still miss frogs that jump or dive out of the way, but a direct hit will secure the frog. Pull the bullfrog off the spear, toss it in your sack, and start looking for another one.

Even if you don't live in an area with bullfrogs, you might still have a way to enjoy frog legs. Where they're legal to harvest, green frogs are a smaller though tasty cousin of the bullfrog. As always when it comes to activities related to hunting and fishing, check your state's or province's rules about the harvest of frogs. Regulations vary widely from place to place, so avoid trouble by making sure you do things the right way.

CLEANING AND COOKING FROG LEGS

When you get home, you'll need to clean your frog legs before you can cook and eat them. Cleaning and preparing your frog legs is a simple process. Here's how to get it done:

1. First, use a pair of scissors or kitchen shears to cut off the feet at the ankle joints. Then snip open the skin on the belly just above the hind legs and continue that cut all the way around the body. Imagine that you're cutting through the skin along what would be the frog's beltline.

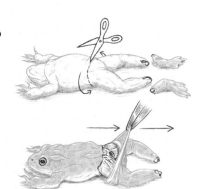

2. Next, use needle-nosed pliers to "take their pants off" by pulling the skin below the cut downward. It should slide off the legs with little effort.

3. Finally, snip off each leg where it's attached to the body at the hip joint.

   To pan-fry your frog legs, rinse them in cold water and then season them with salt and pepper. If you like some spice, add a dash of Cajun seasoning. Next, put the legs in a plastic bag with some flour and shake them around until they're coated. Add a little butter or cooking oil to a frying pan and toss in the legs. Cook them on medium heat for a few minutes then flip them over and cook the other side for a few more minutes. They're done when they've turned a golden brown color. Dip them in ketchup or cocktail sauce and enjoy!

MAKE YOUR OWN GIG

Fish spears, or gigs, have been used by humans for much longer than fishing rods. In many places, spearing remains a legal way to harvest some species of fish. Saltwater anglers use gigs to catch flounder, and freshwater anglers use them for northern pike, suckers, bullfrogs, and several other species. Commercially made gigs have a long wooden shaft and a head that looks like a miniature pitchfork. The heads will have anywhere from three to seven tines, or sharpened points. This design is almost certainly inspired by multi-pronged fishing spears made of wood that were used thousands of years before humans learned how to work with metal. If you're going to get serious about spearing frogs or fish, you'll eventually want to use a metal gig, but in the meantime, here's how to make a simple but very effective wooden one.

Note: You will need adult help or supervision to make this spear, since you'll be working with sharp tools.

What You'll Need

- Two thick, sturdy zip ties at least 8 inches long
- Marker
- Pocketknife
- Handsaw
- Mallet or hammer
- Sharp hatchet or machete

Building Steps

1. Find a straight sapling about 2 inches thick and 6 or 7 feet tall. Cut it off near the ground with your handsaw, then trim the other end with your saw so that the sapling's length is now about a foot taller than you are. This will be your spear.

2. With a marker, draw a vertical line and a horizontal line on one of the cut-off ends of the spear. You should have a perfect cross, with an intersection that divides the end of the limb into quarter circles.

3. Now use your hatchet to make a split at the end of your spear by carefully tapping into one of the lines you drew with the marker. Make the split about 6–8 inches deep. Next, split the limb into quarters using the same process on the second line you drew. These four quarters will be your gigging points. If it is too hard to make these splits with your hatchet, you can also split the ends of the spear by using your handsaw. You'll need an extra set of hands to do this. Have someone hold the spear while you make the cuts.

4. Find a live branch about ¼ to ½ inch thick. Cut two pieces of the branch, each about 3 inches long. These will be the wedges that spread out your spear points.

5. Slide one of these wedges all the way down to the bottom of one of the splits in your spear. You may need to spread out the four splits to get it down all the way, but

be careful. Don't force it too much or you'll break your spear and will need to start over.

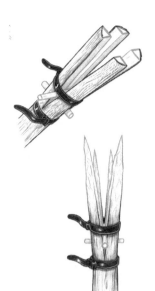

6. Carefully slide the second small wedge down the second split until it hits the first wedge. Your four spear points should now be spread out.

7. Directly below the lower wedge, secure one of the zip ties to the spear shaft as tightly as you can get it.

8. Repeat with the second zip tie just above the upper wedge. The zip ties reinforce your spear shaft against breakage.

9. Now use your pocketknife to carefully sharpen each of the four points.

The gigging points will harden and become more durable if you let the wood dry out for a couple of weeks before using your spear, but you can speed up this process by fire-hardening your creation. All you need to do is hold the pointy end very near (but not in) the flames or coals of a small campfire for a half-hour or so. Just make sure you don't waste all that hard work you put into making your spear by setting it on fire!

Even after you've fire-hardened your fishing spear, you'll need to periodically resharpen the gigging points. Avoid smashing your spear against rocks if you can, or the points may break off completely. If you want your gigging spear to last awhile, remember that it is meant to be thrust, not thrown. Even with the proper care, it won't last forever, and eventually you'll need to make a new one.

CATCH CRAYFISH

There are over 300 species of crayfish in North America. They're found in all fifty states and across much of Canada in freshwater ponds, lakes, creeks, rivers, and even some brackish estuaries where rivers meet the ocean. This is good news for you, because no kid's life is complete without getting pinched on the finger by one of these interesting critters. If you put your mind to it, you could probably make that happen in the next week or so!

Because crayfish live in so many places, they're known by many names—crawdads, mudbugs, crawfish, crawdaddies, baybugs, and yabbies, to name a few. They taste a bit like shrimp. Crayfish serve as a key ingredient in several well-known dishes, though they taste best as part of a simple crayfish boil (see page 248).

Crayfish are mostly aquatic, although they do occasionally leave the water for short periods of time. They belong to a large group of invertebrate animals known as crustaceans. Like insects, crustaceans have a hard exoskeleton, or shell, that they shed and regrow as they get older and bigger. Their relatives include tasty critters like shrimp, crabs, and lobsters. In fact, crayfish look almost exactly like miniature lobsters. Unlike their larger cousins, though, they can't survive in salt water. Depending on the species and location, crayfish can be different shades of olive, brown, orange, or red. They can range in size from less than 1 inch to more than 6 inches long.

Crayfish like to crawl around in and under vegetation, rocks, and submerged mud (hence their "mudbug" moniker) looking for food. Maybe you've already tried flipping over some rocks in a creek or pond to look for them. The key to catching crayfish by hand is swiftly pinning them to the bottom before they can use their powerful tail muscle to scoot backward and escape. Don't worry too much about their fierce-looking claws. They're not powerful enough to do any serious damage, and you can hold a crayfish without getting pinched by grasping them firmly with your thumb and pointer finger on top of their head, behind the claws. If they do get a hold of you, the worst you'll get is a small cut or blood blister.

As fun as it is to sneak around grabbing crayfish by hand, you might only catch a few in an hour of trying. Trapping crayfish, on the other hand, is a more efficient way to capture a lot of them at one time. Check your state's fishing regulations regarding trapping crayfish before you go. In many states, the dimensions of your trap must not exceed 24 × 12 × 2 inches—which just happens to be the size of most inexpensive wire crayfish and minnow traps sold online or in sporting goods stores. If you already have a minnow trap (see page 162), you can use it to catch crayfish; just use a pair of wire cutters to make the small openings about 2 inches wide. Your trap will still work for minnows, but big crayfish will also be able to get inside. Another option is to make your own trap. There are lots of options, from super-simple builds like disposable water bottle traps to 5-gallon bucket traps to versions that look and function just like commercially made traps that you can buy at the store. Search "DIY crayfish traps" online and you'll find something that will work for you. Since you're going to be leaving your trap in place, your local fishing regulations may require your name and phone number to be written on the trap or on something attached to the trap.

In order to coax crayfish into your trap, you'll need some bait. Crayfish are omnivorous scavengers that feed on both animal and plant matter, so they'll eat just about anything. But there is no better crayfish bait than the carcass and guts from a fish you just caught and cleaned—the scent of a dead fish will attract crayfish from a long distance. Stuff the bait inside a disposable mesh produce bag (the kind that's used to package onions and citrus fruit) from the grocery store, and then use a small zip tie to secure it to the inside of your trap. If you don't have a fish carcass, a small can of sardines or cat food with a few holes punched through it will work, too.

Crayfish are mostly nocturnal, so you'll catch more if you let your trap soak overnight. Scout out a spot with some rocks and mud on the bottom where you know crayfish are hiding, and set your trap near shore, in water at least a foot or two deep. If you're trapping in a river or creek, look for spots with little to no current, since crayfish avoid fast-moving water. Don't forget to tie your trap to something onshore. Hopefully when you return, it will be loaded with crayfish.

BUILD A WILDLIFE VIEWING BLIND

You can learn a lot just by watching birds and animals go about their daily lives in their natural environments. If you're in the right place at the right time, you might witness two sibling deer fawns play by chasing each other around in circles. Or you might see a red-tailed hawk snatching a mouse out of the grass, or a black bear scratching its back on a tree trunk. There's always something interesting going on in the natural world.

Many wild animals are very shy of humans, so you might not see them at all if you don't develop your skills as a wildlife watcher. Oftentimes, the best way to see wildlife is to let it come to you. But this won't happen on its own. Animals have very keen senses of smell, hearing, and eyesight. They can easily detect your presence if you don't take the necessary precautions. If you really want to get close to animals, you should conceal yourself behind or inside a simple structure called a blind.

Hunters all over the world use blinds to hide from the animals that they're hunting. In 2022, on a mountainous island off the coast of Norway, forty ancient hunting blinds made out of stacks of rocks were discovered when the glaciers in the area that had buried them for hundreds of years began melting. Here in America, archaeologists have discovered 9,000-year-old stone hunting blinds on the bottom of Lake Huron! That might seem strange, but the people who built those blinds long ago weren't hunting underwater. Back then, the water levels of the Great Lakes were much lower, and the blinds were on dry land.

Blinds are just as useful today, and not only for hunters. Wildlife biologists, wildlife photographers, and bird-watchers all use blinds. Most of the time, they're hiding inside lightweight, portable pop-up blinds that are similar to camping tents. Or they build permanent tower blinds that resemble tree houses built on stilts. These types of artificial blinds work well, but you can take a cue from those ancient hunters and build one yourself. Blinds made with natural materials gathered directly from the landscape blend in with the surrounding environment and do a great job of concealing whoever is inside. They're also pretty easy to build.

The first step in constructing a wildlife viewing blind is to pick the spot where you want to put it. For instance, if you are interested in hunting ducks or geese or watching wading birds like herons or egrets, you'll need to place your blind near a pond, a marsh, or another water source where those birds hang out. If your goal is to see deer, wild turkeys, squirrels, or other woodland critters, you'll need to scout out a forested location. But you shouldn't just build your

blind in any random spot out in the woods. Look for game trails in areas called edge habitat, where thick stands of trees meet open meadows and farm fields. Tracks (page 209) and other signs (page 214) left by animals will also tip you off to good blind locations.

Once you've settled on a general area, you'll need to zero in on the exact spot where you'll build your blind. Ideally, it will be right in front of a big tree or rock that you can sit against. All the better if there are some overhanging branches to give you a bit of cover from rain and some additional concealment. You'll also need to have a good view of the surrounding area. And don't forget about the wind! Since many animals rely on their sense of smell to detect potential danger, you'll want to stay downwind of the place where you most expect to see some critters. That way, your human smell won't be blowing directly toward them. Use your homemade windicator (page 199) to determine the wind's direction. The wind will likely change direction throughout the day, so check it often to make sure you've got the right location. And finally, you'll want to select a spot with plenty of available building materials like rocks, logs, sticks, brush, and clumps of tall grass.

Start your blind by building a small, simple frame with just enough room for you and a buddy to sit down. Stack up sturdy materials to make two short diagonal walls, like the long sides of a piece of pie. The walls should meet in front of where you'll be sitting. The back of the triangle—imagine the crusty part of your pie slice—should be formed by the backrest you selected. The walls should be at the height of your shoulders when you're sitting down. That'll be high enough to conceal your body but low enough for you to see over the top. You can probably get this done without any tools. If not, you might need a hatchet or an axe for cutting branches, and a length of wire or rope for reinforcing the frame. After you've got the frame built, you should "brush in" your blind by adding vegetation that functions as camouflage. Stuff the cracks and gaps in the frame with clumps of grass, dead brush, and leafy branches to make your hideout disappear into the background.

The best times to sit in your blind are early mornings and late evenings, when the sun is just starting to come up or go down. But if you can't make that work, don't worry. You can see some great stuff in the middle of the day as well. The main thing is holding still! Even though you're mostly hidden behind your blind, animals might still detect your movement if you're fidgeting around too much. Noise will also scare them, so talk in whispers if you're with a buddy. Sometimes it only takes 15 or 20 minutes before you start seeing some animals stirring about. Other times it might take an hour or more. Be patient enough, and animals will often approach within a few yards of your blind. Then you can sit back and enjoy the show.

MAKE A WINDICATOR

Many animals rely on their noses for survival. Whether it's for finding food, locating mates, or avoiding predators, an animal's sense of smell is often the most important of all its senses. While humans are pretty good at smelling certain things, such as frying bacon or rotten garbage, that's nothing compared to what animals can sniff out. Black bears are known to have some of the best noses in the entire animal kingdom. Their nasal cavity is one hundred times larger than a human's and contains many layers of tissue, with millions of scent receptors that are capable of smelling food from as far as 3 miles away. Whitetail deer also have a powerful sense of smell that can identify several different odors at the same time. While we can't get into a deer's brain to see what it's thinking, it seems as though they can smell the air and simultaneously pick out the odors of predators, food, and other deer all at once.

No matter how good an animal's nose is, the direction of the wind has a major impact on its ability to pick up smells. A deer can smell a nearby predator only if the wind is either calm or blowing from the predator to the deer. If the wind is blowing away from the deer and toward the predator, the predator's smell will be carried in the other direction and the deer won't be able to smell it. That's why when a deer runs away because it smelled a hunter, the hunter will say that they got "winded."

Whether you're hunting or just hoping to see some wildlife out in the woods, it's a good idea to keep track of the wind direction. Try watching how the leaves on the trees are moving or which way the grass is bent over. Or you might be able to feel the wind brushing against the skin on one side of your face and not the other. Of course, clues like these may not work well when there's only a light breeze. In those situations, you can use what's called a windicator to determine the wind direction. There's nothing complicated about a windicator. It can be any lightweight material that you can toss or release into the air in order to see what direction the breeze carries it.

Dried grass and crumbled-up dead leaves will glide pretty well in a stiff breeze. Very fine, dusty, dry dirt particles are light enough to be carried by the wind, too. There are even better choices, though. If you've ever made a wish by blowing on the fluffy head of a dandelion, you'll know how well those feathery seeds fly around. The reason they're so light and fluffy is so that the wind will disperse them over long distances, allowing the plants to spread to new areas. This makes them the perfect material to use as a windicator.

Other types of plants, like cattails and milkweed, grow a very similar type of seed. You'll find cattail plants growing in wetlands and marshes. The name cattail comes from their soft, dark brown seed pods—they look a bit like miniature versions of a cat's tail. Collect the pods by breaking them off their stalk in late summer when they are dried out but still intact. Later in the fall, each pod bursts apart to distribute over 200,000 fluffy seeds! To use a cattail as a windicator, just pinch a clump of seed fluff off a pod, raise your hand up in the air, and release the fluff to see what direction the wind is blowing.

Milkweed is another great source of windicator material that is found throughout the United States. The name comes from the white milky sap that oozes out of the plant when it is injured. Milkweed plants usually grow near water and have wide oval-shaped leaves and spherical clumps of white, pink, orange, or red flowers. In late summer, the flowers turn into hard, dry tubular or horn-shaped pods full of seeds attached to wispy white floss. This floss makes a great windicator, and using it this way also has an unexpected bonus. Milkweed plants are the one and only food source for monarch butterfly caterpillars. In some places, milkweed plant numbers have declined drastically due to the use of chemical weed killers. Because of this, monarch numbers have also declined, so every new milkweed seed you release gives these beautiful butterflies a better chance for survival in the future.

STALK AN ANIMAL

If you're like most kids, you've probably had some fun trying to sneak up behind a friend or sibling just to scare the living daylights out of them. You might even think you're pretty good at creeping around without anyone noticing you. But if you really want to test your sneaking abilities, you need to try stalking an animal. "Stalk" is just another word for "sneak" that hunters use to describe the process of approaching or following an animal without being seen or heard.

Stalking unnoticed into close proximity to a wild animal is a big challenge. The first line of defense for many animals is their formidable sense of smell. But if their nose fails them, many also have an acute sense of hearing and extremely good vision as a backup defense system. For instance, deer have vision that is believed to be a little blurry compared to ours, but their eyes are still very good at picking up movement, even at great distances. With eyes that bulge out on the sides of their heads, they have a much wider field of view than humans do. We have a field of view of about 180 degrees. Without turning our heads, we can see only what's in front of us.

Deer have a field of view of 310 degrees. They can see in an almost complete circle around their body. Deer also have large, cupped ears that can rotate in different directions at the same time, which allows them to zero in on the source of any suspicious noises. With eyes and ears like that, plus a nose that can smell a person a half mile away, you can see why stalking a deer is so challenging.

Deer aren't the only animals that are tough to sneak up on. Bobcats, coyotes, and foxes all have good eyes, ears, and noses, and they are always on the lookout for larger predators that might steal their food or turn them into a meal. Wild turkeys and many other birds don't use their noses to warn them of a predator closing in. But they can see three times better than a human and pick up even the slightest movements behind their head. Their hearing is so fine-tuned that they can pinpoint exactly where distant noises are coming from. Likewise, squirrels and rabbits do not seem to rely on their noses to detect predators. They are always on high alert, though, and will flee the instant they hear or see something that isn't right.

Squirrels will also warn each other with loud screeches and barks when they detect a nearby predator.

So you've got your work cut out for you if you want to stalk a wild animal. However, outwitting a wary critter by sneaking in close enough to make a good shot (page 243) or take a cool photo (page 85) is certainly possible. It's also exciting and fun to see how close you can get. Here are some tips that will help you out.

- Wear camouflage clothing or natural colors like brown, green, or gray that blend in with the natural environment.
- Scan the area constantly and carefully and try to spot animals from a distance before you begin a stalk. Binoculars are a great tool for finding animals that are far away.
- As you look for animals, walk through the woods very slowly and quietly. Stop frequently to look and listen. You can even sit down for a while and wait for animals to show themselves.
- When you spot an animal, watch it for a while before you begin your stalk. Make sure it is relaxed and unaware of your presence before you make your first move.
- Remember to check the wind direction if you're stalking an animal that has a good nose.
- Before you begin approaching the animal, plan a route that will bring you closer but keep you out of sight as much as possible. Keep brush, trees, hills, and other objects between you and the animal in order to stay hidden.
- Begin stalking when the animal is looking away from you, or feeding, or distracted by another animal. Be stealthy, move slow, and stay low. Crouch, crawl, or slide on your belly to keep out of sight.

- Keep an eye on the animal. If it becomes alert and turns its attention toward you, stop moving and wait patiently for it to lose interest.
- Don't forget to stay quiet. Watch out for dry leaves or sticks that will snap or crack if you step on them.

BLAZING A FAMOUS TRAIL

Nowadays, the word "trailblazer" is usually used as a term for someone who's an innovator in their work. But 250 years ago, being a trailblazer meant that you literally "blazed trails"—meaning you marked routes through the wilderness by notching or marking up trees for others to follow. No one was more famous for blazing trails than the hunter, pioneer, and frontiersman Daniel Boone (1734–1820), who grew up hunting and tending to his family's cattle in the woods of Pennsylvania.

Boone's parents were Quakers who left England to escape religious persecution. Boone was raised in a log cabin many miles away from the city of Philadelphia. He received basic lessons in reading and writing from a family member, but he did not go to school. At the time, violent conflict between European colonists and Native Americans frequently arose over competing claims to land and resources historically controlled by tribal nations. But Quakers were unique among the newest arrivals to North America in that they saw all human beings as equals and lived by a code of pacifism, which meant that they did not believe in war or the use of violence. As a result, they attempted to coexist with Native Americans in a peaceful way. Boone's parents welcomed Native American men and women traveling through the area to stay in their home as guests.

Boone spent much of his childhood wandering the woods. He spent a lot of time with Native people from the local Delaware and Shawnee tribes. He likely learned to hunt by emulating their techniques, at first taking small game and birds by throwing a homemade club fashioned out of a small sapling. By the age of twelve or thirteen, having acquired a rifle of his own, he became a skilled marksman and helped to supply his family with fresh meat from the woods. After the family moved to North Carolina, hunting and extended trips into the backcountry of the western frontier soon became his primary focus. On these long adventures, Boone hunted and trapped animals that could be sold for money in the settlements. In the summer, he'd hunt deer in order to sell the skins. These were turned into leather for clothing. In the fall, Boone hunted black bears in order to sell the meat and fat as food. He trapped beavers in the winter and spring and sold the furs.

Over time, Boone borrowed from Native American traditions and adopted a practice known as the "long hunt." He and his hunting partners would leave home for weeks and months on end in pursuit of wild game. Boone loved the freedom of the woods, the solitude of this lifestyle, and the simplicity of such a close relationship with nature. In addition to his talents with the rifle and his knowledge of woodsmanship, Boone developed remarkable abilities to read sign left by wildlife and to survive on his own in challenging conditions. Even after marrying and starting a family, Boone continued to make his living as a hunter and trapper. He was unable to resist the temptation to explore faraway wild places.

But as more and more colonists settled around Boone's home in North Carolina, the game animals on which Boone depended and the solitude he craved became harder and harder to find. Soon, the allure of the wild landscapes across the Appalachian Mountains, which had served as a natural barrier to expansion by the British colonies, called to him. Game animals like deer, bear, and beaver were more abundant to the west, and the Native Americans who lived there practiced a lifestyle more compatible with his own.

In the late 1760s, Boone's explorations began to push westward into Kentucky. This was the traditional hunting grounds of the Shawnee tribe. In 1773, Boone led a party of more than fifty settlers, including a number of enslaved men and women, on the first attempt to establish a British settlement beyond the Appalachians. Angered by the intrusion into what had long been their uncontested territory, a group of Shawnees attacked members of the expedition. Among those killed was Boone's son James. Although that particular effort was abandoned, Boone was undeterred and returned with another party in 1775 to cut a route that would become known as Boone's Trace. In this he was successful beyond his wildest imagination. Hundreds of thousands of settlers followed in his tracks, forever transforming the wild landscape that had for so long symbolized an escape from the crowding of his previous home.

By the end of his life, Boone was widely recognized for his role in opening the lands beyond the Appalachian Mountains to settlers. But his most celebrated accomplishments cost him a great deal. As the woods were cleared for farms and towns, he lost his favorite hunting grounds and sympathized with Native Americans who had been displaced by white settlement. Some remember Boone as a man who wanted nothing more than to flee Euro-American civilization, while others remember him as a pioneer who helped pave a way for development to reach into the wilds of North America. His story is a reminder that our relationships with nature are often complicated. Those who prefer the solitude of the woods over the bustle of towns bring changes to the woods simply by being there. Our presence alters, forever, the places that we love most.

—By Randall Williams

TRACK AN ANIMAL

From the slimy trails left behind by snails to the clawed footprints of bears, all kinds of creatures leave clues on the ground showing where they've traveled. The art of identifying and following these marks is called tracking, and when it comes to tracking, the San people, or Bushmen, of Africa's Kalahari Desert are some of the best in the world. They can follow the footprints of a single animal through the desert for many days and miles. Even when the tracks of the animal they're following cross the paths of other animals, these trackers can identify the exact animal they are after and stick with it. Tracking remains an important skill for hunters today. But even if you don't hunt, tracking can still teach you a lot about the wildlife in your area.

Tracking actually has two components. The first part of tracking is finding a set, or multiple sets, of tracks and being able to identify what type of animal left them behind. Most mammal tracks fall into one of four different groups—steppers, hoppers, bounders, or waddlers—based on the patterns they create. The stepper group of animals includes coyotes, deer, and bob-cats. When they're walking, these animals leave a line of single footprints with a zigzag pattern. They often place their rear foot exactly where the front foot landed. Hoppers include animals like rabbits, squirrels, and mice that leave a pat-tern with all four feet grouped together. Their larger hind feet often appear in front of the smaller front feet. Bounders such as pine martens, minks, and weasels jump across the ground with their hind feet landing next to, or on top of, the

ANIMAL TRACKS

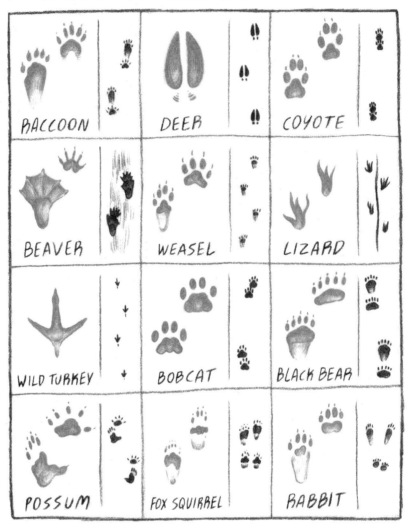

RACCOON	DEER	COYOTE
BEAVER	WEASEL	LIZARD
WILD TURKEY	BOBCAT	BLACK BEAR
POSSUM	FOX SQUIRREL	RABBIT

imprint of their front feet. Their tracks look like a line of two side-by-side footprints. Waddlers like bears, raccoons, beavers, and porcupines have wide, fat bodies and short legs. Their toes often point inward, with the smaller front tracks landing right behind or just next to the inside of the bigger rear track.

These patterns are a great starting point for identifying animal tracks, but there are many other clues you should consider. For instance, an animal's tracks will always look different when it's running. The tracks will be farther apart, and the feet may appear wider or more spread out. You might also see bits of dirt or snow that were kicked up by the fast-moving animal. Water-dwelling mammals such as otters, mink, beaver, and muskrats often make slide marks with their bellies when entering or exiting the water. In the snow, these short-legged animals all leave tail marks and belly marks in addition to footprints. And some animals, like coyotes and foxes, have footprints and track patterns that are almost identical. The only difference between them is the length of their stride (the space between the front and back prints) and the size of their feet. Sometimes completely different species have tracks that look similar! Telling the difference between a mountain lion, a bobcat, and someone's pet dog can be really tricky if you don't have much tracking experience. (Here's a hint: Canines, or members of the dog family, have tracks with claw marks. Felines, or members of the cat family, do not leave claw marks, because they walk around with their claws retracted inside their toes.)

Once you've identified a track, the second step in the tracking process is to follow in the animal's path. You have the best chance of doing this if you've found a very fresh set of tracks. It's easiest to find and follow tracks in places with soft dirt or mud, or when there's an inch or two of new snow. In these conditions, fresh tracks will have very sharp, crisp edges. Older tracks will appear to have a worn-out look with crumbled or rounded edges.

You can use recent weather conditions to help you age tracks. For instance, let's say it stopped snowing an hour ago and you find a set of tracks on top of the new snow. Then you know you're looking at a very fresh track. Or let's say it hasn't rained in a while and all you're seeing are tracks preserved in dried mud. You'll know those tracks are at least as old as the last time it was muddy. After all, the tracks were made when the ground was wet and soft.

Certain conditions can make tracking difficult. You can easily find and follow tracks in deep powder snow, but you may have trouble identifying what animal made them or which direction they're moving because the loose snow collapses on top of the tracks. Tracking is also tough through tall grass or when there's a thick layer of dead leaves on the ground. You'll have to find where the grass or leaves have been cleared away by wind or the passage of

THE WIDE WORLD OF TRACKING

You can track many other creatures besides mammals. Birds like grouse, pheasants, and turkeys spend most of their time on the ground. They have feet with three evenly spaced front toes and one toe in the back. Each toe has a sharp little claw on the end. You can recognize duck or goose tracks in the mud by spotting the imprint of their webbed feet, which they use to propel themselves through the water. If you're really paying attention, you might even see where a lizard has left tracks with all four feet and its tail, or where a snake has slithered across the sand.

The track guide on page 210 shows a few examples of tracks you might be looking for. But in order to get really good at identifying different footprints, it's a good idea to get yourself a field guidebook about animal tracks or an app that helps you identify them. Carry these resources with you in the woods so you can reference them when you come across a track you don't recognize.

animals and hope to uncover a hidden track on the ground. Identifying tracks in loose sand can be challenging, too, but at least you can follow them. It's much harder to track an animal across rocky ground. Rocks can make it hard to find even a single track, let alone enough tracks to follow the animal. But sometimes you'll get lucky. It's not uncommon to find a muddy footprint on a rock, made after an animal crosses a creek and then steps on a rock with wet feet. You never know what you'll find when you start looking.

If you do have good tracking conditions, following them a short distance usually isn't too difficult. Following them over long distances is more challenging. Move slowly, carefully scanning the ground as you piece together a path from one track to the next. Every now and then, stop and try to anticipate where the animal could be headed. Most animals will follow the path of least resistance by walking along game trails, fence lines, or shorelines. They'll usually try to go around obstacles, too. Stick with it for as long as you can. If you lose the track, ask yourself some questions. Which route would you take? Where do you think the animal is going and why? Maybe get down on your hands and knees and carefully examine the ground in the direction that you've guessed the animal might have gone. If you still can't find the next track, the animal may have turned in an unexpected direction. Try walking in a small circle around the last track you found to see if you can find another. If that doesn't work, walk a larger circle. Look for other types of sign (see page 214) that might help lead you along. Tracking requires focus, so stick with it. The farther you follow the tracks, the more clues you'll encounter. You might even catch a glimpse of the animal. Then you'll know for sure what you've been following!

READ ANIMAL SIGN

When police detectives are investigating a crime scene, they search for evidence left behind by criminals. You can search for that same type of evidence when you're scanning a piece of habitat for wild animals, because—just like criminals—animals leave behind evidence as they go about their daily lives. Trackers refer to this evidence as animal sign, and it can include things like poop, tufts of hair, feathers, or even little bits of leftover meals. For instance, a bloodstain in the snow showing where a red-tailed hawk killed a rabbit would be regarded as hawk sign.

Think about the sorts of sign you leave around your own home. Did you track some mud into the house on the bottom of your shoes? Are some of your toys lying around? Are there some crumbs from your last snack on the kitchen table? These are all details that a good tracker might notice in trying to figure out who's been passing through your home.

Some types of animal sign can point to a specific kind of critter. Shed or molted snakeskins are diagnostic. That is, a snake expert can look at the molted skin and tell what kind of snake left it behind. So are birds' nests. A bird scientist, known as an ornithologist, could look at an old nest and tell you what kind of bird built it. Some animals leave behind all sorts of sign. Take deer, for instance. It's common to find clumps of deer hair on fences where the deer jump over or crawl beneath the wires, and you can learn where and what deer have been eating by noticing where they nipped the buds and twigs off shrubs. When they lie down in the grass, leaves, or snow, deer make oval-shaped depressions called beds. And during

ANIMAL SIGN

DEER HAIR	ACORN SHELLS	BEAVER CHEWINGS
CRAYFISH REMAINS	BEAR CLAW MARKINGS	RABBIT POOP
BUCK RUB	SNAKE SKIN	TURKEY FEATHERS

the fall, male deer use their hooves and antlers to dig out patches of bare dirt called "scrapes." They pee in the scrapes in order to let female deer (and other bucks) know that they're in the area. Remember how the bucks rub their antlers on trees before shedding them every winter? That behavior shreds the bark and leaves a very visible scar, called a buck rub, on the tree.

Animal poop, or scat, is one of the most common types of sign you're likely to find. At first, different types of animal poop all might look the same. Deer and rabbit poop, for instance, appear very similar from a distance. But on closer examination, you'll find that deer poop is oval and rabbit droppings are spherical. Scat can even tell you how long ago an animal was around. Wet, shiny poop means it's fresh, while dry, crumbly poop could be months old. Scat can also tell you what an animal has been eating, and when it was eating it. In the late summer, red fox scat will often contain a lot of grasshopper legs. In the winter, when grasshoppers are unavailable, fox poop might be made of hair and small mammal bones. Whitetail deer that are eating fresh grass and forbs (a type of flowering plant) in the summer will have clumpy, blackish poop with pellets that are joined together. Deer that are browsing on shrubs and trees in the winter will leave behind piles of loose, single pellets that look woody or fibrous.

Not all evidence left behind by animals is as obvious as tracks or scat. Sometimes you'll need to think like a detective to figure out what kind of animal made a particular bit of sign. This process of solving mysteries is called reading animal sign. In order to read sign, it's important to analyze what you're seeing. Say you find an oak stump in the woods that's covered in busted-up pieces of acorn shell. You pick up one of the larger pieces of shell to find small tooth marks on it. There's a good chance you're looking at a spot where a squirrel was having a snack. While mice usually eat acorns in burrows or hollow logs where they can hide from airborne predators such as owls, squirrels like to eat in open places where they have a clear view of their surroundings. But there's a problem: chipmunks also like to eat acorns while sitting on stumps. So you take a look high up in the treetops. Do you see any squirrel nests, which are made from bundles of leaves about the size of a pillow? Or do you see any holes high in the trees that are about as big around as your fist? If the answers to these questions are yes, then you've found some additional evidence supporting your idea that squirrels have been eating acorns on the stump. On the other hand, a much smaller hole going underground beneath the stump might suggest chipmunks. If you still can't make up your mind about what kind of animal left behind the sign you're seeing, maybe it's time to construct a blind (see page 196) so that you can get an eyewitness view of the action.

Sometimes you'll discover animal sign that you can't even see. You probably know that beavers use their powerful jaw muscles and long, sharp incisors to chop down trees. But did you know they have glands near the base of their tails that emit an oily substance called castor? Castor produces a powerful, sweet aroma. If you're walking along a stream or lake and think you're smelling perfume, it's probably because a beaver has marked its territory by secreting castor on a little pile of mud along the water's edge. You might smell another type of animal sign if you're walking through the woods in the Rocky Mountains and detect a barnyard odor that reminds you of horses or cows—not like the smell of manure, but more like the animals themselves. What you're probably smelling is a herd of elk, or at least a herd of elk that recently passed through.

There's no end to the amount of animal sign you'll discover if you start paying close attention to your surroundings. Just remember, use your eyes, ears, and nose. The more sign you find when you're out in the woods, the more you're learning about the animals that live there.

SHARPEN YOUR POCKETKNIFE

A pocketknife, sometimes called a jackknife, is the type of knife where the blade folds into the handle for safe and convenient storage. This is an essential tool for anyone who spends a lot of time outside. You can use a pocketknife to clean fish and small game animals, cut fishing line, remove splinters, whittle sticks for roasting hot dogs, make wood shavings for fire tinder, cut rope, peel and slice apples, and dozens of other jobs. Once you start carrying a pocketknife around, you'll wonder how you ever got by without one.

Pocketknives come in many different sizes, styles, and configurations. The ideal pocketknife blade should be made out of stainless steel, so it won't rust, and it should be between 3 and 4 inches long. That might seem like a short blade length, but it's all you need to do a bunch of different jobs. Just make sure to get one with a safety locking mechanism that prevents the blade from collapsing onto your fingers while you're using it. These types of pocketknives are often known as lockback knives. You can't go wrong with a locking folder made by Buck Knives. They're good knives at a good price.

If you're looking for something that can do more than just cut things, you might consider a good multi-tool. You can get a multi-tool that has a saw, file, screwdrivers, scissors, and a good pair of needle-nose pliers with a wire cutter. The Leatherman Rev comes with a knife blade and thirteen other useful tools. Leatherman makes a lot of other good multi-tools as well.

Just remember, owning any kind of pocketknife is a big responsibility. They're one of the most helpful tools you can carry, but there are some places where they don't belong and you can get in trouble for having one. Never bring your pocketknife to school or inside a government building. You can't carry knives onto airplanes, either, so if you're traveling with one, always pack it inside your checked baggage.

Remember, too, that knives can also cause serious harm if they're handled carelessly. Never walk or run with a knife in your hand. When you're using a knife, cut away from your body whenever possible. You'll hear a lot of people say that dull knives are more dangerous than sharp knives. What they mean is that a sharp blade will cut smoothly with little effort, while you have to force a dull blade to cut things. This can cause either your grip or the blade to slip, which could lead to cutting yourself. But don't go thinking that a sharp knife is necessarily safer. As you can imagine, sharp knives can cut you quick and easy. Regardless of which is safer, it's a no-brainer that sharp knives work better and are more fun to use. If you use your knife regularly, you'll need to sharpen it regularly.

People have been sharpening knives and other tools with naturally occurring minerals and rocks like quartz for thousands of years. This type of sharpening stone is still used today. There are also more modern sharpening stones made from aluminum oxide, ceramics, carbides, diamond-coated steel, and other synthetic materials. Natural sharpening stones work very well, but they are heavy, so they're better for home use. If you want a lightweight sharpener to carry in your backpack, get a Work Sharp Guided Field Sharpener. No matter what type of sharpening stone you're using, they all work basically the same way. The knife blade's edge is scraped along an abrasive surface to remove a small amount of metal from the blade and reshape the rounded, dull edge into a thin, razor-sharp edge. Here's how to use one.

- Most sharpening stones have sharpening surfaces on both sides. One side is coarse, and the other side has a finer texture, or grit. Start your sharpening with the coarser side facing up.
- If you're using a natural whetstone, dribble some water or mineral oil onto the surface. This lubricates the stone, which helps it work better. This step isn't necessary with most synthetic stones.
- Carefully use a black Sharpie to darken both sides of the edge of the knife. Mark just the cutting edges, not any other part of the blade.

- Holding the knife with the blade facing away from you, position it at about a 20-degree angle to the surface of the stone. Only the cutting surface of the blade's edge should touch the surface of the sharpening stone. (The Work Sharp Guided Field Sharpener mentioned above has a built-in angle guide, which makes it very easy to use.)
- Begin gliding the edge forward along the surface of the stone, following the curve of the edge from the base of the blade all the way to the point.

- Don't press down hard. Just a little bit of pressure will do the trick.
- Flip the knife over and repeat this process on the other side of the blade. This time you'll be pulling the knife toward you along the surface of the sharpening stone, so be careful.
- Continue alternating knife sides over the coarse side of the stone several times until the edge is shiny and the black Sharpie markings are gone.
- Use the Sharpie to darken both sides of the blade's edge again.
- Now flip the sharpening stone over and repeat the entire sharpening process on the fine side.
- Check the blade for sharpness by cutting a piece of paper. The knife should slide through the paper, making a smooth, clean cut with almost no effort.

Make a habit of sharpening your knife every time it's used for any tough task like whittling sticks, cleaning fish and game, or cutting rope. Otherwise, without regular sharpening, it gets too dull and will be very hard to get sharp again. You should also wash your knife in warm water and dish soap now and then. And if you see any rusty spots, spray it with WD-40 and wipe off the rust. Or, if the rust is thick and heavy, use a penetrating oil like Liquid Wrench and scrub the knife with an old toothbrush or a pad of steel wool. A well-maintained pocketknife will last you a lifetime, or at least until you drop it over the side of a boat or lose it in the woods!

MAKE A BLOWGUN THAT SHOOTS GREAT

Paleoanthropologists who study the hunting weapons used by ancient humans believe that different cultures around the world invented blowguns at different times. If you've ever shot a spitball through a drinking straw, you're familiar with the principle of a blowgun. Hunters in Asia, South America, and Africa used these weapons to deliver small doses of poison into animals that they hunted for food. Their poisons were made from toxins extracted from plants and animals. In Africa, some tribes made a poisonous concoction of mashed-up spiders, scorpions, and snake venom. Other African tribes used dried red ants as a poison. The Yagua, a tribe of hunter-gatherers who live in the jungles of Colombia and Peru, used blowgun darts that were sharpened with piranha teeth and dipped in a poison called curare. The poison is made by boiling the bark of certain species of trees. In small doses, it paralyzes the hunter's prey. They used curare in the hunting of monkeys, sloths, birds, and tree porcupines.

Because poisons are often slow to act and can cause pain, they are regarded by most modern-day hunters as an inhumane way of harvesting animals. Some Indigenous hunters living in remote jungle areas of the Amazon and Congo still use poisons for hunting today, but they are strictly illegal as a hunting tool in the United States.

It is possible to harvest small game with nonpoisonous blowgun darts, but they lack the power required to be a truly effective hunting tool. Different kinds of weapons get their power in different ways. Firearms get their energy from the combustion of gunpowder. The small explosion of gunpowder inside the gun's chamber releases hot gas, which creates so much pressure that it forces the bullet out of the barrel at a very high speed. Bows get their energy by harnessing the strength of the archer's arm and back muscles, which are used to bend the body of the bow by exerting pressure on the bow's string. When the archer releases the bowstring, the energy generated by the archer's muscles is transferred to the arrow and the arrow takes flight. Blowguns, on the other hand, are pneumatic. That's a word for something that is operated by air under pressure. In this case, the pressure is created by the user's lungs, diaphragm, and mouth. With a big and sudden huff, air is blown into the blowgun's barrel and the pressure sends the projectile flying. However, a person can't generate nearly as much energy with their breath as they can with their arms. So blowguns are weak compared to bows, and extremely weak compared to firearms.

As crazy as it sounds, some states have banned blowguns altogether. If you built a homemade blowgun to do some backyard target practice in California, you'd actually be breaking the law! This is too bad, because blowguns are a great way to develop aiming skills and hand-eye coordination that will come in handy when you start hunting with bows or firearms. They're also a ton of fun, and a great way to study and understand the skill sets used by Indigenous peoples around the world.

Once you determine that it's legal for you to make a blowgun (don't worry, in most places it's okay) you and your parents need to decide what type of dart you'll be allowed to use. You can make two types of darts using most of the same household materials. One kind is pointy and will be capable of sticking into cardboard boxes and dartboards. The other kind has a blunt tip that won't stick into anything.

Regardless of your dart type, you need to start by making your blowgun. It's as simple as getting a 3-foot section of ½-inch PVC pipe. It is usually sold in 10-foot sections, which cost about $5. But you might be able to ask the folks at your local hardware store or places such as Home Depot if they have a shorter section you can buy. Either way, they'll probably be able to cut your piece of PVC pipe to the proper length. If not, it's easy to cut it with a standard hacksaw or even a carpenter's wood saw. To finish the blowgun, take a pocketknife or a piece of sandpaper and scrape away any PVC shavings so that the ends of the pipe are nice and smooth.

What You'll Need

- Sheet of standard printer paper
- Roll of clear packing tape
- Scissors
- Hot glue gun
- For a pointy dart, you'll need a small nail that's about 1 or 1½ inches long—a 4d nail made from 12½-gauge wire would be perfect
- For a blunt-tip dart, you'll need a small fishing sinker—size #4 (1⁄12 ounce) or #5 (1⁄16 ounce) would be ideal

Building Steps

1. Roll the piece of paper into a tight cone. The small end of the cone should come to a fine point; the big end of the cone will have a diameter around 2½ inches. Secure the cone in place, so that it doesn't unravel, with a small piece of tape. Then measure up about 4 inches from the point of the cone and cut it off. You can discard the piece you cut away. You just want the small end of the cone.

2. Wrap the cone in packing tape. Do a careful job, so the tape doesn't have a lot of wrinkles.

3. Take your hot glue gun and put a couple of squirts of hot glue inside the cone, so that the glue lands down in the point.

4. For the pointy dart: Working quickly, before the glue dries, pass the nail down through the glue so that the tip of the nail comes out of the paper dart's point. Press on the head of the nail gently (a pencil or pen might help) until you feel it seat against the inside of the cone. Then add another squirt or two of glue to help hold the nail in place.

5. For the blunt-tip dart: Working quickly, before the glue dries, press the sinker down into the glue so that it comes to rest in the point of the cone. Then add another squirt or two of glue to help hold the sinker in place.

6. Place the dart, point first, into one end of your blowgun. Press gently until the walls of the cone are pressed firmly into the tube. Now take your scissors and cut the cone so that the diameter of the wide end is exactly the same as the diameter of the inside of the PVC pipe. Once it's cut, you should be able to push your dart inside the blowgun, with the wide end of the cone forming a tight seal against the walls of the tube. It's now ready to use.

To fire your blowgun, get a large cardboard box to use as a target. A box that comes up to your knees would be good, in case your aim is a little off. Take a Sharpie or a piece of tape and make a bull's-eye in the middle of the box.

For your first shot, stand back about 8 feet from your target. Press the end of the tube that holds the dart firmly against your lips like you're giving it a kiss. Now look down the tube and aim it toward the center of your target. When ready, push out all your air in a quick, single puff. Blow as hard and quick as you can. The dart will pass through the tube and fly out. Hopefully you'll get a bull's-eye. As you practice and get better, you can move farther and farther away from your target as you explore your efficacy and maximum range. Soon you'll be daydreaming about stalking the jungles of the Amazon with Yagua hunters while you watch the treetops for something tasty to eat.

MAKE YOUR OWN BOW

You might think of archery as an old-time way of hunting that re-quires a lot of skill. When you compare archery equipment to mod-ern firearms, that makes sense. Arrows fly much slower than bullets, and they don't travel nearly as far. What's more, bows are generally much harder to aim than guns. Using them effectively takes a lot more practice. Once upon a time, though, a bow and arrow were cutting-edge technology. Before the invention of the bow, hunters used different sorts of hand-thrown spears. If you wanted to kill a big animal to eat, you had to get really close. You might throw the spear a short distance or else jab it directly into your target. Bows made it possible to kill animals that were twenty or thirty steps away, or even more. And they were far more powerful than spears. In the early 1800s, a man named Anthony Glass traveled westward from Louisiana and stayed with members of the Wichita tribe in Texas. One day, Glass watched fifty of his hosts kill an entire herd of forty-one buffalo without the use of guns. He described how they made bows with wood from a type of tree called Osage orange. The bows were so strong that they could send an arrow into one side of the 1,000-pound buffalo and the arrow would come out the other side and stick into the dirt. That's strong!

Today, some archers still shoot bows made from Osage orange. But most modern bows are made out of combinations of synthetic materials like fiberglass, plastic, carbon fiber, and even lightweight metal alloys. Regardless of what they're made out of, all bows work basically the same way. When an archer pulls the bowstring back, the flexible, curved limbs of the bow bend, which builds up stored energy. When the archer lets go of the string, the limbs snap back to their original position, instantly releasing all of their stored energy as the string shoots forward and propels the arrow through the air.

If you're interested in archery but don't have a bow of your own, you don't need to worry. It's pretty easy to build a basic beginner bow and arrow setup with the same kind of hardware store PVC pipe used to build the simple blowgun on page 222. PVC pipe is strong and springy, so it works great for bow-making. Using the following building instructions, you can be shooting arrows in no time.

What You'll Need

You'll find most of this stuff at any hardware or home and garden store.

- A 48-inch piece of ¾-inch PVC pipe
- 6 feet of brightly colored 550 paracord or similar utility cord
- Electrical tape

- Matches or lighter
- Black Sharpie
- Tape measure
- Scissors or pocketknife
- Small hacksaw or Dremel tool
- A small rattail file or a piece of 80-grit sandpaper

You'll need arrows, too, but building them yourself is incredibly difficult and time-consuming. Instead, for about $20, you can buy a dozen durable fiberglass training arrows that come with blunt practice tips already installed. Arrows around 28–30 inches long are about right for most kids. You can find them on Amazon or at online archery shops such as 3riversarchery.com.

Building Steps

You'll need help from a parent or older sibling to build your bow.

1″

48″

1″

1. Start by using your tape measure to find the middle of the PVC pipe and use the Sharpie to draw a line there.
2. On each end of the PVC, you need to mark where you'll cut the grooves that hold the bowstring in place. Using the Sharpie, draw two 1-inch lines on opposite sides of each end of the PVC pipe. It is important that the marker lines on each end of the PVC pipe line up with each other.
3. Using the marker lines as a guide, use the hacksaw or Dremel tool to cut the notches in the ends of the PVC pipe. The notches should only be as wide as your string, so about ⅛ inch wide. You'll have two notches on each end of the PVC pipe,

for a total of four cuts. This step is easier if you can secure the PVC pipe in a vise at a workbench.

4. If the edges of the cuts are rough and sharp, use a rattail file or sandpaper to smooth them out.

5. Now tie two overhand loop knots about 36 inches apart in the paracord. Each loop should be about 2 inches wide. Make sure the knots are good and tight.

6. Put a loop of the paracord into the notches on one end of the PVC pipe. Next, stand up the PVC pipe with that end on the ground. Now, bend the top end of the PVC pipe down slowly until you can slip the other loop in the paracord into the notches on the top end of the PVC pipe.

7. Using the electrical tape, make a grip about 6 inches long around the middle of the bow. The top of the grip should line up with the mark you made in the first step. Use as many wraps of tape as you need to build up a comfy grip.

8. Next, use the tape measure to find the middle point of the bowstring. Use the Sharpie to make a mark there. This mark is where you'll nock, or attach, an arrow to the string. The nocking mark should line up pretty closely with the top of the grip.

9. Test your bow by drawing the string back without an arrow nocked. If it's too hard to pull it back, take the string off and make another one with the loops a little farther apart. If it feels like it's way too easy to pull the string back, make another one with the loops a little closer together.

10. Once the bow feels right, go ahead and cut off any extra cord that you don't need, but leave an inch or two so that you can continue to make adjustments. Use your matches or lighter to burn the ends of the cord so it doesn't fray.

Shooting Your Bow

Before you start shooting your bow, you should line up a safe place to practice. If you have a big backyard, that will work as long as you're careful and don't recklessly shoot arrows into the neighbors' yards. Remember that most of the safety rules that apply to shooting guns (page 237) also apply to archery. Shoot in a safe direction away from houses and other buildings. A bow is not nearly as powerful as a firearm, but it can still inflict grave injuries if it is used carelessly.

A PVC bow isn't designed for hunting. Some kids have successfully used them for squirrels, rabbits, and grouse, but they're mostly meant for target practice. You can buy archery targets, or stuff a big cardboard box full of newspaper or old bedsheets and draw a bull's-eye on the outside. Hay bales make good archery targets, too. But there's another way to practice with a bow that's even more fun. It's called stump shooting. That's where you walk through the woods and pick out targets like old, rotting stumps and logs.

But first you need to know how to use a bow. If you're right-handed, hold the bow in your left hand with the arrow resting on top of your hand on the left side of the bow. Pull, or draw, the string and arrow back in one smooth motion with your right hand. If you are left-handed, hold the bow with your right hand and draw with the left. Grip the string and arrow with your first three fingers; your pointer finger goes above the arrow and your two middle fingers below. The string should rest in the first joint below the tips of your fingers. When you draw the bow, try to bring it back to the same place every time. This is called finding your anchor spot. Some people draw back until they touch the corner of their mouth or until their thumb hits their ear. Having a consistent anchor spot will make you a more accurate archer. Modern compound bows used for hunting deer and other big game animals have sights that help the user to aim precisely and shoot accurately at different distances, but you'll be shooting instinctively, without a sight. This is just how bowhunters did it hundreds of years ago.

Start by shooting at a target that's just 4 or 5 yards away. To shoot instinctively, draw back, look down your arrow shaft at your target, and release the string as soon as it feels like you're lined up right. You probably won't be too accurate at first, but with some practice, you'll start to get a feel for adjusting your aim. When you can consistently hit a target the size of a paper plate, move back to practice at 10 yards, and then 20 yards. That's about as far as you can expect to be reasonably accurate with a PVC bow. If you become an ace at that range with a homemade bow, you might have to convince your parents to let you get a real bow and join an archery club. And if you dream of becoming a bowhunter someday, you're already well on your way to success!

BECOME A DEADEYE

You've probably heard the saying "Practice makes perfect" at least a hundred times. And just like hitting a curveball or playing the piano, it takes a lot of practice to become a deadeye with an air rifle or firearm. Recently, a team of long-range target shooters in Wyoming set a new world-record rifle shot by hitting an 8-inch bull's-eye from 7,774 yards away. That's over 4 miles! The catch is that even though these guys are expert marksmen, it took them more than a year of planning and practice and sixty-nine tries to finally hit the target.

Target shooting is a ton of fun all on its own, and it's essential if you dream of becoming a hunter someday. The shots that you'll be taking as a small-game hunter are much, much shorter than that world-record shot of 7,774 yards, but that doesn't mean hitting them will be easy. Although small game animals are typically taken at ranges of less than 50 yards, there's a strict rule in hunting that you should never take a shot at an animal unless you're confident the result will be a quick, humane kill. Otherwise, you'll probably miss or, even worse, end up with a wounded animal that gets away. That can leave you feeling really bad, as you caused it harm but weren't able to utilize it as a food resource. That's part of why you shouldn't even consider going hunting until you've put in enough time practicing that you can consistently hit what you're aiming at. And before you can begin practicing with firearms, you and your parents will have to come to an agreement that this is something you're responsible enough to do, and only with adult supervision.

Obviously, you'll need a rifle to shoot. Hopefully your adult shooting and hunting mentor has one that you can use with them. That way, you can see if you like target shooting before you make the commitment of getting your own rifle. If you do need to get one for yourself, you and your parents will need to decide what is best for you. Many parents who aren't comfortable with their kids having an actual firearm will at least let them have an air rifle. An air rifle is a pneumatic, or air-powered, rifle that propels a BB or a small lead pellet with a burst of air. Although they are capable of quickly killing animals like squirrels and rabbits, air rifles aren't as powerful as firearms, which ignite a charge of gunpowder to create a contained explosion that propels bullets with great speed and force. Air rifles are completely unregulated, and you can just order them online from Amazon or buy them at Walmart. There are no age restrictions to owning an air rifle. There are many kinds out there, but a .17- or .22-caliber air rifle from Gamo or Beeman will get you started.

If you can talk your parents into letting you have an actual firearm, you definitely want what's called a .22LR, which is a small-bore rifle. Your parents will have to buy the firearm, since you can't buy one yourself from a gun store until you're eighteen. So a parent will be the actual owner. In order to buy the rifle from a gun store, they'll need to answer some questions and submit to what's called a background check to make sure they'd be a safe and legal gun owner. If they've been in major trouble with the law, they might not be eligible to own one, and you'll have to stick with air rifles. Whichever way you go, both styles of rifles are relatively quiet and don't produce recoil, or kick, when you shoot. They are also inexpensive to shoot, so you can do plenty of practicing and become a real sharpshooter.

Whatever you get, there's a good chance it'll come with a telescopic sight, or scope. If not, you'll want to get one from a sporting goods store. You can install the scope using the owner's manual that comes with the rifle and/or scope, or they'll set it up for you and explain how it works at the sporting goods store you bought it from. Scopes make aiming at distant targets easier, and they can be easily adjusted so your shot hits exactly where you're aiming.

Once you've secured access to a rifle, you'll need to get a few things. Safety is first and foremost when shooting any type of firearm, so make sure you have eye and ear protection. For just a few bucks, you can pick up some shooting glasses and earplugs at the nearest sporting goods store. You'll also want some paper targets. Sporting goods stores and Amazon will have a ton of options you can look at. Or you can make your own target by drawing a thumbprint-sized circle in the middle of a piece of paper with a marker. Color the circle in so you can see it clearly from a ways off.

Now you have to find a place to shoot. Ask around with any friends and family who might enjoy shooting to see if anyone has a safe place where they like to go target shooting. If not, no big deal. You can always go shooting at a local shooting range. Some shooting ranges are open to the public, while others are private and require a membership fee. What's nice about shooting ranges is that they're all set up with target stands and shooting benches that you can use. Some even have staff range officers who keep an eye on everyone to make sure they're following all the rules and being safe. Many private ranges also offer beginner shooting classes with professional instructors, and some even offer loaner firearms to practice with. You can find nearby shooting ranges with a quick search on the internet or a visit to the local branch of your state fish and game agency.

You want to start out by shooting short distances. Around 20 yards is great. That'll help you get the hang of it. Some shooting ranges have their target stands set up at a minimum distance of 50 yards. But if you talk to someone who works there, or ask another shooter for help, you'll get set up with a stand at a shorter distance. While you practice, keep in mind that consistency is the most important thing. Hitting the center of the bull's-eye might feel great, but it doesn't matter at all if you can't do it over and over again. Once you can get five shots in a row into a 2-inch circle at 20 yards, move the target out to 30 yards. Then go to 40 and 50 yards as you get better. If your goal is to hunt squirrels (page 238), you should be good enough to hit a 1-inch circle. If you can do that consistently at 50 yards, you'll be able to take shots at that distance when you're hunting. If you can only do it at 20 yards, then limit your hunting shots to that distance until you get more skilled. If it seems hard, don't worry. Learning to be a true deadeye is a lifelong pursuit. Enjoy the journey. Practice, practice, practice. And keep dreaming of squirrel soup (page 252).

FOLLOW THE RULES OF GUN SAFETY

Target shooting and hunting can provide some of the most fun and exciting experiences around. You shouldn't be afraid of handling and shooting guns as long as you treat them with care and respect. Like many tools, guns are safe when handled properly, but they can be extremely dangerous when mishandled. Never, ever handle or shoot guns without adult supervision, and always practice the following rules of safe, responsible shooting. These rules are mandatory!

1. Always treat every gun as if it were loaded.
2. Always keep the barrel of the gun pointed in a safe direction.
3. Never assume the safety will prevent the gun from firing.
4. Always be sure of your target and what is beyond it.
5. Never point the gun at anything you don't intend to destroy.
6. Always keep the gun's safety on until you are ready to shoot.
7. Always keep your finger off the trigger until you are ready to shoot.
8. Always keep the gun unloaded until you are ready to use it.
9. Learn how to safely operate the gun you are using.
10. Make sure you are using the proper ammunition and that the barrel is free of obstructions.

GO SQUIRREL HUNTING

If you've put in your time at the shooting range and want to try your hand at hunting, you first need to look into your state's rules about youth hunters. Some states have a minimum hunting age of ten or twelve, but in others there is no minimum. No matter where you live, all new hunters are required to take a hunter's safety and education course. You may be able to hunt for a year or two with an adult mentor before completing the course. Even after you've completed your hunter's safety certification course, there's a chance you might need to be accompanied in the field by an adult hunter until you're sixteen years old. There are many other hunting regulations you'll need to understand and follow, but the most important rule to remember is that safety (page 237) always comes first.

Let's assume you're ready to follow the rules and that you have an adult mentor to take you hunting. What should you go hunting for? There are lots of options, but squirrels are the ideal quarry for new hunters. First, you don't have to purchase a lot of expensive, specialized gear to hunt them; all you really need is a .22 rifle or a decent air rifle. Next, squirrels are very common throughout the country, so there are very likely some good opportunities to hunt them near you. Most states have long squirrel hunting seasons with generous bag limits, too, so you'll have plenty of chances to bring some home to eat.

There are many kinds of squirrels. Some live in underground burrows, but the squirrel species that are targeted by hunters are known as tree squirrels. You'll find lots of different subspecies within that category, but here's a basic rundown of what's out there. Fox squirrels and eastern gray squirrels are abundant in the eastern two-thirds of the United States. Fox squirrels, the biggest tree squirrels in North America, get their name from their fur—they're colored like red foxes, with reddish orange highlights. Gray squirrels are a little smaller than fox squirrels. They are usually gray, but it's not unusual to see one that is jet black. (These are called black-phase gray squirrels.)

In the northern and western United States, plus across Canada, there's an abundant little squirrel called a pine squirrel. In some areas, it's known as a red squirrel. Pine squirrels' color can range from red to brown, and they are quite a bit smaller than gray squirrels and fox squirrels. Yet another type of squirrel, the Abert's squirrel, lives in the Ponderosa pine forests of the southwestern United States. Abert's squirrels have tufts on their ears that look like little horns. In California and Oregon, you can hunt western gray squirrels, which are a tad bigger than their eastern cousins but look just about the same.

All of these species spend a little time on the ground, but for the most part they are arboreal, meaning they live in trees. So if you want to be a good squirrel hunter, you need to be good at identifying the different kinds of trees squirrels like. Pine squirrels get their name from the fact that they eat pine nuts, the seeds inside pine cones. You should look for them in coniferous forests. Fox squirrels and gray squirrels prefer stands of deciduous hardwood trees like oaks, hickory, beech, hazelnut, black walnut, and other nut-bearing varieties. They will also occasionally venture out from the woods a short ways into farm fields to eat corn, soybeans, and grains. This is especially true of fox squirrels, which seem to be more comfortable exposing themselves to airborne predators like hawks and owls. Gray squirrels, on the other hand, like to stay in thicker cover.

There are tons of good squirrel hunting places on public lands such as national forests, state game lands, and wildlife management areas. What's cool about these places is that anyone is allowed to go hunting there, as long as they have a license and follow the rules. Farms with a mix of crop fields and woodlots are an even better place to find squirrels, but you'll need to politely ask the landowners for permission to hunt on their property. Don't let that intimidate you, though—you'd be surprised by how many farmers and other large landowners are more than happy to let kids do some squirrel hunting.

Once you've found a likely spot, there are a couple of different methods you can use to hunt squirrels. You can sit and wait for squirrels to come around, which is called ambush hunting. Or you can do what's called still hunting, which—contrary to what it sounds like—actually means to sneak through the woods very slowly and quietly.

Ambush hunting is a good option when you know exactly where some squirrels have been hanging around. It's not a bad idea to build a blind (page 196) or two in the area, so you have a good place to hide and wait. Otherwise, all you need to do is sit down with your back against a big tree where you have a clear view of the surrounding area. Generally, mornings and evenings are better times to hunt squirrels than the middle of the day. You need to watch carefully while you're hunting. Sometimes all you'll see at first is what looks like a furry bump on a branch, a wiggling tail, or a small head peering around a branch. When a squirrel appears inside your effective shooting range (we talk about that on page 236), wait for it to sit still before you take your shot. If you hit it, grab it and return to your seat to wait for another one to show up. If you miss and the squirrel disappears, don't give up. It'll likely be back in the same area the next day.

The nice thing about still hunting is that you get to see more places and scout out new hunting grounds to come back to. Because you're slowly creeping through the woods, you can turn this way and that to check out any ponds or fields or big trees that might interest you. And by covering more ground, you might see more squirrels than you would sitting in one spot. When you're still hunting, plan on spending as much time standing still as you do walking. A good strategy is to lean against a tree and carefully watch the surrounding treetops for any sign of squirrels. You should listen for squirrels, too. They often give themselves away with their barks and chirps or by rustling through the leaves on the ground or in trees. After several minutes of watching and listening, slowly move along to another tree and do the same thing over again. If you find a great spot, you might decide to try an ambush hunt the next time you come to the area.

Still hunting tends to work best when deciduous trees still have their leaves on them. The leaves prevent the squirrels from seeing far away, giving you a better chance of slipping up close to them without getting noticed. Later in the year, when the leaves fall, the squirrels will be able to see you coming from far away. Also, only the wariest squirrels are still alive at that time of year. The rest have been eaten by predators like weasels, hawks, owls, bobcats, raccoons, foxes, feral house cats, and hunters like yourself. High in the branches, the survivors have learned to retreat into their nests at the first sign of danger. When hunting these crafty squirrels, you might have to switch to ambush hunting.

If you want to improve your skills as a squirrel hunter, there are a couple of other things you can try. Store-bought squirrel calls that mimic the noises squirrels make can work pretty well in the right situations. If you're not seeing any squirrels, a call may pique their curiosity enough to get them to leave the confines of their nest and present you with an opportunity. You can order a squirrel call online or find one at your local sporting goods store. If you see a squirrel vanish up into a treetop and you can't find it again, you should first walk around the tree a few times and look very carefully. A pair of binoculars is a helpful tool for studying the branches in search of any tufts of fur that might give the squirrel away. If you still can't find it, the squirrel might be moving around the tree as you move, always keeping the tree trunk between you. If a squirrel is using this trick against you, there's a good way to use its behavior to your advantage. Stand on one side of the tree and toss a big rock or a dead branch over to the ground on the other side of the tree. Be ready to shoot when the squirrel gets scared and scurries over to your side. If you're lucky and take careful aim, you'll be rewarded with a very special treat at dinnertime.

AIM FOR THE VITALS

Before you go hunting, you should know that shooting at an animal is much different from shooting at a target. This is especially true for beginners without a lot of experience. It's easy to stay calm when you're shooting at a piece of paper, but you'll get excited and maybe even a little nervous when you're shooting at an animal. That excitement can cause you to miss your shot. Knowing exactly where to aim will help you stay calm and focused.

First, when you are shooting at an animal, the main goal is always to make a quick, clean kill. Second, you want to hit the animal in a spot that doesn't damage too much meat. Hunting, after all, is about bringing home some delicious wild food to share with your friends and family. Depending on the species, you'll need to hit a vital organ like the brain, heart, or  lungs to accomplish these goals. Take the time to study anatomy and ideal shot placement for different game animals so you know the exact location of their vital organs. For instance, you should aim for the head on a squirrel or rabbit. On a deer, however, you should aim for the rib cage just behind the shoulder. You can even practice by shooting at targets that show the locations of vital organs for different game animals.

And remember, you must be able to clearly see an animal in order to make an accurate shot. Never, ever shoot at something that's moving that you can't identify, or through thick brush that obscures your view of your target. Be patient and wait for the animal to expose itself. It's better to let your quarry get away than to take a shot at an animal you cannot clearly identify.

CLEAN A SQUIRREL

A couple of centuries ago, it was normal to live without access to fresh meat from grocery stores and restaurants. Many people either hunted or raised their own animals for food. If a hunter's luck was bad, or a farmer's animals were stolen or died of starvation, their family would go hungry. Back then, pretty much everyone, including kids, knew how to butcher the rabbits, chickens, deer, cows, and other animals that they lived off. These days, the skills required to butcher meat are largely forgotten among the general population. All that work is done by professional meat cutters. In the United States and Canada, not even farmers and ranchers are involved in processing their livestock into food. Instead, their animals are usually shipped to faraway factories where they get turned into the things we eat. Hunters are an exception to this, as it's common for them to have the skills and tools required to extract clean, edible pieces of meat from something that's covered in fur or feathers and full of internal organs and bones.

When it comes to small game like squirrels and rabbits, hunters often refer to the butchering process as "cleaning." This includes everything required to get the animal ready to be cooked and eaten. You'll be removing the internal organs and skin, as well as other inedible portions such as the feet and tail. If you've never done it, you might be intimidated by the thought of cleaning an animal. But there's nothing gross or scary about turning an animal into a meal. After all, every meat product you've ever eaten, including hot dogs, Chicken McNuggets, hamburgers, and even marshmallows (yes, marshmallows) went through a similar process. It's a worthwhile skill to master, and it is not that difficult. What's more, the process is basically the same no matter what kind of animal you're working on. If you know how to clean a squirrel, then it'll be no big deal to clean a rabbit or even butcher a deer. Just make sure you don't wait too long to field dress any game animal or bird. The sooner you get the skin off and the guts out, the sooner the meat will begin to cool. This prevents the meat from spoiling. It's best to work outside or in the garage. Wear disposable nitrile gloves so your hands stay clean. If you're at home, you'll want a cutting board to work on and a garbage bag to dispose of the guts and other inedible parts.

Here's how to field dress a squirrel using the "shirt and pants" method:

- Make sure your knife is sharp (page 218) before you start. It's not completely necessary to have kitchen shears, but it's a lot easier to snip through tough pieces of hide and bone and remove the feet and head with shears than to cut through that stuff with a knife.

- Make the first incision with your knife through the squirrel's hide on the middle of its back. Using either your knife or shears, carefully extend this cut all the way around the middle of the squirrel's body.

- With one hand, grasp the squirrel firmly just above its back legs. Use the other hand to begin peeling off the "shirt" portion of its hide toward the head. Squirrels have a tough hide, so it takes some effort to pull it away from the underlying flesh.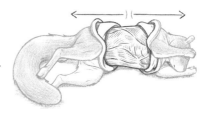

- Peel the squirrel's shirt off over the shoulders up to the neck and down the front legs to the feet.

- Next, grab the squirrel around the shoulders and remove its "pants" using the same technique. Make sure you get the hide off all the way down to the feet and the base of the tail.

- Now use your kitchen shears to cut off all four feet, the tail, and the head. You should be left with a fully skinned body and legs.

- Use your knife to make a very shallow cut from the squirrel's sternum (the bone in the middle of the rib cage) down through the belly to the anus. Don't cut too deep or you'll puncture the stomach and intestines. That can make a mess.

- Now use a couple of fingers to reach all the way inside the rib cage. Pull the heart and lungs toward the stomach and intestines. Continue pulling all the internal organs back toward the anus. Everything should all come out in one big lump. Snip the large intestine near the anus and dispose of the gut contents.

- After that, you'll need to cut the squirrel into five edible portions. This is best done with kitchen shears. Start by separating the legs from the body at the hip and shoulder joints. The piece you want is the middle of the body, which is called the saddle.

- Next, prepare the saddle by snipping off the rib bones, the hip bones, and the bony shoulder and neck area. Discard those pieces. You should be left with a thick, meaty chunk surrounding the spine.

- There will probably be some pieces of hair stuck to the squirrel meat. Remove as much as you can and then rinse all five pieces of meat in cold water until they're clean.

Your squirrel is now recipe-ready, meaning it's ready to cook. One fox or gray squirrel is just right for one hungry kid, but you'll probably need two pine squirrels per person. They're great in Squirrel Noodle Soup (page 252), prepared just like fried chicken, or in gumbo. If you're not going to eat the meat within a couple of days, wrap it in freezer paper or put it in a vacuum-sealed plastic bag and store it in the freezer.

COOK YOUR CATCH

Turning your catch into a tasty meal that your whole family can enjoy is the best way to celebrate a successful fishing or hunting trip. Your parents probably do most of the cooking in your house, but don't be afraid to try cooking for them instead. Even if you get the kitchen messy, you can probably talk them into helping you clean up and do the dishes. Of course, you may need a little help with the cooking here and there, but with these three simple recipes, you'll be able to make some delicious food that is the ultimate reward for your efforts.

Crayfish Boil

Have you ever heard of a crayfish boil? It's a very popular type of celebration in the American South, especially in Louisiana. (In Louisiana, they call them crawfish.) People do crayfish boils during the holidays, at football game tailgating parties, and at backyard barbecues. They might cook up 30 or 40 pounds of crayfish to feed just ten people. If you've trapped a few crayfish, you can have your own version of a crayfish boil at home. It's not hard, either. Boiling is a very easy technique, so it's a good way of cooking things if you don't have a ton of experience.

You can keep the crayfish you trapped alive in a cooler full of water and ice for a day, or two days at the most. Before you cook your crayfish, throw out any that are dead. You don't want to eat those because they could make you sick.

- Get a big pot for boiling water. If you have a dozen or so crayfish, 1 gallon of water will work. Toss in ½ cup salt. Or, better yet, toss in ¼ cup salt and ¼ cup Cajun seasoning. If you have a lot of crayfish, they might not all fit in the pot, so you'll need to boil more water or else cook your crayfish in batches.
- Carefully dump them into the boiling water. They'll die instantly and begin to turn a bright reddish orange color.
- Boil them for about 10 minutes.
- Turn off the heat and let the crayfish soak in the water for another 10 minutes. When they're done, carefully transfer the crayfish into a colander to cool off.
- While the crayfish are cooling, make a quick side dish by cooking some ears of corn in a pot of boiling water for several minutes.

Just like shrimp, all the meat on a crayfish is inside the tail. After your crayfish have cooled off, pull the tail from the body and peel off the shell. Dip your crayfish tails in a dish of melted butter and dig in! If you're feeling adventurous, you also can suck the juice out of the head just like they do down south.

Fried Fish

Fried fish is delicious. People eat it all over the world, and just about every culture has its own version. They call it fish and chips in England. In Japan, there's seafood tempura. In America, people do fish fries with everything from bluegills to catfish to grouper. The crunchy coating on the outside and moist, flaky fish on the inside are the perfect match of texture and flavor. If you've ever bitten into a piece of crispy fried fish, then you already know how good it is. If you haven't, then here's your chance to give it a try.

This particular preparation for fried fish works well with whole scaled panfish or panfish fillets. Plan on cooking a few whole panfish or a half dozen panfish fillets per person so that everyone gets a taste. You can also use any other fish with mild, white flesh. If you're working with large fillets, like those from big catfish, slice them into "fish fingers" about the size of a Chicken McNugget before frying.

- Pour about 1 cup of milk into a bowl or small baking dish, crack an egg into the milk, and scramble up the egg with a fork.
- For the breading, you can use flour, fine-ground cornmeal, breadcrumbs, or panko crumbs. You can also make good breading by smashing up pretzels, saltines, or Ritz crackers. Put 1 or 2 cups of the breading in another bowl or baking dish.
- Pat your fish dry with some paper towels and lightly season it with salt. You can also add a little pepper, Old Bay, or Cajun seasoning.

- Pour canola or peanut oil into a large frying pan. You want it to be about ½ inch deep.
- One piece at a time, dip the fish into the egg/milk mixture. Then roll it in the coating. This part can get kind of messy, so have plenty of paper towels on hand.
- While you're dipping and coating the pieces of fish, turn the stove's burner to medium-high to get the oil in the pan hot. This will take a couple of minutes. If you have a candy or deep fat thermometer, you want your oil between 365 and 375 degrees.
- After all the fish are breaded, use a pair of tongs to lay them in the hot oil. Cook for 3 minutes and then gently flip the fish with your cooking tongs. Cook them for another 3 minutes on the other side. You want them nice and crisp but not burned. When they're done, they should be golden brown.
- Remove the cooked pieces of fish using your cooking tongs and lay them on a plate that's covered with a few pieces of paper towel. The paper towel will let the extra oil drain away from your fish. Make sure to let them cool off before you grab one. That hot oil can burn your fingers or tongue.

Cut a wedge off a lemon and squeeze a little of the juice over the fried fish. You can eat it as is or dip the fish in ketchup or tartar sauce. After a couple of bites, you'll be wanting to plan your next fishing trip.

Squirrel Noodle Soup

Who doesn't love a steaming bowl of homemade chicken noodle soup? It is the perfect meal for warming up after a day of stomping around outside in the rain or snow. And if you're a hunter or know someone who is, you can make a great pot of chicken noodle soup by using squirrels instead of chicken. To be honest, it's hard to tell them apart when used in this recipe. You can serve it to friends and then surprise them when you tell them what they just ate.

Ingredients

4 cleaned squirrels (pages 244–247)

1 medium onion, chopped into little pieces the size of your fingernail

2 carrots, sliced thin

2 celery sticks, sliced thin

4 garlic cloves, minced up

1 tablespoon each salt, black pepper, dried sage, thyme, rosemary, and parsley

4 quarts unsalted or low sodium chicken stock (16 cups)

1 bag egg noodles

Cooking oil (olive or canola)

Preparation

1. Season each piece of squirrel with salt and pepper.
2. In a large soup pot, add 2 tablespoons cooking oil and brown the squirrel pieces over medium heat. After each piece has browned, remove from the pot and set aside.
3. Add another tablespoon of cooking oil to the pan and add the

onion and cook until translucent. Add the carrots, celery, and garlic and cook until they begin to soften.

4. Put the pieces of squirrel meat back in the pot and add all the seasonings. Pour in the chicken stock and stir to combine everything.

5. Bring the soup to a boil, then turn down the heat down to low so it's gently simmering. Cook uncovered for roughly 3 hours, or until the meat is fork-tender.

6. Use tongs to lift out each piece of squirrel. Let it cool off and use your fingers or a fork to shred the meat off the bones. Toss the bones in the trash and put the shredded meat back in the pot.

7. In a separate pot, cook the bag of egg noodles according to the directions on the package.

Ladle a healthy portion of soup into a bowl and add as many noodles as you like! You'll be able to feed your whole family and still have leftovers. And don't hesitate to use rabbit, pheasant, grouse, wild turkey, or even chicken instead of squirrel meat for this noodle soup recipe. The results will be almost as good.

IV

GARDEN AND HOME

Kids who love outdoor exploration (that means you!) don't need to travel far from home in order to get outside and have adventures. You can birdwatch from your backyard, a balcony, a fire escape, or even just by looking out your window. And you can continue to hone your outdoor skills by putting together a few homemade tools that'll help you understand the weather conditions in your home habitat. And then there's gardening. It's one of the very best ways to engage with the natural world, and this section will teach you exactly how to do it. When you dig into these projects, you'll learn that nature is always very close. Sometimes, it's as close as the inside of your own home.

MAKE A WEATHER VANE

The highest wind speed ever recorded at the earth's surface was 253 miles per hour. A wind that fast would easily beat a NASCAR driver in a race. This amazing gust of wind occurred in 1996 on Barrow Island, Australia, during a typhoon. The weather event beat the previous record of 231 miles per hour, set on the summit of New Hampshire's Mount Washington in 1934. Try to think about what that wind would feel like. A 20 mph wind can easily carry away your umbrella at the beach. A wind blowing 200 mph faster than that could carry away pretty much everything you own!

While wind speed is an important part of any weather forecast, meteorologists also pay careful attention to wind direction. Imagine if you were a bush pilot in Alaska who had to fly 400 miles to deliver medicine to a remote village during 40 mph winds. If that was a tailwind, blowing in the direction you're flying, you'd be there in just 3 hours. But let's say it was a headwind, blowing straight into your plane. The trip would now take close to 7 hours. Wind direction can also tell you what weather to expect in the future, from rain showers and slight temperature changes to hurricanes and tornadoes. Winds blowing from the north tend to bring colder weather, including snow or hail in the wintertime. Winds blowing from the south tend to bring warm and humid conditions, which might mean rain. Obviously, these conditions can have a big impact on what sorts of outdoor activities you should plan.

You can get an idea of which way the wind is blowing by simply using your senses. Noticing the feel of the wind as it moves across your skin or the way it rustles the leaves in a nearby tree is a good way to find out. But if you want to know more about how the wind typically behaves over time, you can build a weather vane to watch its movements around your home. The instrument was first invented by the Greek astronomer Andronicus in 48 BC. That weather vane was made of bronze and built to look like the Greek god Triton, the ruler of the sea. Farmers and fishermen used the invention to plan their harvests or fishing trips. President George Washington, who famously loved to record weather patterns, had a dove-shaped weather vane made out of copper—you can go visit it at Mount Vernon, in Virginia, where it still tops the cupola of the Founding Father's home.

Your weather vane will be made of cardboard, but it'll be just as effective. Eventually, you might be able to use it to predict the weather, especially in combination with the barometer on page 260.

What You'll Need

- Pencil with an eraser on one end
- Drawing compass

- Piece of cardboard
- Scissors
- Ruler
- Markers
- Bit of construction paper
- Clear packing tape
- Drinking straw
- Superglue
- Thumbtack

Building Steps

1. Use your pencil and drawing compass to mark a circle on the cardboard that's about the size of a paper plate, then cut around the circle with your scissors.

2. Draw two intersecting lines across the circle, using your ruler to evenly divide your pie into four slices. Then mark your cardinal directions (north, east, south, and west) at the ends of your intersecting lines. It's nice to use different colors for these.

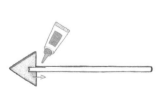

3. Make your flag. Cut a small triangle out of construction paper—the base of the triangle should be 1 to 1½ inches wide. Cover both sides of the flag with packing tape to waterproof it. Then use your scissors to cut a small slit down one end of the straw. Use a bit of superglue to secure the paper triangle into the slit.

CATCH A CRAYFISH, COUNT THE STARS

4. Gently punch the thumbtack through the center of the straw. Swivel the thumbtack around a bit to make sure the arrow glides, then press the thumbtack into your pencil's eraser. Blow on your flag to make sure it swivels in response to air pressure; if it doesn't, try raising your thumbtack a bit so that the flag has more room to move.

5. Press the tip of your pencil into the center of your cardboard circle. Keep pressing until your pencil goes midway through the cardboard. Now you've built a weather vane. You can waterproof the cardboard by covering it up with tape.

Using Your Weather Vane

To use your weather vane, take it outside along with a magnetic compass or a smartphone with a compass app. Look up the cardinal directions using your compass or phone, then position your weather vane so that the markings are pointing in the right direction. Take wind readings on a regular schedule, or whenever you get the urge, and write down your findings in a journal. Over time, see if you can answer the following questions: What is the dominant wind direction where you live? Does it change seasonally? What direction do storms generally come from? What wind directions tend to precede clear weather?

To really advance your skills, make the barometer on the following page. By measuring *both* wind direction and air pressure, you'll be on your way to becoming your family's in-house meteorologist.

MEASURE YOUR
ATMOSPHERIC PRESSURE

Have you ever ridden on an airplane and felt something strange happening inside your ears as you lifted up into the skies? If so, what you experienced was the effect of a rapid change in atmospheric pressure. When your ears pop, that's your body's way of adjusting the air inside your ears to match the pressure inside the plane. The term "atmospheric pressure" refers to the weight of the air in our atmosphere. It might not seem like it, but the air molecules all around us have weight. The combined weight of all those trillions of air molecules really adds up. At sea level, your body is holding up almost 15 pounds of weight in air! The higher up you go, like in a plane or climbing a mountain, the more the air pressure generally decreases. You might be wondering why you don't actually feel like you're holding up the weight of the air. It's partly because you're used to it, and partly because the pressure in our lungs has evolved to match the air pressure outside our bodies. A person usually becomes aware of atmospheric pressure when there's a sudden change. In fact, flying in a jet would actually be a lot worse if the planes weren't equipped with devices that control the atmospheric pressure inside the cabin. There's no such luxury when you're climbing a big mountain. There, the decreased atmospheric pressure and the reduction in oxygen might make you dizzy, tired, and short of breath until you gradually get used to the new conditions.

One way to measure the pressure of the atmosphere is with a unit of measure called a millibar. Millibars are part of the metric

CATCH A CRAYFISH, COUNT THE STARS

system. They're sort of confusing. It's the amount of pressure that it takes to move a certain object over a certain distance in a certain amount of time. Specifically, a millibar is the amount of pressure it would take to move an object weighing one gram the distance of one centimeter in one second's time. The average atmospheric pressure at sea level is about 1,000 millibars. On the summit of Mount Everest, which is the highest mountain on earth, the average air pressure is about 300 millibars.

Atmospheric pressure has a major impact on weather. In times of high atmospheric pressure, the weather is usually warm and calm. During low atmospheric pressure, the weather is usually rainy and windy. The weather gets stirred up when there are major changes in atmospheric pressure. A sudden change can cause high winds, hurricanes, rainstorms, and more. If you want to start understanding the weather and learning how to predict it, you should make your own barometer in order to track local changes in atmospheric pressure. Traditionally, scientists have used glass barometers filled with a pool of mercury to take their measurements—the mercury expands as air pressure increases, pushing the silver liquid up the vial. You'll be making a much simpler barometer out of a glass jar and a cut-up balloon.

What You'll Need

- Balloon
- Pair of scissors
- Quart-sized glass canning jar
- Thick rubber or elastic band that fits around mouth of jar
- Drinking straw

- Pen and a piece of heavy-duty paper
- Tape

Building Steps

1. First, cut off the neck of your balloon and throw it away.

2. Stretch your balloon tightly over the mouth of your jar, and place the rubber band tightly over the rim of the jar to secure the balloon. The balloon will rise and fall as air pressure changes.

3. If your straw is curved, cut off the curved part. Tape the straw to the top of your balloon, so that it sticks out horizontally. This is your air pressure gauge.

4. Now, make a simple chart to record your findings. Cut your paper into a vertical strip. Stand the strip up next to your barometer, and draw a marking at the level of the straw. Now

draw two other markings an inch above and below the first. Add a sun to the top of your chart, and some rain on the bottom.

Here's how your barometer works. When you placed the balloon over the jar, you trapped some air inside. If the air pressure outside of the jar increases (high pressure), it will weigh down on the balloon and cause the tip of the straw to rise up. If the air pressure outside of the jar decreases, the air inside of the jar will rise up in response. As the balloon rises, the end of the straw will drop down. Go ahead and watch your barometer and then look up the weather forecast for the next hour or so. Do you agree with what the meteorologist is saying?

GAUGE YOUR RAINFALL

If you really hate the rain, you might consider moving to Arica, Chile. The city is on the Pacific Ocean in the northern part of the country. It lies in the Atacama Desert. During a recorded period of 43 years, Arica averaged just .02 inches of rain per year. That's about the thickness of the average adult's thumbnail. Outside of the city, in the core of the desert, there's a place where it didn't rain for 500 years. If you love rain, on the other hand, maybe you should move to Mawsynram, India. They have an average annual rainfall of 467.4 inches. That's 39 feet of rain, which is about as high as seven grown-ups standing on top of one another.

Obviously, the rainfall in your own home habitat sits somewhere between those extremes. But what is it, exactly? Since rainfall varies so much from place to place, it's possible that no one actually knows how much rain you get at your home. You can solve this mystery by creating your own rain gauge. Once you've built your rain gauge, you can begin to track how precipitation changes over time. How does this year's rainfall compare to the long-term average? How does it compare to the highs and lows that set past records? How much rain does it take for the local streams and rivers to rise and turn muddy? After a good rain, do you notice that grass grows greener and you start to hear more insect noises? These are all great questions to ask yourself once you start monitoring your local rainfall.

What You'll Need

- Empty 2-liter plastic soda bottle
- Scissors
- A few small rocks
- Glue
- Masking tape or packing tape
- Ruler or measuring tape
- Sharpie
- Mineral oil (optional)

Building Steps

1. Cut the top off the bottle and set it aside. Make the cut right where the straight walls of the bottle begin to narrow in toward the cap.
2. Place a layer of small rocks at the bottom of the bottle. These will act as an anchor.
3. Flip the top of the bottle over and glue it into the bottom half, so it looks like a funnel.
4. Fill the bottle with water up to the top of the rocks.
5. Cut a 6-inch-long piece of masking tape and, for the moment, stick it to the ground. Lay your ruler alongside your tape, and mark off measurements at one-inch intervals. Stick the tape to the side of your bottle, lining up the zero on the number line with the top of the rocks and water inside of the bottle.
6. Find a spot for your rain gauge where it'll be under open sky but out of the way of foot traffic.

Now you're ready to record rainfall. Check your gauge after a rain, and record the date and your measurements before emptying the gauge. If you want to let the rain in your gauge build up over a longer period of time, you can put a few drops of mineral oil into your bottle. The mineral oil will float at the surface of the water and create an evaporation barrier. When you record the rainfall, just make sure to ignore this oil and record the measurement where the water sits.

MAKE WIND CHIMES

You probably already have the tools and supplies you need to turn wind into music. Sounds a bit like a magic trick, right? In fact, wind chimes *are* a bit magical. You might forget they're there until a gentle breeze blows, and then suddenly you're treated to a beautiful and unpredictable tune. In China, wind chimes are thought to keep evil spirits away and bring good luck to a house. They've been around for a very long time. Archaeologists have found early examples made of bones, shells, and bamboo. Store-bought wind chimes are usually made of metal, but playing around with different materials will yield different soundscapes. You might want to try making a couple of variations, to see how they play together.

Your beachcombing finds can be good things to use in your wind chimes. Seashells, sea glass, small stones, driftwood, little bits of metal, and old fishing line can all be used as chime material. But any natural environment can yield good finds for use in a wind chime, from animal bones to twigs to flat rocks. There's lots of stuff from home that can be incorporated, too, from buttons to bottle caps to soup can lids and more.

Here's a simple chime that you can adapt to any materials you might find.

1. First, prep your noisemaking materials. Use a thin nail and a hammer to make holes in items like seashells and bottle caps (position your shells or caps on a workbench or a piece of scrap wood), or have an adult help you use a drill. Buttons

don't need any help—you can just thread them onto your chime through the button-holes.

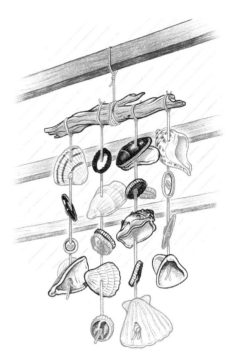

2. Create the individual strands for your chimes—you want at least three—by cutting several pieces of fishing line, yarn, or twine to about 2 feet in length.

3. Thread or tie your noisemaking materials onto these strands at regular intervals. As you work, tap the various pieces together to see which ones make a cool noise. When you find a good combination, position the pieces on the wind chime so that they'll bang together when the wind blows. If you have some larger objects that might catch more wind, place them at the bottom of the string. That'll help the wind chime work even during lighter breezes. To hold the pieces in place, you can use hot glue, knots, or a combination of both. Make sure to leave some extra length at the top of the strands for tying them off.

4. Tie off your chimes to an anchor. You can wrap and knot them around a piece of driftwood or a stick, or thread them through an empty can with a hole punctured in the bottom.

5. Hang your chimes on a tree branch, or from the eaves of your roof.

You might have to adjust your wind chime's location in order to find the right spot. If it's getting too tangled up, it might be too windy. If you don't get any good sounds, it's probably not windy enough. Also consider adjusting the position of your objects and swapping them out with replacements in order to find the perfect combination of noises. You'll know you've got it right when you start looking forward to a nice breeze, so that you can hear the magical sounds of the wind.

MAKE YOUR OWN ART SUPPLIES

You've probably stained a shirt or two by accident with raspberry juice. And you've probably made stains on the knees of your pants by playing in the grass. It happens to everybody! But did you know you could harness the staining power of berries and grass and other natural substances and put them to good use as art supplies? It's a practice that's been around ever since people started painting on the walls of caves. Our ancient ancestors used to mix the ashes from their campfires with animal fat or even their own spit to make paints. They would travel for many miles to retrieve iron-rich rocks called ochre that would create reddish-colored hues when used like a crayon. Native Americans traditionally used various roots, berries, and barks to paint their faces, adorn canoes and totem poles, and decorate ceramics. Until modern times, paints used across Europe and the United States were still made from natural materials. For instance, the leaves of a plant from the bean family called *Indigofera tinctoria* could be fermented to make a bright blue pigment called indigo. It was commonly used to dye denim. That's how blue jeans came to get their color, and their name.

Some natural pigments are stronger than others. Mashed up tomatoes will produce a nice watery red, but a beet that's been cut in half will lay down a much brighter color. Look around your backyard, your neighborhood park, or a nearby trail for other potential sources of pigment. It might be hard to keep yourself from eating them, but a handful of wild berries can produce beautiful colors. Brown and green colors are easy to find in nature—you can use mud as paint, or a piece of bark as a crayon. Grab a handful of grass and smudge it directly on your paper. Would you believe that even animal poop has been used as a traditional paint source? It's true, but don't try this yourself. Poop can harbor a lot of harmful bacteria.

An Earth Artist's Palette

Use as many of these ideas for paints and dyes as you like, and then try to come up with your own inventions. If you make a bunch of different colors at once, you can create a painter's palette, then mix and match to create different tones.

Ashes and burnt sticks. Mix up some ashes from your campfire with a bit of vegetable oil or lard (water will work, too), and use it for grays and blacks. Or char the end of a stick and use it like a crayon!

Beets. Pick a few beets from your garden (or grab some from the fridge), then clean and slice them in half. Carve a simple design like a heart, a star, or an initial into your stamp, and simply press it onto paper to activate.

Berries. Pretty much any berry will make a pigment in its own color.

Egg whites. Use a whisk to whip an egg white until it thickens, then add a little water over the top of it and place it in a covered container. Let it sit overnight, drain off the liquid, then use the egg white as varnish over your finished artwork. It'll add a gloss and help preserve the colors.

Eggshells. Grind up and mix with water or oil for white.

Flowers. Crush dried flower petals and mix with water, or rub the heads of fresh flowers directly onto paper.

Grass. Smudge grass onto paper for a bit of green, or boil in water and leave to soak overnight to create a nice supply.

PRINT A FISH

The whole body of a fresh fish may sound like a strange thing to bring to the arts and crafts table. But covering a fish with ink to produce a textured print is actually a traditional Japanese art dating back to the 1800s. Back then, owners of fish markets would hang their fish prints around their shops or stalls as a way to advertise their catch. The technique is called *gyotaku*—*gyo* translates to "fish," and *taku* means "rubbing." You can still see such prints in some fishing shops in Japan today, and fishing tournaments around the world will sometimes feature *gyotaku* artists who'll print the winner's catch for them. Maybe someday you'll win a fishing tournament. If you do, you won't need someone to print your fish for you. You'll know how to do it yourself.

The cool thing about *gyotaku* is that you can make multiple prints off a single fish. It's kind of like making pancakes, where the second or third one will be better than the first. As excess ink is blotted off by your consecutive printings, you may find that your prints reveal more and more detail.

The only special materials you'll need are rice paper and *sumi* ink, which are both easily found online or at craft or art stores. Just make sure it's rice paper for crafts you're looking at, and not the edible kind of rice paper used for cooking. You can also use any soft, uncoated paper that can be molded around your fish. If you've got some fabric you're willing to sacrifice, that'll work great as well. *Sumi* ink is a traditional Japanese ink made from burnt pine mixed with vegetable oil and animal glue. You could also use a nontoxic acrylic paint. *Gyotaku* is traditionally made with black ink, but use whatever color you like. Make sure to print your fish within 24 hours of catching it, and keep it well iced up to the time when you're ready to start. That way, the fish will still be good to eat once you're done creating your artwork.

What You'll Need

- A whole, unscaled fish
- Paper towels
- Scissors
- Rice paper (several sheets or a roll), or pieces of fabric from old pillowcases or sheets
- Clean, old towel or a few sheets of newspaper
- *Sumi* ink or a nontoxic acrylic paint in a color of your choice
- Clean paintbrush

Printing Steps

1. Prepare your fish. Rinse the outside of the fish to clean it, and scrape away any slime. Then dab the fish dry with clean paper towels. If the fish has already been gutted, fill its stomach and gills with paper towels so that fluids won't seep out onto your print. Place the fish on a plate or baking tray, loosely cover it with paper towels, and leave it in the fridge overnight to continue drying out.

2. Prep your workstation. Cut your paper or fabric to a size that will leave plenty of room for a border around your fish. Pour some ink or paint into an old mug, and lay newspapers or a clean, old towel on top of the kitchen counter or a table. Lay your fish on top.

3. To ink your fish, dip your paintbrush in your ink and sweep it over the surface of the fish until it is completely inked on the upward facing side. Don't oversaturate your fish with ink, or you'll get a bunch of black blobs on your paper. Pay attention to the fins—get them nicely coated so that they'll stand out on your print.

4. Wash and dry your hands if they've got ink on them. Then gently lay the paper or fabric over the fish. Carefully smooth and mold the paper or fabric over the surface of the fish with your hands. Don't let your canvas wriggle around, or you'll smudge your print. Just press it straight down with gentle touches.

5. Once the paper has been pressed to all surfaces of the fish's side, it's time to lift the piece of paper away and check out your *gyotaku*! How does it look? If some parts look too dark and don't show enough detail, try again on a fresh piece of paper or fabric—there should be less ink on the fish this time around.

Once your *gyotaku* dries, you may want to add some color—watercolors or colored pencils make a nice complement to the technique since they won't cover up your ink. Another cool thing about *gyotaku* is that you can use the same technique on any number of treasures from the natural world, from seashells to plants and flowers. Some artists combine different elements to create a full scene. Play around and see what you come up with! Just don't forget that your fish will begin to spoil if it's out of the fridge for more than an hour or so. When you're done with your *gyotaku* prints, rinse the ink off the fish and then gut or fillet the fish (see pages 179–182).

Get it back in the fridge and cook it that day or put it in the freezer for later use. In the future, when you look at your artwork, it will remind you of a great catch and a great meal!

....

SPROUT SOME BEANS

Long before Europeans came to America, Native American farmers were growing crops to feed their families. They had three primary crops that they raised: corn, squash, and beans. These plants were known as the Three Sisters because of the way they cooperated with each other. The corn and beans were planted together on small mounds of soil. The squash was planted between the mounds. As the cornstalks grew, they acted as a trellis for the beans to climb. In turn, the roots of the beans changed the soil in a way that helped the corn grow even higher and the squash grow bigger. For its part, the squash leaves shaded the ground so that the soil remained moist. The leaves also helped prevent the growth of weeds.

Today, people still grow and eat the crops known as Three Sisters. Corn on the cob and breakfast cereals such as cornflakes are made from ancestors of the same corn grown by Native Americans. Believe it or not, a byproduct of corn called ethanol is added to the gasoline that we burn in our cars. Halloween pumpkins and pumpkin pie are made from the same squash species raised by the Indigenous peoples who lived in present-day Mexico. Beans are everywhere, too. The refried beans you eat with nachos and burritos are made from pinto beans. Pinto beans were domesticated in Peru and used widely by Native Americans for thousands and thousands of years.

If you live in a warm, sunny climate, you can plant the Three Sisters in your garden using the same methods as Native American farmers. Regardless of where you live, or even what time of year it is, you can also do a really cool thing with beans right in your own kitchen. Have you ever heard of bean sprouts? As soon as a bean starts to grow into a new plant, the first thing it does is produce a sprout. If properly cared for, the sprout will eventually turn into a bean plant. But you can also eat the bean sprouts instead of planting them. They're super good for you and they taste nice and crunchy. Some bean sprouts need to be cooked. These can be added to stir-fries or soups. There's a bean from Asia, called a mung bean, that makes a sprout you can eat raw. They are great on sandwiches and salads. The best part is, it only takes a few days or so to make bean sprouts.

What You'll Need

- Wide-mouth glass canning jar
- Canning jar ring
- Piece of cheesecloth or window screen big enough to cover the mouth of the jar
- About 2 tablespoons mung beans

How to Sprout a Bean or Seed

1. Place the mung beans in your glass jar and fill the jar half full of water. Place the screen over the jar and screw on the ring lid.

2. After 8–12 hours of soaking, rinse the beans well, drain them, and place the jar upside down and at an angle so that water can keep draining out. There are special holders made for this purpose, but you can also just place your jar in a bowl.

3. Visible sprouts that look like little tails coming off the beans will begin to emerge within a couple of days. Rinse and drain the sprouting beans—remove the lid, fill the jar with water, recap with the lid, drain the beans, and return the jar to its upside-down angle. Do this two or three times a day until the sprouts are 1–2 inches long. This should take two to five days.

4. Remove the sprouts from your sprouting jar with clean hands or a spoon. Rinse them, and add them to sandwiches, salads, or stir-fries. Dry any sprouts you're not using on paper towels, and store in the refrigerator in a bowl covered in plastic wrap. Poke a few small holes in the plastic for airflow, and use within 3 days.

So what just happened? By placing the beans in water, you were waking them up from a long nap. The water activates enzymes (a type of chemical) inside the seeds, causing stored energy to begin to be released. As that energy builds up, pressure inside the bean causes it to burst open its coating! The sprout emerges and lives off the bean's stored energy. In order to keep growing beyond a sprout, it would need to be placed in soil.

PLANT A VEGETABLE GARDEN

There's not a living thing on earth that doesn't affect its ecosystem in some way or another. Beavers cut down trees to create dams on creeks and rivers. The dams make beaver ponds, which provide protection for the beavers as well as homes for fish and water-loving birds. Prairie dogs, a type of ground squirrel in the West, build "towns" that cover many acres of land. The critters are valuable prey species for predators ranging from badgers to red-tailed hawks to black-footed ferrets. Sometimes, though, prairie dogs can eat so much of the surrounding grass that their town turns to a sandy desert and they have to leave or face starvation until the vegetation recuperates. Even bacteria and fungi affect their ecosystems. When a dead animal or tree rots away in the woods, that's bacteria altering their ecosystem.

Obviously, there's no creature on the planet that alters its ecosystem as much as humans. Many ecologists say that we're living in a period of time called the Anthropocene Epoch. That first word comes from the Greek words *anthropo-* (human being) and *-cene* (new). It means that humans are now the dominant force that shapes the climate and other aspects of the environment on earth. The word "Anthropocene" is usually used in a negative way, to describe how human activity has caused the mass extinction of plants and animals through our endless quest for modernity. Luckily, there are still plenty of positive ways to affect your personal ecosystem. Making a vegetable garden is a great example.

Whatever type of garden you grow, you'll be contributing to the world of living things around your home while also getting an opportunity to play in the dirt. More important, you'll be taking over some of the responsibility of producing your own food. And not only do gardens create great food that tastes way better than anything that comes from the store, but small backyard gardens can help improve everything from the air we breathe down to the quality of the soil we walk on. All gardening requires some work before you get the reward of fresh veggies, but the work isn't terribly difficult. There is, however, a lot of trial and error that goes into gardening. Not everything you plant will work out. Some things will die no matter how hard you try to keep them alive. Other things will shock you by how quickly they grow and how big they get. Every one of your successes and failures will teach you something new about the world.

Assess Your Garden Plot

Before you start digging a garden in your backyard, there are some important things you'll need to consider.

The sun. One of the first steps in planning a garden location is to pay attention to the sun. Most vegetables need at least 6–8 hours of direct sunlight per day. Some veggies will take all the sun they can get. Others, such as kale and lettuces, will need a little bit of shade for at least some of the day, especially in very hot and sunny regions. So you'll need to choose your planting spots depending on where your crops will get the light they need. You can find the ideal growing conditions for the plants you want to grow on their seed packets or by doing a quick internet search.

Your soil. Not all dirt is alike. In fact, there is a ton of difference between the dry, sandy, crumbly dirt of a southwestern desert and the dark, moist soil of a midwestern forest. Even two adjacent backyards can have very different soil depending on how the land was cared for and used. The condition of your soil will determine what plants grow well. Thankfully, you can adjust your soil to make it a better place for the types of vegetables you want to grow. You can do a quick assessment of your soil by testing its pH—"pH" stands for "potential hydrogen," and it will let you know how acidic your soil is. Very acidic soil contains lots of hydrogen and has a low pH; very alkaline, or basic, soil contains little hydrogen and has a high pH. Neutral soil has a pH of around 6 or 7. Generally, neutral soil is the best for growing most vegetables. Buy a soil testing kit online or at any garden store and you'll find out very quickly what kind of soil you have. Depending on your test results, you can get different kinds of soil amendments to adjust the soil.

No matter what you're working with, one of the best things you can do for your garden is build a compost bin, which you'll learn how to do on page 298. Compost adds nutrients and beneficial microbes to garden soil and helps it retain moisture, all of which will increase your garden's productivity.

Your frost dates. Plants need temperatures warm enough to facilitate growth. Temperatures below freezing (32°F) will kill most vegetables or cause them to become dormant (go to sleep). Some garden plants, such as kale and broccoli, like cool temperatures and can still grow when nighttime temperatures are below freezing. Other veggies require temps at or above 70°F or else they won't grow. When gardeners talk about their growing season, they're usually talking about how many days they have between the last freezing temperatures in the spring and the first freezing temperatures in the fall or winter. These are called frost-free days. In Orlando, Florida, gardeners get more than 300 frost-free days. In Fairbanks, Alaska, you'd be likely to get less than half that amount. It's good to know the average first and last frost dates of the year in your area so that you know when and what to plant. You can look up your frost dates online, using your zip code. Keep in mind, though, that these are just estimates. A surprise late frost in May or June could kill your garden well before your first harvest. Likewise, an early frost in August or September will shorten your gardening season by several weeks. Keep a close watch on the weather throughout the growing season and cover your garden with tarps or blankets if there's even a small chance temperatures will dip below freezing.

Your garden design. How you design your garden depends on what you're working with. If you only have a small amount of space, you might consider building a trellis (page 289). If your soil is very hard and dry, go with a raised bed filled with store-bought topsoil (page 295). Many vegetable gardeners opt for raised beds because the containers give some protection from hungry garden marauders such as rabbits or certain insect pests. But if you've got good soil and enough room, you can skip the raised beds and plant directly in the ground. Whatever you decide, it's a good idea to start small if this is your first garden. Gardens are often measured in square feet. That is calculated by multiplying the length of the garden by the width. A garden measuring 6 feet by 6 feet—that's about the height of a grown man—would be 36 square feet. That's plenty big enough to get started. Even half as many square feet would make a nice garden.

ESSENTIAL GARDEN TOOLS

Outfitting your garden doesn't need to be expensive, but you will need a few tools to get going. Check to see what you've got lying around, and look around at yard sales or thrift shops where you can pick things up for cheap or even for free.

- Wheelbarrow or 5-gallon buckets
- Spade or shovel
- Trowel
- Hoe or steel rake
- Garden hose with watering wand
- Watering can
- Twine
- Tall wooden poles or stakes
- Tomato cage supports
- Garden shears

Select Your Crops

Once you've gotten your garden space and tools, it's time to decide what exactly you want to grow. Some plants are more difficult to grow than others. They may need lots of attention or specialized care. Maybe they're susceptible to pests or diseases, or maybe they're very picky about how much water they get. Other plants seem to grow pretty well as long as they get some basic care and attention. Here are five of those easy veggies that you should know about.

Green beans. They will grow in about 45–60 days depending on the variety. Estimate around 1–4 plants for a good serving of beans every week.

Leaf lettuce. You can start harvesting lettuce in 21–28 days (that's fast!), depending on the variety. It's a cut-and-come-again plant, meaning that the more you harvest, the more it will grow. So one plant can give you repeat harvests. Cut the outside leaves (always leaving two-thirds of the plant there) and it will grow new leaves for you to cut later in the week. Suggested varieties: Black Seeded Simpson for the South; most other lettuces will do well in the North. A really fun variety of lettuce is called Freckles. It produces green leaves that have purple dots.

Squash or zucchini. These beautiful plants grow fast and produce edible flowers that will attract pollinators. Early Yellow Crookneck is a favorite for both its flavor and how fast it grows.

Baby tomatoes. These take up a little space and will need to be staked, but they produce well in hot and dry weather and will keep producing when temperatures drop (as long as there isn't a frost) in the fall. The Supersweet 100 variety is loved for its flavor and productivity, and Black Strawberry is a favorite for its beauty and productivity.

Radishes. Easy and fun to grow, these will usually be some of the first plants to pop up in your garden. Radishes are typically harvestable throughout the year (spring, summer, fall—though they taste best in cooler temps) and you can get a crop from seed to harvest in 30 days.

Carrots. These veggie-garden favorites are a great pick for raised beds (page 295). They do their best work in cooler temperatures when not much else is growing. They're also easily one of the neatest plants to harvest—pulling them out of the ground is tons of fun.

Planting and Harvesting

Once you've gotten your soil in order, identified your frost dates, and chosen your plants, you're ready to start planting. Planting and harvest times depend on where you live and on what you're growing; check the seed packets or look online to find out. Summer squash varieties are planted and harvested in the spring and summer. Winter squash varieties like acorn squash and butternut squash are planted in the spring but won't be ready to harvest until the fall. Some plants will give you repeat harvests within a growing season—tomatoes (depending on the type), peppers, and squash are a few examples. If you want to ensure a continuous supply of veggies that only produce once, such as radishes and peas, you'll need to do what's called succession planting. This means you spread out several plantings of these vegetables with a few weeks in between, so that you'll have veggies ripening throughout the harvest period.

Some garden plants are perennial. After you plant them, they continue to come back every spring. Strawberries, asparagus, and rhubarb are all examples of perennials. Annual plants only have a single life cycle. Once they have fruited, they die off. You have to replant or reseed them every year if you want them to come back. Annual garden plants include tomatoes, lettuce, potatoes, and cucumbers. You should plant what you like, but it's fun to try a mix!

Usually, you'll be planting two or three seeds for every plant (not every seed will become a plant). Your seed packets will include instructions on how deep to plant and how much space to leave around each seed. Lots of beginner gardeners tend to overdo it and put their seeds and plants too close together. When that happens, they do not grow well. The saying "less is more" is true for gardening.

Water your plants. Water is key for a plant's photosynthesis—the process of converting the energy of sunlight into food. During the growing season, plants need enough water to keep the soil and roots moist but not wet. For most plants, that is roughly 1 inch of water per week. They'll need more if it's hot and dry, and less if it's rainy.

One way to know if your plants might be thirsty is to stick your finger in the soil and see if it feels moist. It's possible to overwater your plants, so don't overdo it. Around three times a week is usually a good schedule. To get a sense of how much water your hose is depositing, try placing your rain gauge (page 263) in your vegetable garden to see how long it takes you to get to 1 inch with your hose on the spray setting. In rainy weeks, factor the amount of water you see in your rain gauge into your overall calculations.

Watch for weeds. Weeds are those unwanted and pesky plants that grow without being planted. Their seeds are carried by wind, birds, and other garden visitors. Weeds typically grow quickly, stealing important space and nutrients from everything else in your garden. No matter what you're growing, you'll want to do some regular weeding—that means pulling these unwanted plants out of the ground. You don't want to simply cut them off. They'll just regrow. Instead, make sure you pull the root along with the stems and leaves in order to remove it. Always pull a weed slowly and gently, so that the plant doesn't break in half. If the soil is hard, you may need to dig around a bit with your trowel to loosen the weed's roots.

Protect your crops. The big, wide world of bugs is a very important part of every gardener's life. There are a lot of bugs, like butterflies and bees, that are good for plants (learn more about them in the sidebar on pages 287–289). But there are also lots of bugs that will eat their way through your garden. They can steal your harvest and sometimes kill your plants. To keep them away without the use of chemical pesticides, you can plant some dual-purpose garden heroes in your vegetable patch or raised bed. Marigolds are a great choice: Their edible flowers attract wasps that prey on harmful garden insects, and their roots repel certain kinds of worms that can do damage to plants below the ground. Nasturtiums have edible flowers that make a beautiful addition to salads, and they function as trap plants that draw bugs to them instead of to the vegetables in your garden. Garlic and onions are staples in most kitchens, and their strong odors repel harmful insects. If you're still losing too many of your fruits and veggies to creepy-crawly freeloaders, see if you can make a game of just spotting the bugs and picking them off by hand.

Your vegetable garden will probably be tempting to bigger pests as well. To keep birds away from your strawberries or tomatoes, you can install some garden netting. You might also try harvesting your tomatoes before they're ripe—just as they start to turn from green to red. That way you'll get them before your competition does! Mice, chipmunks, squirrels, and rabbits are notorious garden thieves. Once they find a good food source, they'll make a habit of raiding your garden. They can wipe out your lettuce or strawberry patch in no time. Garden netting will help, but you may need to resort to erecting a small fence if the problem is really bad. Or else you can try setting a live trap in order to catch the vegetable thieves. Then you can release the critter out in the woods and far away from your garden.

No matter how much research or planning you do, you should expect plenty of failures. Over time, you'll start to build up knowledge about what plants tend to thrive in your garden. It helps to take notes, so consider starting a gardening journal. Record your first and last frost dates, your seeding dates, your harvest dates, and notes about the weather. If you want to get super technical, you can draw a diagram of what you planted where. That way, if you want to try switching things around, you'll have a record of how your various garden designs worked out. Don't get too frustrated if you lose one of your crops to an early frost or an army of bugs. The joy of biting into even a single carrot that you grew with your own hands will make up for any plant that you lost along the way.

Last but not least, make sure you and your family actually eat your harvest! If you're producing more than your kitchen can handle, try pickling (page 303) and give some away to friends and neighbors. Sharing the bounty is a big part of the joy of vegetable gardening.

SAVE THE POLLINATORS!

One of the many wonderful things about gardens is that they give you a chance to leave your own personality on a small patch of ground that is swarming with life. You can make all the rules. Is your favorite color orange? Then go ahead and plant some marigolds. Or is it purple? If so, did you know that you can plant tomatoes that will ripen into a shiny purple color? If you like carrot sticks but hate radishes, you can ban radishes from your vegetable garden and grow nothing but carrots. No matter what you're planting, though, you can always make decisions that will be helpful to nature.

One of the best ways that your garden can support nature is to be a good home for butterflies and bees. These are very important insects because they are pollinators. While feeding on the nectar produced by flowers, the bugs

move pollen from the male part of a flower to the female part of a flower. That process is called pollination, and it's essential to the plant's ability to produce seeds, fruit, or young plants. About 30 percent of the food we eat is pollinated by insects such as bees and butterflies, from corn and broccoli to almonds and apples. In a way, pollinators even produce the meat that we eat, because those animals eat plants that rely on pollinators. But as the world has gotten more and more covered in concrete, the loss of natural habitat has been very difficult for pollinators such as bees and butterflies. Changes in modern farming practices have also reduced their populations.

The biggest thing you can do to encourage visits from pollinators is to avoid using pesticides. While they're great at killing off those marauding grubs that eat your tomatoes, they also indiscriminately kill off the sorts of bugs and insects that benefit your garden and the planet. You can also help attract pollinators by planting some brightly colored flowers.

Pollinators love bright flowers just as much as we do! It's a great idea to plant flowers that are native to your area; look them up online so that you can help encourage a diversity of insects to visit and thrive. Many conservation organizations, such as Pheasants Forever, produce pollinator seed packets that are custom made for specific locations. Visit their website to learn more.

Lastly, you can let your garden run a little wild. Insects of all kinds like it when things get a bit overgrown. That way, they can hide from predators and find places to shelter from the wind. So give them some safe space by letting your garden or lawn get a little messy with some scattered patches of high grass or other thick vegetation. That will help turn your garden into a thriving ecosystem that's full of life. And when it comes to putting your own personality into a patch of ground, that's the coolest thing you can do. Be proud and show the world that you love nature!

BUILD A GARDEN TRELLIS

Here's a fun and simple building project that will add lots of room to your family's garden without actually making it bigger. A garden trellis allows certain plants to grow up high, making use of space (the air above your garden) that otherwise wouldn't get used at all. Some plants, like pole beans or snap peas, are meant to climb. The taller they grow, the more blossoms they produce and the more food you get. Other plants, such as cucumbers, don't necessarily need to climb but are more than willing to do so if you help them out. That way, they'll be up off the ground and not taking up space that could be used by plants that are incapable of climbing, such as carrots or potatoes.

Another benefit of a trellis is that it can help provide shade for vegetables that don't like too much sun, such as lettuces and kale. So, if you can, choose a spot for your trellis where it will provide shade for other plants during the hottest parts of the afternoon. This trellis design is simple. You don't need much room for it. It's based on the same teepee shape you used to create the shelter on pages 79–81. You might already have the materials you need.

What You'll Need

- 3–5 straight saplings, branches, or bamboo poles, about 6 or 7 feet tall
- Rope
- Thick twine
- Scissors
- Spade or shovel

Building Steps

1. Lay the poles for your teepee structure alongside each other on the ground.
2. Connect the ends of the poles with a piece of rope. At a point about a foot from the end of the poles, make a loop around each individual pole, then a loop around all three. These tied-up ends will be the top of your teepee.
3. Stand up your teepee on a flat patch of soil in your garden space. Go ahead and clear away any weeds first. It'll be easier to do that now. The arrangement of the poles should form a circle. To make the structure stable, keep the poles roughly equidistant (about the same distance apart).
4. Mark the place where you want each pole to sit. Then move the pole out of the way and dig a hole about a foot deep. Set the end of the pole in the hole and pat down the dirt around it.
5. Now, create a twine trellis around the teepee—this will help

support your plant stems as they grow. Cut several lengths of twine that are more than long enough to encircle your structure. Start at the bottom, about 6 inches off the ground, and wrap the twine all the way around the structure. It's sort of like wrapping lights around a Christmas tree. For extra security, weave the twine in and around each stick as you wrap it. Then go up about 12 inches and do another wrap of twine. Repeat that process every 12 inches until you reach the top.

Now that you've created your trellis, it's time to plant some pole beans, snap peas, or cucumbers. Plant three seeds at the bottom of each pole, water them, and then watch them climb. Your plants will likely grow up the teepee on their own, but if you have a wild vine that strays from the teepee, you can just gently grab it and wrap it around the twine. Be patient, and pretty soon you'll be serving your family an amazing dinner.

SAVING THE SOIL OF THE SOUTH

Imagine someone calling you by a name that only tells a little bit about who you really are and the amazing things you've accomplished. What if you were known only by the color of your skin or hair or for how well you threw a ball? It might make you feel like less than who you really are. You are certainly much more than your hair color or how good an athlete you might be.

This was the case for the extraordinary scientist and conservationist George Washington Carver (c. 1864–1943). He was an African American scholar who became famous for creating hundreds of uses for peanuts and similar pea-like plants known as legumes. But he was known as "The Peanut Man."

George Washington Carver was born in Missouri as an enslaved person. The exact date of his birth is unknown. He was owned by another person at birth and then kidnapped along with his mother and sisters when he was still just a baby. Although slavery was abolished in 1865, George lived during a time when the freedom and rights of Black Americans were under violent assault. As a teenager, George saw a man murdered because of the color of his skin. Imagine the sadness and fear a person would feel upon seeing such a terrible thing happen. In spite of this and other misfortunes, George persisted.

Growing up in the fields, forests, and prairies of the Midwest, young George was drawn to wildness and fell in love with botany (the study of plants). He was particularly interested in the ways that soil supports plant growth. He very much wanted to study ecology (how living things interact with their environment) and also art and music. He was quite accomplished at all of these things, but he was not allowed to attend most schools because his skin was black. By the laws of the time, a system of oppression and division called Jim Crow, these schools excluded anyone not white.

Discrimination clawed at the devoted student like a vicious predator, and George struggled with a stutter that he would eventually conquer. But he did not let any of that keep him from discovering his potential. Eventually, he became the first Black American to graduate from and teach at Iowa State University. As a professor at Iowa State and later Tuskegee Institute (now University) in Alabama, George became an expert at researching how different crops (including peanuts, but many others, too) could be used not only for food but also to create textiles, paper, and plastic, as well as medicine and lots of other things we use daily. He also studied how poor farming practices harmed the land. He began to help farmers save their soil by showing them better techniques. He showed them how to plow in a way that followed the natural contours of the land in order to prevent erosion, or wearing away of the soil. He also taught farmers to sow cover crops like alfalfa after a harvest to nourish the soil and hold it in place.

Professor Carver earned tremendous respect as an agronomist and even garnered the praise of President Theodore Roosevelt. Congress called upon him to ask his advice on agricultural matters, and he was celebrated in Europe for his knowledge of the most up-to-date farming practices. Although Professor Carver couldn't attend most schools in the southern United States, he spoke to students and other researchers at many of the same colleges that wouldn't accept him as a student or professor. In helping others who didn't fully respect him, he saved the soil of the South for everyone—whether they looked like him or not.

People called him the Peanut Man, but George Washington Carver was so much more than that. He was his own kind of explorer and hero. He didn't traverse broad expanses of wilderness, summit lofty peaks, or navigate raging rivers. But he overcame obstacles that were just as daunting and dangerous. Prejudice and hate were the stormy summits that he conquered. Finding respect as a Black scientist was the rugged frontier that Professor Carver had to cross. Today, the barriers of bias and prejudice still exist, but they are easier to overcome because of his brave work.

—By J. Drew Lanham

MAKE A RAISED GARDEN BED

There have been a couple of times in this book when we've learned about the paleoanthropologists who study ancient fossils and tools, but the study of anthropology also includes topics like the development of agriculture. That's the science and practice of raising crops and livestock, and anthropologists believe that humans invented it around 10,000 years ago. The invention had enormous impacts on how humans lived. Before agriculture, most people in the world were at least semi-nomadic. They traveled from place to place throughout the year as they hunted, fished, and searched for wild plant foods. With agriculture, people began to live in one single place throughout the year in order to take care of their crops and livestock. Eventually, towns and cities were built around these agricultural communities. That's how the world started to look the way it looks now. Today, even though most people are no longer involved in agriculture, we still have our habit of staying put. We tend to live in the same building all year round and don't move from place to place.

Thinking about our human history, it makes sense why some people love their gardens so much. Maybe, deep down, gardens make people happy because they're a reminder of those long-ago times when we humans had to care for and protect little patches of ground in order to get food. You might want to explore this connection for yourself by making your own garden. One of the easiest ways to do this is to build a raised bed. You can make them just about anywhere. Even if your backyard is too rocky and dry to dig up, you can put a raised bed on top of that dry ground. And if all you have access to is a patch of concrete or a wooden deck, that's no problem. You can build your raised bed right on top of it. Raised beds give you a chance to create ideal soil conditions, including adequate drainage, and they'll warm up more quickly after a frost than the rest of your garden will. And last but not least, they do a nice job of keeping weeds and some critters away.

You've probably seen raised beds built out of wood. Those are great, but there's a quicker and cheaper way to make one. Follow along to find out how to convert a galvanized stock tank (the kind that's used to give water to livestock) into a garden plot that will last through many, many harvests. The biggest question is how big your garden should be. A great size to get you started would be a 100-gallon stock tank that measures about 2 feet wide, 2 feet tall, and 4 feet long. That's a versatile size that will fit in many spaces. But you can get other shapes, too. Round stock tanks range in size from just 3 feet in diameter to huge ones with an 8-foot diameter. Just make sure to get a grown-up's help and measure your space before you start shopping for a tank. It'd be a real pain in the butt to get a tank home and then realize it doesn't fit!

What You'll Need

- Galvanized stock tank (available at places like Home Depot, Lowe's, or local farm and ranch supply stores)
- Electric drill with ⅜- or ½-inch drill bit
- Enough gravel to make a 3-inch-deep layer in tank
- Piece of landscape fabric big enough to cover bottom of tank
- Enough sticks, branches, and pine cones to make a 12-inch-deep layer in tank
- Enough potting mix or garden soil to fill tank
- Compost

Building Steps

1. Flip the tank upside down.
2. Drill a bunch of holes in the bottom so that water can drain out of the tank. For every square foot, you should have at least two holes.
3. Place the tank where you want your garden to be. If you're building your raised garden bed on a hard surface such as wood or concrete, you'll want to lift it up a bit so that the water can easily drain away. You can set the stock tank on a row of pressure-treated wooden slats. Getting it off the ground just ½ inch or so is all it takes.
4. Put a 3-inch layer of gravel in the bottom. This helps with drainage.
5. Lay a sheet of landscape fabric over the rocks. This will keep the soil from clogging up all those nice holes you drilled.

6. To save money on soil, fill the trough with a 12-inch-thick layer of sticks, branches, and pine cones. (They will eventually biodegrade.) Place these loose parts in the trough, spacing them far enough apart that there's room for soil to run between them. No need to pack this layer tightly. Just throw it in there!

7. Fill up the rest of the trough with a mix of garden or potting soil and high-quality compost. You'll want three parts garden soil to every part of compost.

Good luck, and get growing!

TURN GARBAGE INTO GARDEN GOLD

Here's a crazy fact: On average, each person in the United States wastes over 200 pounds of edible food every year. Imagine all of that wasted food as a pile of bread. Every person's pile would have 2,400 slices of bread in it! In fact, experts estimate that about a third of the edible food produced in the United States ends up rotting in landfills. That's a lot of wasted energy! If you want to contribute to the health of the planet, one easy way to do that is by only taking or ordering as much food as you can eat. You can also be thoughtful about using your leftovers rather than just throwing them away. Another great idea is to compost your kitchen waste. You'll be reducing your household's contribution to landfills while also benefiting the plants in your yard or garden.

Composting is the process of turning plant or food waste into fertilizer by letting it decompose. Decomposition is a totally natural process. It's what happens to dead plants and animals that are left on the forest floor—eventually, they break down into small particles and turn into nutrient-rich materials that help other plants grow. By composting, you're just helping decomposition work in a faster and more productive way. The material that is produced through composting is known as compost.

You may be used to thinking of bacteria as a bad thing. After all, we wash our hands with soap and clean our cuts with disinfectant in order to kill harmful bacteria. But bacteria are also incredibly important and helpful life-forms. During the composting process, bacteria feed on our rotting food waste and help turn it into its simplest parts. These parts include nitrogen, carbon, potassium, and phosphorus. When these things are fed into the soil, they can be put to use by nature to build new life. Healthy soil is filled with good nutrients, and it isn't too dense, too loose, or too dry. Compost can help with all of that. And here's the good news: Making your own compost is super simple.

Start by setting up an outdoor compost bin. You can buy really fancy compost bins that work great. But you can also make your own compost bins that work just fine. For the method described here, it's best if you make two of them that sit side by side.

What You'll Need

- 20 feet of chicken wire fencing that is 24 inches tall, with 1-inch mesh (or something close to these dimensions)
- Tin snips, or heavy-duty scissors suitable for cutting the wire fencing
- Zip ties
- Four sharpened wooden or metal stakes, approximately 3 feet long

Building Steps

1. Cut two 10-foot lengths of chicken wire and form each into a cylinder shape. Use your zip ties to "stitch" the cylinders together at their seams. Each cylinder will be about 3 feet across and 2 feet high.
2. Place the cylinders in an out-of-the-way place in your yard where you want to do your composting. If you have a vegetable garden, it's a good idea to put your compost bins nearby.
3. Anchor each compost bin in place with two stakes. The stakes should be positioned across from each other and driven into the ground. Secure the bins to the stakes with zip ties.

Now it's time to start composting. First, get a countertop container that you can keep in your kitchen to hold leftover food scraps. You want something that can hold about ½ gallon of food scraps. You can buy nice stainless steel compost buckets at the store, but pretty much any tub or bucket will work. It's best if it has a lid, in order to keep away fruit flies or other pesky bugs.

Fill that container with edible kitchen scraps. Apple peels and cores, celery tops, onion skins, coffee grounds, eggshells, and vegetable trimmings are all great for your compost bucket. Avoid any kind of meat. As meat degrades, it can attract harmful bacteria that will contaminate your compost. Also avoid citrus peels, banana peels, and dairy products; those things take way too long to decompose. (See below for other things you'll need to avoid.) Every few days, whenever your bucket gets a little stinky or fills up, take it outside and dump it into your compost bin.

It's not just food scraps that can go into your compost bin. Your yard is also likely to have a lot of great items to add. You can put grass clippings, leaves, and pulled-up weeds into your compost bin, and even certain kinds of manure. (More on that below.)

Every time you add something new to the bin, you should stir it up with a shovel or pitchfork. Since composting takes time, you'll eventually need to stop adding items so that everything in the bin has time to decompose. After all, if you add new kitchen scraps every day, you'll always have something in there that's not done yet. So once you fill your first bin up, you'll want to start filling the second bin so that the first one can do its work. But don't forget to keep stirring that first bin every week or so. Depending on where you live and what time of year it is, it might take weeks or months before your compost is ready. (If you live in the North, where there's lots of snow and ice, your compost bin will just sit there and do nothing until the weather warms up in the spring.) But don't worry! Eventually, you'll discover that you no longer have a bin full of food scraps and grass clippings. Instead, you'll have a nice layer of compost at the bottom. It will feel like a rich, loose soil that you can run through your fingers. Just go ahead and spread this magical material over the soil in your garden and stir it in a little bit. Your garden will love it!

The Rules of Composting

Now that you have some ideas about what to compost and why, here are some general rules that will help keep your compost healthy.

Feed it. Keep gathering those kitchen scraps and feed your compost bin regularly. Don't forget the eggshells and your parents' coffee grounds. Compost bins love those things.

Poop and manure. Do not add any poop from household pets, or poop from animals that consume meat. Manure from chickens, turkeys, rabbits, and cows is fine.

Other no-nos. Don't add diseased plants, burned charcoal from barbecues, cooking oil, or leaves and husks from black walnut trees.

Cover your scraps. Don't leave fruit and vegetable scraps on the surface of your compost heap, or you could attract insects, pests, and maybe even larger hungry critters. Bury fresh scraps under older compost.

Aerate your heap. Introducing fresh oxygen to the materials in your compost bin can increase the speed of decomposition. Bacteria need oxygen to do their work! To aerate your compost bin, stir it up really well every week or two.

Welcome mold and worms. The earthworms and nightcrawlers that are naturally present in your garden will gravitate to your compost, and that's a good thing! Whenever you find a worm, carefully bury it in your compost bin. Hungry worms are terrific decomposers, and their castings (that means worm poop!) make a rich fertilizer for your garden. The way worms tunnel through soil also helps aerate both your garden soil and your compost pile. In fact, worms are so good at composting that some people actually buy them for their compost bin. Check out worm bin or vermicomposting instructions online if you're interested. It's also normal to see some mold in your compost. That's a sign that helpful fungi are hard at work decomposing your waste.

PICKLE A CUCUMBER

A calorie is a way of measuring the energy in food. A single plain M&M candy has just over 4 calories in it. That's enough energy to move your body the length of a football field. Not all foods have the same amount of calories in them. A cup of M&Ms has over 1,000 calories in it, while a cup of cucumber has only 16 calories. One of the reasons that cucumbers have such a small amount of energy is that they're pretty much made out of water. In fact, cucumbers are 96 percent water.

By now you might be wondering, what good are cucumbers? If they hardly have any energy, why would anyone bother eating them? Well, there's a one-word answer to that question: pickles! One of the reasons that cucumbers taste so good when they're turned into pickles is that a bunch of the water inside the cucumber is being replaced with a much tastier mixture of salt, sugar, vinegar, and spices. You've certainly tried pickles before, and there's a good chance that you love them. If so, you should know that it's incredibly easy to make pickles from scratch right inside your own kitchen.

For starters, you want to make sure you've got the right kind of cucumbers for making pickles. English or Persian cucumbers work best for this kind of recipe. The ingredients listed below will give you a good starting point for making pickles, but don't be afraid to add some of your own personality by adjusting the seasoning. You can add whole coriander seeds, mustard seeds, and bay leaves. You can swap in some chopped onion for the garlic, or use both, or neither. Some people like to add fresh dill, or a bit of heat from sliced jalapeños or crushed red pepper.

Ingredients

1½ cups white vinegar (or ¾ cup each water and vinegar, if you
    don't want such a sour pickle)
½ tablespoon salt
2 tablespoons sugar
1½ cups water
3 cloves garlic, sliced (optional)
1 pound cucumbers, sliced into thin rounds

Preparation

1. Bring the vinegar, salt, sugar, water, and garlic to a boil in a small saucepan.
2. Simmer for 10 minutes.
3. Let the pickling liquid cool completely. (You can pour it carefully

into a glass measuring cup and stash it in the fridge to speed this along.)

4. Meanwhile, place your cucumbers in a glass jar or container with a lid.

5. When the liquid is completely cool, pour it over the cucumbers, seal, and refrigerate. Let them sit at least two hours before eating.

The pickles that you just made are called refrigerator pickles, because they need to be stored in your refrigerator. It's best if you eat them over the next few days. If you want to make the kind of pickles that can sit on a shelf in your pantry for years, you'd need to sterilize your canning materials in boiling water and then pasteurize your pickles to prevent the growth of harmful bacteria. That's a lot more complicated and requires some specialized tools, but it's still a fun project to graduate to if you catch the pickling bug and want to get more serious.

By the way, you can also use this recipe to pickle carrots, beets, onions, and green beans. Pickled vegetables make great additions to salads, and pickled onions taste great on a burger (and they won't stink up your breath like raw onions do). However, if you're pickling these other vegetables, don't wait for the liquid to cool before pouring it over your vegetables. You'll need the hot liquid to partially cook your firmer veggies in order to soften them up.

PRESERVE YOUR SUMMER BERRIES

Have you ever heard that squirrels are able to memorize the places where they bury their nuts? Well, that isn't just a legend. In a study on eastern gray squirrels, researchers discovered that the squirrels are more likely to return to caches of nuts that they made themselves than they are to find caches of nuts made by other squirrels. Also, the gray squirrels seemed to remember the places where they buried a lot of nuts more reliably than they remembered the places where they buried only a few. And here's a final thing about squirrels that might be especially surprising. It seems as though gray squirrels will periodically dig up their caches of nuts just to check on them. They'll remove a nut from underground, examine it, and then bury it right back where they found it.

The practice of burying nuts in a bunch of different places is called "scatter hoarding." That's what gray squirrels do. It's different from the strategy used by a slightly smaller species of tree-dwelling squirrels called pine squirrels. They bury their caches of seeds and nuts in just one or two specific areas. This strategy is called "larder hoarding." Larder hoarding is similar to what we humans do. Instead of storing little bits of food all over the place, we like to keep all of our food in one single location. Chances are, you and your family store your food in a refrigerator and on pantry shelves right inside your kitchen.

We all know the sense of comfort that comes from having a good supply of food all stashed away for later. It's especially nice when you have the pride of knowing that you gathered some of that food all by yourself in the wild—just like the squirrels do. If you did a good job of foraging for berries over the summer, you can actually store some of that fruit for later inside your own kitchen by using different preservation techniques. These include making jam and dehydrating your own fruit leather snacks.

Wild Berry Refrigerator Jam

Making a jar of jam that you can store on a shelf for months or years is a fairly complicated project that requires a grown-up's assistance and special equipment. But here's a pretty easy jam for wild berries that you can store right in your fridge. It doesn't require any special gear, and you can probably make it all on your own. You just need some fruit, sugar, salt, and lemon.

1. Wash your berries and measure how much you have. For every 3 cups of berries, you'll need to measure 1 cup of sugar, a pinch of salt, and 1 tablespoon of lemon juice.
2. Place berries in a medium or large saucepan over medium heat, and add the sugar, salt, and lemon juice.
3. Mash ingredients together with a fork or a potato masher. Stop mashing when you like the consistency—some people like a smoother jam, some like more texture.
4. Bring to a boil and cook for 20 minutes or until somewhat thickened.
5. Let the jam cool on the stove, then scoop or pour the jam into a container with a tight-fitting lid. You can store the jam in a covered jar or container in the refrigerator for up to 3 weeks. You can also freeze the jam and store it for up to a year.

Fruit Leather

The fruit leather you buy at grocery stores is actually very easy to make at home. Unlike jellies and jams, which require the use of sugar for preservation (microbes love moisture, and sugar sucks the moisture out of the fruit), fruit leather is dehydrated in the oven with just enough sugar for taste. Besides the fruit, all you'll need is your oven, a blender, a saucepan, and a couple of simple ingredients.

1. Preheat your oven to its lowest temperature setting (usually 170 degrees).
2. Wash your fruit and measure how much you have. For every 2 cups of fruit, you'll need ¼ cup water, a teaspoon of lemon

juice, and a tablespoon of sugar. (You may want to add a touch more lemon juice and sugar if you think it tastes better that way.)

3. Place your fruit in a large saucepan and add the water. Bring to a simmer, cover, and cook on low heat for 10 minutes. While the mixture is still simmering, mash it up with a fork or a potato masher.

4. Add the lemon juice and sugar. Taste the mixture to see if you're happy with the results. Just make sure that you don't add too much. Once you get to 2 tablespoons of sugar for every 2 cups of fruit, stop there! Continue to cook for another 5 minutes, stirring occasionally, until the mixture has thickened and the sugar is dissolved.

5. Let cool, then transfer fruit mixture to a blender or food processor. Puree until smooth.

6. Line a rimmed baking dish with parchment paper. Pour the mixture into the tray. Stop pouring before you get past a quarter-inch of thickness. Either save the remaining mixture for a second batch or pour into a second lined tray.

7. Bake overnight, 8–12 hours, until the mixture is no longer sticky to the touch.

8. Let cool, then roll the fruit leather up in its parchment paper to store. Stash it in a lidded jar or a ziplock bag; it'll keep for about a month on a shelf or six months in the fridge.

MAKE A COBBLER

Want to be the hero of your family's dinner table? Try making a fruit cobbler with some berries or other fruit that you picked yourself. According to food historians, the cobbler is a modified version of a pie made with any available fruit and an easy crust on top. When English colonists first came to America, they were used to baking pies in the brick ovens they'd had back in England. But in their new home, they had to do all their cooking on open fires. So they learned to skip the bottom layer of the pie crust and just pile the fruit into the pan. As the fruit bubbled and cooked, it would steam the crust on top of the cobbler as the fire's heat turned it golden brown.

Cobblers remain one of the easiest desserts to make, so they're a good choice for beginners. Any fruit you can get your hands on should work—whether it's foraged, purchased, frozen, or home-grown. You can serve your cobbler à la mode, which is a French term that means "trendy" or "fashionable" in France but that means "served with ice cream on top" in America. If you have any cobbler left over, it's a tasty breakfast when served with some warm milk poured on top. (You might have to set your alarm for extra early in order to beat the rest of your household to the leftovers!)

Ingredients

¼ cup butter

¾ cup flour

¾ cup white or brown sugar (or any combo of the two)

1 tablespoon cinnamon

1 teaspoon baking powder

¼ teaspoon salt

¾ cup milk

2 cups fresh fruit, chopped and peeled as needed

Steps

1. Preheat oven to 350°F.
2. Put the butter in an 8-by-8-inch or 9-by-9-inch baking dish and place in preheating oven until melted.
3. While butter is melting, add all of the dry ingredients to a bowl and combine well with a fork. Add milk and mix until smooth.
4. Once the butter has melted, take the pan out and add the fruit to the pan directly on top of the butter. (Some people sprinkle a little sugar or cinnamon on top of the fruit at this point, but it's optional. If you do, just add a little bit, 1 to 4 tablespoons—fruit contains its own natural sugars.)
5. Pour the batter on top of the fruit, making sure that all of the

fruit is covered with batter. It's okay if a little fruit sticks out, but you don't want a big patch of fruit hanging out with no batter on top of it.

6. Bake until the batter is lightly brown and any visible fruit is bubbling, about 45–60 minutes.

- -

GROW A JACK-O'-LANTERN

You might not think of a Halloween jack-o'-lantern as being scarier than a haunted house, but knowing the history of jack-o'-lanterns could change your mind. The tradition of carving creepy faces into pumpkins for Halloween may have derived from the ancient Celtic wartime ritual of chopping off your enemy's head and displaying it as a gruesome trophy. Now that's spooky! If you love jack-o'-lanterns and wish the Halloween season lasted longer, you can extend the scariest day of the year into a period of several months by growing your own pumpkins in your garden. At harvest time, you can carve the scariest face possible on your biggest pumpkin and then place it on your doorstep in order to frighten away your enemies!

Growing pumpkins requires a frost-free growing season (see pages 279–280) of 2 or 3 months. Once harvested, your pumpkins should last for another 2 months or more. So your start date will depend on the climate where you live. Generally, you'll want to plant your pumpkins outside around the 4th of July if you live in a warm southern climate. If you live in the northern half of the country, plant after the last frost, which usually occurs in late spring to early summer.

First, pick out seeds for the pumpkin variety that you want to grow. There's a type of pumpkin that's actually called jack-o'-lantern, and you can buy the seeds online or at most garden stores. Jack-o'-lantern plants produce three to five pumpkins per plant, whereas smaller varieties might grow more pumpkins per plant. On planting day, make a mound of dirt about as big as the pillow on your bed in a sunny spot in your garden. Pick a spot where your pumpkins will have plenty of room to grow! Each pumpkin seed will shoot off what's called a runner. These are long, vinelike growths that might spread out anywhere from 6 feet to 20 feet away from where the seeds are planted. Don't worry if you need to plant near a fence, because the runners will climb right over it. So put your pumpkin mound somewhere where there'll be space for the pumpkins to spread out, either on the ground or vertically. If you're low on space, you can plant smaller varieties and grow them up a trellis (page 289).

You should plant three seeds right on top of the mound. Place them in a little triangle shape with the seeds just a couple of inches apart under an inch of soil. If you want to build more than one mound and plant more seeds, make sure to separate your mounds by about 6 to 8 feet. Pumpkins drink a lot, so water the plants a few times a week. The first thing you'll see will be the leafy runners. Eventually your pumpkins will begin to form. They start as orange blossoms that will develop a little green bulb on the end. The pumpkins will grow and grow for a month or more before they stop growing and begin to turn from green to orange. You can pick them at this point. Leave them outside, in the sun, so they can harden and finish turning color. Then, you can store your harvested pumpkins in a cool, dark, dry place. Now all you've got to do is get busy carving just before Halloween.

Note: If your pumpkins are not done growing but the weather forecast is calling for a strong frost, go ahead and pick them and put them in your garage or somewhere where they won't freeze. Don't worry if they're still green. They will turn orange after a few weeks.

SAVE YOUR SEEDS

When you're carving up your jack-o'-lantern and you get to the part where you pull out the guts from the middle, save the seeds! They are good for both snacking and planting. To save some as seeds, wash a dozen or so in cool water until all the pumpkin mess is gone. Then set them out to dry. You can just lay them on a paper towel by a kitchen or bedroom window and that should do it. Once they're dry, just put them in an envelope, label them, and then forget about them until it's time to plant again next spring.

For making a crunchy snack, give the seeds a good rinse in cold water and then spread them out on a screen or baking sheet overnight to dry. Next, preheat your oven to 350°F. While the oven is warming, toss the seeds in a little melted butter (olive oil will work, too) so they get a nice coating of oil. Now sprinkle them with salt and pepper or any type of seasoning that you like. Your family's favorite steak seasoning will work just fine. Spread the seeds on a baking sheet and roast them in the oven for 15–25 minutes, tossing them every 5 minutes until they're golden brown all over. They might not be as good as your Halloween trick-or-treat candy, but they're still pretty darn good!

CUT DOWN A CHRISTMAS TREE

Most people buy their Christmas trees from gardening and land-scaping stores or special Christmas tree lots that pop up around town during the holidays. Most of these trees come from Christmas tree plantations. The top producing states in the U.S. are Oregon, North Carolina, Michigan, Pennsylvania, Wisconsin, and Washington. On average, it takes a plantation about seven years to grow a tree that's 6 or 7 feet tall. The growers harvest the trees ahead of the Christmas season and then haul them away on trucks to supply dealers.

Buying one of these Christmas trees is convenient, but there's not much excitement in it. If you want to turn your annual hunt for a Christmas tree into a bigger adventure, you and your family can head into the woods and cut down your own tree with a saw. How you do this will depend on where you live.

As a first step, check to see if you live near a national forest that allows the public to harvest wild Christmas trees. Start your search at Recreation.gov, a website of the U.S. Forest Service. If you're not familiar with your local national forest, you can find it there. Once you know the name of your national forest, type it into the search bar along with the words "Christmas tree permit." Hopefully, you'll be directed to a web page where you can buy your tree permit for a small fee. (Costs range from $5 to $20, depending on your national forest.) For example, say you live in Salt Lake City, Utah. You'd want to search "Wasatch National Forest Christmas Tree Permit." From there, you'll find what you need.

If you're not within driving distance of a national forest that allows the harvest of Christmas trees, you might not be totally out of luck. It's worth going online to search for local Christmas tree farms that offer "you cut" Christmas trees. It might not be as exciting as going to a national forest, but it's still a super cool experience to select and cut down your own tree.

A good thing about Christmas tree farms is that you don't need to worry about what kind of tree to cut down. After all, they're in the business of growing Christmas trees so they'll have the right species of trees planted. If you go to a national forest, you'll need to identify the proper types of evergreen coniferous trees such as pines, firs, and spruces. These are generally triangular-shaped trees that produce cones and feature fragrant, needle-shaped leaves. Your permit might have additional rules, such as size limits on trees or instructions about not cutting trees too close to campgrounds or roads. Keep in mind that you probably won't find the perfectly shaped Christmas trees that you see for sale in town. Those get lots of care, including pruning and fertilizer treatments. Wild trees are less perfect, but their wildness more than makes up for it. Remember, beauty is in the eye of the beholder. If you can find a Christmas tree with the right shape that's anywhere from 6 to 10 feet tall, you're in luck! And make sure to check the tree's trunk. It has to be straight enough to fit into your Christmas tree stand. For tools, bring a handsaw, plenty of rope, and a sled or plastic tarp. Once you saw the tree down, you can tie some rope to the trunk and then pull the tree back to your vehicle. If the ground is rough or rocky, you might want to lay the tree on your sled or tarp so that it doesn't get too banged up while you're dragging it. You don't want to knock off a bunch of branches or needles if you can avoid it. Unless you've got a family pickup truck or a car with a really big trunk, you'll need some extra rope or cord to secure the tree to the top of your vehicle.

Before you leave the forest or tree farm, there's one last thing you need to do. Go ahead and collect a bunch of fallen pine cones. When you get home, you can spray-paint them silver or gold for display around the house, or use them as decorations to hang on your Christmas tree. Look out for the fallen boughs of conifer trees, too. You can take a few home and turn them into wreaths, or simply lay them on a table or mantel for some holiday flair.

After the holidays, you'll need to do something with your Christmas tree. Some towns have Christmas tree collection sites where you can drop your tree off to be composted or turned into mulch. Old Christmas trees make a great habitat for bugs, birds, and other small critters. You can toss the tree on top of your backyard brush pile (page 326), where it'll get used by local critters. You can also use your saw to cut the tree's trunk and branches into 12-inch pieces of firewood and kindling that can be used next summer when you build a campfire. If you use your imagination, you can get even more adventure from your tree than just going into the woods to cut it down.

WHY WE WATCH BIRDS

Did you know that it's still possible to discover new species of birds? That's what happened when researchers set out on a 6-week expedition to a cluster of Indonesian islands in 2013. The Taliabu grasshopper-warbler, the Peleng fantail, the Togian jungle-flycatcher, and the Taliabu snowy-browed flycatcher were just a few of the bird species and subspecies they cataloged and described.

There's a lot you can learn by watching birds, even if you're not trekking into the jungle to find new species. You can study birds' migration patterns by watching for their arrival in your own backyard. And if you're in the right place at the right time, you can observe some of the mating rituals that make birds so interesting to watch—you might see them fan out their colorful wings or tail feathers to attract mates or wield their feet and wings in fights to defend their territory. Spotting bird nests is another worthwhile pastime. If you find one, you'll know where to go in the coming weeks in order to watch the young hatchlings as they learn to fly and feed themselves.

These are the same kinds of observational techniques used by ornithologists. (That's the official name for someone who studies birds.) But that wasn't always the case. The practice of studying wild birds in their natural habitat was pioneered by the naturalist and ornithologist Florence Merriam Bailey (1863–1948). She published the very first field guide to American birds, *Birds Through an Opera-Glass,* in 1889. At the time, it was common for scientists to kill the birds they studied in order to dissect them or add them to museum collections. Florence was no stranger to the practice—she'd grown up "collecting" birds the same way. But she felt there was much more to learn by simply watching birds go about their lives. "Ask him for his compass," she said of the belted kingfisher, a blue-gray bird with a spiky crest that is commonly found along streams and shorelines. "He needs no trail. Follow him and he will teach you the secrets of the forest." The opera glass mentioned in her book title was an early version of binoculars, used mainly during opera and theater performances so that audience members could get a better view of the stage. The specially designed field glasses that came later were larger, less delicate, and more powerful. Florence used the information she gathered through hers to create hundreds of colorful drawings that helped beginning bird-watchers identify species in the field.

You can probably guess how she felt about the craze for hats adorned with bird feathers (and sometimes whole birds) among the women of her time. The fashion statement was responsible for nearly wiping out many coastal bird species, which were hunted without any meaningful regulations to preserve the populations. Florence organized crowds of hundreds to protest against the hat makers. Eventually the activists prevailed, and their work, together with the efforts of like-minded lobbyists, led to the passing of the Lacey Act in 1900. The act outlawed the interstate movement of wildlife that was killed illegally, meaning a poacher who killed a shorebird in Florida could face federal criminal charges if they tried to move the bird across state lines in order to sell it in New York. The act was followed in 1918 by the Federal Migratory Bird Treaty Act, which helped save many bird species from extinction. In 1908, a bird was named in Florence's honor: the *Parus gambeli baileyae,* a subspecies of the mountain chickadee.

If, like Florence, you find yourself getting really into birds, start a bird-watching journal to document your findings. See how many species you can spot in your neck of the woods. Get to know their calls, and see if you can recognize them by their song. If you like to draw, learning to sketch wildlife is a terrific way to stretch your skills. Maybe one day your field guide will make history, too. As Florence Merriam Bailey taught us, there is so much to be learned by simply watching.

BECOME A BACKYARD BIRD-WATCHER

There are more than 10,000 species of birds on earth, with over 2,000 that can be found in North America. What's amazing is that every species of bird in the world evolved from meat-eating dinosaurs like the velociraptor. It makes sense when you look at pictures of birds like the cassowary, shoebill stork, or California condor. They kind of look like dinosaurs. But even sparrows that are small enough to fit in the palm of your hand and weigh just a couple of ounces are the descendants of one of the most fearsome predators to ever roam the earth.

Based on fossil records from 150 million years ago, the *Archaeopteryx* is one of the earliest birdlike creatures. It was about the size of a crow, with sharp teeth like a dinosaur and feathers like a bird. However, it is unknown how *Archaeopteryx* used its feathers. Did it use them for flying, for gliding, or simply as insulation to keep warm? Maybe someday you'll be part of a team of scientists who answers this question. We do know, however, that the first examples of modern birds were flying at least 60 million years ago. Since then, birds have become one of the most diverse types of wildlife on the planet.

The variety of birds that we have is crazy. We have giant birds like the ostrich, which can be taller than an NBA basketball player and can weigh nearly 300 pounds. We also have tiny birds such as the bee hummingbird, which is the size of your thumb and weighs less than a penny. Depending on the species, a bird's diet might consist of fruits and seeds, or it might prey on insects, fish, other birds, rodents, or even monkeys. Some birds, like vultures, eat only rotting animal carcasses. Ducks and geese that migrate to the best places to eat and raise their young may fly thousands of miles every year. Other birds, like ground-dwelling ruffed grouse, will live their entire lifetime on 10 acres of ground (a football field takes up a little more than 1 acre of space). Birds like the woodcock have feathers with dull, muted colors that act as camouflage. Others, such as tanagers, blue jays, and cardinals, have wildly colored iridescent plumage. Bird calls are highly variable, too. From the high-pitched screech of a red-tailed hawk to the soft cooing of a mourning dove to the thunderous gobble of a male wild turkey, the range of noises birds make is astounding. And these amazing creatures are found on every continent in every possible environment. Birds live in blazing hot deserts, frozen Arctic tundra, jungle rainforests, and the open ocean. They're also comfortable around farms, neighborhoods, parks, and skyscrapers.

In fact, whether you live in the country, the suburbs, or the middle of a large city, there are probably some birds in your backyard right now. And even if you live in an apartment or a condominium complex and don't have a backyard, there are certainly some birds nearby. It probably won't take you very long to spot one if you step outside. Go take a look and you'll discover why bird-watching is one of the most popular outdoor activities in the world.

In the United States alone, as many as 45 million people of all ages and backgrounds consider themselves bird-watchers. Many of these folks take their hobby very seriously, traveling across the country and even the world in search of new birds. Some spend years hoping to catch a glimpse of a single rare species. They might also participate in challenges to see how many different species they can record in a single 24-hour period. The Cornell Lab of Ornithology conducts Global Big Day bird-watching competitions every year. On May 14, 2022, teams of bird-watchers from around the world recorded a total of more than 7,600 different species. The winning team, from Colombia, spotted 1,538 bird species!

Of course, you don't have to participate in competitions to be a bird-watcher. In fact, most birders don't travel the globe or participate in competitions looking for rare, exotic species of birds. They're more interested in the birds they might see while they're camping, hiking, or fishing. Or, better yet, just hanging around at home.

Unlike with a lot of other hobbies, you don't need a bunch of special gear or clothing to be a backyard bird-watcher. There are a few things you'll find helpful, but again, they aren't essential. Having a bird feeder or birdhouse in your backyard will help draw in avian visitors. Store-bought bags of bird food typically contain nuts and seeds that are eaten by a wide variety of birds. You can also put out sugar-water

feeders for hummingbirds. Pieces of fruit and chunks of animal fat will get the attention of other species. Birds will also enjoy some clean water in a birdbath during periods of hot, dry weather. Birdhouses can be bought or built. Some house structures will appeal to several types of birds, while others are designed for a specific species.

Binoculars are a helpful piece of equipment. A small pair of 7- or 8-power binoculars will allow you to closely inspect birds. A notebook is handy for jotting down the species, number, and dates of your bird sightings. A bird guidebook, such as *The Sibley Guide to Birds* or the *National Geographic Field Guide to the Birds of North America,* is super helpful for identifying the birds that you see. There are some excellent bird-watching phone apps, too. The Merlin Bird ID app tells you what birds you might see in your area. The app can also ask you simple questions to help you identify birds. The app analyzes pictures you take of birds, and can even listen to birdsongs in real time to determine what species is making them. Pretty cool!

Another great app is eBird. This app records your sighting in a worldwide scientific database that stores important information like how abundant different species of birds are, what kind of habitat they prefer, and what their migration patterns are. When you use the eBird app, you are engaging in what's called citizen science. That means you're a member of the general public who is working together with professional scientists to make discoveries about birds and their behavior. You can also join hundreds of thousands of other bird-watchers in the Great Backyard Bird Count. Over a four-day period every February, participants are asked to log all of their sightings at birdcount.org or in the eBird app. Every bird counts, whether you spot a couple of English sparrows at your bird feeder, a flock of Canada geese flying high overhead, or a pheasant that runs across the road in front of your school bus. The results of this population survey are posted in real time, so you can keep track of what's going on worldwide and in your local area.

The Great Backyard Bird Count is timed to take place in late winter, before many birds begin traveling to new areas on their annual spring migration. But the spring and fall are great times for bird-watching, too. That's when billions of birds are migrating. They could be traveling to or from places as far away as the Canadian Arctic or the jungles of Central America. You just might get to see a bird you never expected to encounter in your area. Of course, it is always fun and fascinating to keep track of the regular visitors to your backyard. You might get to watch a nesting pair of birds raise their offspring from eggs to baby chicks. Or you may learn to recognize an individual bird by the way it looks or behaves.

The coolest thing about bird-watching, though, is that there's always more to accomplish. It'd be nearly impossible for a single person to see all of the more than 10,000 bird species in this world. But there's no reason you can't try! Start looking now and keep a record of your discoveries. How many birds can you find, and how far will your quest take you?

CREATE A BACKYARD BRUSH PILE

Did you know that you have the power to welcome wild creatures into your backyard? Just like you, animals like the comfort and security of a shelter. A flat, wide-open yard doesn't give them many options for hideaways that can provide cover from predators and a break from the weather. In more natural habitats, they've got underground burrows as well as hollow trees and stumps where they can hide out and rest. Thankfully, it's easy to improve the wildlife habitat in your yard by creating a brush pile. A brush pile is just what it sounds like—a pile of sticks, logs, and brush that'll hopefully become a hangout for insects, squirrels, chipmunks, birds, mice, rabbits, and garter snakes. You might even get lucky and see your brush pile being used as a nesting spot or a den site by birds or other animals.

Think of your brush pile as a work in progress. You can always add to it whenever you want. In the end, you'll want enough to create a pile that's a few feet high and at least as long as a grown-up is tall. But before you start, give some thought to where you want to put it. If you have a large yard, pick a location where it won't get in your way when you mow the lawn or play outdoor games. Try to put it in the "gamiest" place you have, meaning the place where there's the greatest likelihood that animals will find and use it. Near trees or a hedgerow would be great. All the better if you have a pond, creek, or ditch. But don't stress out too much if you don't have a super location. After all, a brush pile is meant to create habitat. Once you build it, it'll hopefully become a focus of wildlife activity.

It's best to start your brush pile with some bigger stuff on the bottom in order to create a base. You want the base to include enough space for animals to move around under there. Some thicker logs will do the trick for the first layer. It's best if the logs are as thick as your upper leg. Lay them out in a row with a foot or so of space between them. Then make a second layer with logs set perpendicular to the first so you have little cubes of space for the animals to hide in. Do this criss-cross pattern another time or two. It's okay if the second or third layers are made from smaller logs or branches. Once you've gotten a couple of layers of criss-crossed logs, you can start throwing on any branches or brush that you can find. Keep going until you've got a nice mound of brush with lots of little tunnels and holes near the bottom where critters can come and go. Whenever you find more brush, go ahead and add it to the top of the pile. That way, you can keep your brush pile in good condition even as the old brush decomposes.

If you have plenty of room, go ahead and make more than one brush pile. That way, you can give animals the opportunity to hop from one hiding spot to another. If you have a bird feeder or birdhouse nearby, you'll probably have even more birds using your brush pile while they hunt for nesting material, food, and hiding places. As smaller animals move in or start to make regular visits, you may notice that they attract the attention of predators like hawks or weasels. You might be in for a predatory showdown!

The adventure of a brush pile is that you can't control or anticipate what kind of visitors it will attract. It's not impossible that a skunk or a family of noisy raccoons might move in. Some hornets could build a nest in there, too. Less intrepid adventurers might be scared off by these possibilities. But a bit of discomfort, danger, and some potential for stink are just part of the highs and lows of connecting with nature!

THE STORY IN A TREE

You can tell the age of a tree by counting the rings on its stump. Some people can look at those rings and feel as though they're hearing the stories that an old tree is whispering. The conservationist Aldo Leopold (1887–1948) was one of those people. For him, an oak felled by lightning and then chopped into firewood was not just a dead tree or a fuel source to warm his home. Leopold recognized that long ago, an acorn had fallen from a parent tree. That acorn then survived an almost certain death by hungry rabbit, and the tree that grew from it had weathered many decades' worth of storms. It had survived severe drought and nearby fires, and countless instances when human interference might have caused its death. It was a student of history, witness to a long-ago war. It had seen the last of the passenger pigeons, once the most common birds in North America, go extinct due to unregulated hunting.

Leopold encouraged everyone to look closely at nature and to think about the ways all of its parts are connected. In the 1930s, during the period known as the Great Depression, he purchased an abandoned farm near the Wisconsin River. The land had been neglected, the dry soil had turned to sand, and the old cornfield was filled with weeds. Leopold, who worked for the newly established U.S. Forest Service, set out to bring this small patch of ecosystem back to life. He had a dream of bringing back the native plant species that had once thrived on the land, and kept detailed diaries recording the blooming schedules of the beloved wild plants whose seeds he'd sown. The family camped outdoors when they visited on weekends and holidays. The Leopold children kept pet squirrels and had raccoons living with them inside the dilapidated barn they called "The Shack." Their days were spent repairing the barn, fishing, hunting, and working the land. When there wasn't work to be done, there was always exploring afoot. "In January one may follow a skunk track, or search for bands on the chickadees, or see what young pines the deer have browsed, or what muskrat houses the mink have dug," he wrote in *A Sand County Almanac,* a collection of essays that inspired generations of naturalists, young and old alike. What do you see when you take a walk on a cold January day, when the world might appear to have gone to sleep?

Leopold had already had a significant impact on the wild spaces of the United States before he purchased his shack. In 1924, his advocacy led to the creation of the first national wilderness area, the Gila Wilderness in New Mexico. In a wilderness area, there could be no roads, no logging, and no further development. This new type of protective designation would become very important for protecting wild spaces from human interference.

Throughout his career, Leopold had a tremendous influence on the protection of wild lands all across America. He believed that humans cannot ignore the reality that our activities change the landscape. Because of this, he taught people to consider *how* and *why* they chose to alter the natural world. His hope was that we'd learn to do it as carefully and responsibly as possible.

ACKNOWLEDGMENTS

My name, Steven Rinella, is on the front of this book. But that only tells about a third of the story. Throughout this entire process, I worked hand in hand with my collaborative partners, Savannah Ashour and Brody Henderson. From big ideas to detailed execution, they were involved in everything that you've seen and read within these pages.

Other colleagues at MeatEater lent their hand on this project whenever needed, including Kylee Archer, Katie Finch, Spencer Neuharth, Janis Putelis, Will Norris, Bridget Noonan, and Tracy Crane. Thanks also to Misty Newcomb, Karl Malcolm, Califia Suntree, and Claudia Sorsby for helpful additions and corrections.

For the conservationist profiles, I'd like to thank Randall Williams, J. Drew Lanham, and Debra Magpie Earling. And for the beautiful illustrations, thanks to Max Temescu. (Max, you're a hard worker and you don't give up. We appreciate that.)

Thanks to everyone at Penguin Random House, especially my editor, Ben Greenberg, as well as Kaeli Subberwal, Caroline Cunningham, Nancy Delia, Tom Perry, Erin Richards, and Ayelet Durrant. Thanks also to Keith Urbahn and Megan Stencel at Javelin for additional help in getting the word out.

Finally, thanks to my literary agent, Marc Gerald. (Marc, I think we just hit the twenty-year mark.)

INDEX

geologists, 139–40

giardiasis or "beaver fever," 90

Glass, Anthony, 227–28

"Grand Adventurer, A" (Williams), 172–75

Grand Canyon, 174, 175

Grand Canyon National Park, 19

Great Backyard Bird Count, 324–25

Guide to Common Freshwater Invertebrates of North America, A (Voshell and Wright), 120

• • • • •

halibut, 167

hawks, 130–31, 196, 214, 240, 242, 277, 322, 328

Hevel, Gary, 111, 112

hiking

apps for, 52–53

follow a game trail, 35–38, *36*

footwear and apparel, 53

health benefits, 51

make a walking stick, 26–30

plan for, 51–53, *53*

purify water, 90–93, *90*

research on line, 52

trail guides, 7, 52

walk in a straight line through the woods, 22–24, *23*

what to do before starting out, 9

what to do if you get lost in the woods, 24–25

Hiking Project (app), 52

Huffman, L. A., 85

hunter-gatherers, 96

hunting

adult mentor for, 238

aim for the vitals, 243, *243*

ambush or still hunting, 240–42

blinds, 196

identify your target, 243

practice target shooting first, 234

rule of quick, humane kill, 234, 243

rules of gun safety, 237

safety certification course, 238

squirrel hunting, 238–42

stalk an animal and, 204

state's rules for youth hunters, 238

stay downwind from wildlife, 198, 200

track an animal and, 209

hydrogen peroxide, for cleaning collected bones or skulls, 138–39

• • • • •

iNaturalist (app), 27

Ingstad, Helge, *The Land of Feast and Famine*, 76

insects

in aquatic environments, 110

for bait, 164

biting, stinging, or poisonous, 113

build a bug hotel, 111–13, *112*

caution before picking up, 110

find a new species, 113

flip a rock to find, 109–11, *109*

how many in a backyard, 111

identifying, 113, 120

importance for life on earth, 151–52

what bug-like critters are non-insects, 112

where to look for, 110

Inuit peoples, 82, 133–34, 149

• • • • •

jack-o'-lantern

how to grow a pumpkin, 312–14

saving the seeds, 314

tradition of carving pumpkins, 312

journaling

bird-watching journal, 320, 324, 325

rain gauge records, 265

waterproof notebook for, 6–7

weather vane readings, 259

• • • • •

kick nets, 116–20, *116*, *119*

catch aquarium specimens, 124

catch hellgammites for bait, 164

how to make, 117–18

how to use, 118–19

identify what you catch, 120

what to wear, 118–19

knife sharpening, 219–21, *220*

knives, 218–21

brand recommended, 218

care and cleaning of, 221

for cleaning animal skulls, 136

for fishing, 171

lockback knife, 218

pocketknife or jackknife, 136, 171, 218–19

knots, 71–73

blood knot, 72, *72*

bowline, 72, *72*

clinch knot, 72, *72*

clove hitch, 73, *73*, 79

double half-hitch, 72, *72*, 80, *80*

timber hitch, 72, *72*

• • • • •

lakes, ponds, rivers, and streams

catch crayfish, 193–95

catch panfish, 176–78, *179*

creatures in cold, clear streams, 51

creatures in weedy ponds, 51

"drop-offs," 124

insects in, 110

make a kick net, 116–20, *116*, *119*

paddle a canoe, 44–47, *44*

stock a home aquarium, 122–25

trail guides for, 54

use a bathyscope, 50–51

use a beach seine to catch minnows, 164

use a minnow trap, *158*, 162–64

where to look for small fish, 124

See also fishing

Land of Feast and Famine, The (Ingstad), 76

Lanham, J. Drew, "Saving the Soil of the South," 292–94

Lapland, Ice Restaurant, 82

lean-to shelter, 76–78, *77*

Leatherman Rev, 218

leopards, 39

Leopold, Aldo, 329–31, *329*

A Sand County Almanac, 330

Letters to a Young Scientist and *Naturalist* (Wilson), 152

Lewis and Clark expedition, 105–6

PocketMacros (app), 120
pompano, 165
poop (scat)
    as animal signs, 216
    composting with, 302
pooping outdoors, 73–74, *74*
porcupines, 39, 127, 210, 222
Powell, John Wesley, 172–75, *172*
pumpkinseeds (fish), 176, 177–78
pumpkin seeds (plant), 314

· · · · ·

Quakers, 206

· · · · ·

rabbits, 36, 203
    poop (scat), *215*, 216
    protect your garden from, 286
    tracks, 209, *210*
rain
    build a rain gauge, 264–65
    keep records of rainfall, 265
    regions with highest and lowest
        amount, 263
raised garden beds, 280, 296
    how to make, *295*, 296–98
redfish, 165
riptides, 43
rockhounding, 139–42, *141*
    apps and guidebooks, 142
    find agates, 141–42
    find artifacts, 143–44
    find rocks on the beach, 148
    find rocks in your area, 142
    local clubs, 142
rocks and minerals, 140–42
    agate, 141–42, *141*
    basalt, 140
    chalcedony, 141
    coal, 140
    igneous rock, 140
    limestone, 140
    marble, 140
    metamorphic rock, 140
    mica, 140
    obsidian, 140
    petrified wood, 141–42
    pyrite (fool's gold), 140
    quartz, 140, 141
    quartzite, 140
    sandstone, 140

sedimentary rock, 140
semiprecious gemstone, 141
shale, 140
types of rocks, 140
Roosevelt, Theodore, 57–60, *57*,
    294
rope, best all-purpose, 6
rose hips, 108

· · · · ·

**"Sacagawea Survives" (Earling),
    103–6**
Sand County Almanac, A (Leopold),
    330
"Saving the Soil of the South"
    (Lanham), 292–94
scouring rush, 67
shelters, 75–81
    A-frame, 78–79, *79*
    lean-to, 76–78, *77*
    teepees, 79–81, *80*, *81*
Sibley Guide to Birds, The, 324
Silent Spring (Carson), 115
"Silent Spring, The," 114–16
situational awareness, xviii
SkySafari (app), 19
SkyView (app), 19
sleeping bag, 56
sleeping pad, 56
sleep under the stars, *55*, 55–56
snacks, 5
    how to roast pumpkin seeds,
        314
    using as tinder, 64
snow fortress, 82–84, *83*
solar still, *90*, 91–93
space blanket, 7, 25
space pen, 6–7
squirrel hunting, 238–42
    ambush or still hunting, 240–42
    build a blind for, 240
    clean a squirrel, 244–47, *245*,
        246, *247*
    cook a squirrel, 247
    firearm for, 238
    gear for, 238, 242
    regulations for hunting, 238
    store a cleaned squirrel, 247
    target practice for, 236–37
Squirrel Noodle Soup, 252–53

squirrels, 203–4, 239–40
    Albert's squirrel, 239
    black-phase gray squirrels, 239
    burying nuts, 306–7
    climb trees like a squirrel,
        39–41, *39*
    eastern gray squirrels, 239, 240,
        247, 306, 307
    fox squirrels, 238–40, 247
    pine squirrels, 239, 247, 307
    protect your garden from, 286
    signs of, *215*, 216, 217
    tracks, 209, *210*
    tree squirrels, 39, 238
    western gray squirrels, 239
stalking an animal, 202–5, *203*
stars and constellations, 14–22
    Acrux, 18–19
    apps, 19
    asterisms, 14
    Betelgeuse, 17, 18
    Big Dipper, 15–16, *15*
    Castor, 17, 18
    Gemini, 17–18, *18*
    Gacrux (star), 18–19
    Little Dipper, 16
    for navigation, 14–19
    North Star, 15, 16, 20–21
    Orion, 16–17, *17*
    Pollux, 17, 18
    Rigel, 17
    Sirius, 17
    Southern Cross, 18–19
    stargazing tips, 19
Star Walk (app), 19
Steripen, 91
STOP (stop, think, observe,
    plan), 24
"Story in a Tree, The," 329–31
sun, 11–12
    make a sun compass, 11–13, *13*
sunfish, 159, 164, 176, 177–78
sunglasses, 7, 49, 87, 171
sunscreen, 7, 53
surf perch, 165

· · · · ·

target shooting, 233–37
    air rifle or rifle for, 234–35
    rules of gun safety, 237

ABOUT THE AUTHOR

STEVEN RINELLA is an outdoorsman, writer, wild foods enthusiast, and television and podcast personality who is a passionate advocate for conservation and the protection of public lands. Rinella is the host of the television show and podcast *MeatEater;* his most recent book is the *New York Times* bestseller *Outdoor Kids in an Inside World.* His writing has appeared in many publications, including *Outside, Field & Stream,* and *The New Yorker.* Rinella lives in Bozeman, Montana, with his wife and their three kids.

themeateater.com
Facebook.com/StevenRinellaMeatEater
Instagram: @stevenrinella and @meateater